Praise for Goth Craft

"*Goth Craft* is a sexy and serious A–Z of dark culture's collective tribal identity. More than just a demented 'Preppy Handbook' for a different era, *Goth Craft* goes beyond mere fashion, taking readers deep into the magickal currents of this emerging subculture. Fascinating."

—Richard Metzger, host of *Disinformation* and editor of *Book of Lies: The Disinformation Guide to Magick and the Occult*

"Don't let your assumptions fool you—*Goth Craft* is a lovingly written and carefully researched piece of work. It covers the intersection of Gothic subculture and Pagan spirituality from every conceivable angle, and manages to be both fun and eye-catching along the way."

—Michelle Belanger, author of *The Psychic Vampire Codex* and editor of *Vampires in Their Own Words*

"With *Goth Craft*, Raven Digitalis pierces the melancholy skin of the dark culture and unveils the beating heart of Goth. More than a fad, more than a romantic fashion statement, more than a global cultural phenomenon, Goth is a living art form whose canvas is the human body, and whose inspiration is Magick."

—Lon Milo DuQuette, author of *The Magick of Aleister Crowley*

"Raven Digitalis' book deserves to be on the bookshelf of anyone interested or involved with magick, ritual, and the Goth subculture. *Goth Craft* not only brings the reader the complete history of both subcultures but weaves together a fascinating dark Pagan tome that will inspire the reader to rediscover themselves by bringing their inner selves out into the open. My highest recommendations!"

—Corvis Nocturnum, author of *Embracing the Darkness: Understanding Dark Subcultures*

"At once a field guide to the Goth scene and a cutting-edge approach to Neopagan spirituality, *Goth Craft* offers a practical guide to magic for fans of contemporary dark culture as well as a glimpse of an unfamiliar subculture for those who think the word 'Goth' means the guys who sacked Rome. Highly recommended."

—John Michael Greer, Archdruid and author of *The New Encyclopedia of the Occult*

"Raven intelligently addresses and explores the Goth's personal lifestyle choices and expression of their Craft. Non-Goths can enjoy this volume too; it is a fascinating insight into a very colorful and creative community."

—Fiona Horne, author of *Bewitch a Man* and *L.A. Witch*

"An insightful, honest, and spiritual exploration of the intersection of Witchcraft and Goth culture not only for those who have a foot in each of these worlds, but also for those explorers on one side, seeking to know the ways of the other."

—Christopher Penczak, author of the Temple of Witchcraft series

Michelle's Book

"Maybe not all Witches are Goths, and vice versa, but for those who are, *Goth Craft* is a wonderful guide to combining these two subcultures. Rather than shying away from controversy, Raven covers sex, drugs, and gender identity with a thoughtful, open mind. I have no doubt that this book will fill a popular niche in both subcultures, and I heartily congratulate Raven on an excellent first publication."

—Lupa, author of *A Field Guide to Otherkin* and co-author of *Kink Magick: Sex Magick Beyond Vanilla*

"Raven provides an intriguing cross-cultural representation of Goth and Witchcraft. He shows how elements from the Goth subculture can be successfully incorporated into everyday magical practice, while at the same time managing to be stylish."

—Taylor Ellwood, author of *Inner Alchemy* and co-author of *Kink Magick: Sex Magick Beyond Vanilla*

"*Goth Craft* expertly dispels common misunderstandings and brings us to the shadow's edge, revealing the beauty of what dwells within the sacred night."

—Raven Grimassi & Stephanie Taylor, authors of *The Well Worn Path* and *The Hidden Path*

"Written with practical insight and ingenious flair, *Goth Craft* is a darkly illuminating guidebook that will be at home on any seeker's shelf, especially if that seeker happens to have a penchant for black eyeliner, nocturnal cloaks, fishnet, and dramatic jewelry. Seeded with anthropological anecdotes and humorous asides, *Goth Craft* enlightens and entertains as well as offering up everything you'll ever need to know about Gothic culture today, and its ongoing love affair with the mysterious and magickal. I cannot recommend this book highly enough."

—Kala Trobe, author of *The Witch's Guide to Life* and *Magick in the West End*

"For far too long, our modern magickal systems have avoided the darker aspects of occultism. If it wasn't sweetness and light, then it simply did not exist; and students were taught that anything that made them 'uncomfortable' was not for them. Thankfully, this is beginning to change as a new generation of 21st century occultists come of age. *Goth Craft* by Raven Digitalis is an important addition to this new generation, whether or not you consider yourself a Goth."

—Aaron Leitch, author of *Secrets of the Magickal Grimoires*

"I applaud Raven for tackling such a challenging topic and doing so in such an eloquent manner. *Goth Craft* will make a fine addition to the libraries of those of us who go bump in the night or are just curious to know what does!"

—John J. Coughlin, author of *Out of the Shadows: An Exploration of Dark Paganism and Magick*

"For a great many magickal folks, Hallowe'en has always been our favorite holiday; indeed, we often say that we're the kind of people who like to leave our Hallowe'en decorations up all year long! We love the dark spooky stuff, and Raven's *Goth Craft* is a book many of us have always longed for."

—Oberon Zell-Ravenheart, co-founder of the Church of All Worlds and author of *Creating Circles & Ceremonies: Rituals for All Seasons and Reasons*

The Magickal Side
of Dark Culture

Goth
cRaFt

RaVeN DiGiTaLiS

Llewellyn Publications
Woodbury, Minnesota

About the Author

Raven Digitalis (Missoula, MT) is a Neopagan Priest of the "disciplined eclectic" shadow magick tradition Opus Aima Obscuræ, and is a radio and club DJ of Gothic, EBM, and industrial music. With his Priestess Estha, Raven holds community gatherings, conducts Tarot readings, and provides a variety of ritual services. From their home, the two also operate the metaphysical business Twigs & Brews, specializing in magickal and medicinal bath salts, herbal blends, essential oils, and incenses. Raven holds a degree in anthropology from the University of Montana and is also a black-and-white photographic artist.

To Write to the Author

If you wish to contact the author or would like more information about this book, please write to the author in care of Llewellyn Worldwide and we will forward your request. Both the author and publisher appreciate hearing from you and learning of your enjoyment of this book and how it has helped you. Llewellyn Worldwide cannot guarantee that every letter written to the author can be answered, but all will be forwarded. Please write to:

Raven Digitalis
℅ Llewellyn Worldwide
2143 Wooddale Drive, Dept. 978-0-7387-1104-1
Woodbury, MN 55125-2989, U.S.A.
Please enclose a self-addressed stamped envelope for reply,
or $1.00 to cover costs. If outside U.S.A., enclose
international postal reply coupon.

Many of Llewellyn's authors have websites with additional information and resources. For more information, please visit our website at http://www.llewellyn.com.

Forthcoming Book by Raven Digitalis

Shadow Magick Compendium
(Llewellyn Publications, 2008)

First Edition
First Printing, 2007

Book design by Donna Burch
Copyediting by Andrea Neff
Cover design by Kevin R. Brown
Editing by Jason Louv
Interior illustrations by the Llewellyn Art Department
Llewellyn is a registered trademark of Llewellyn Worldwide, Ltd.

For a complete list of photograph credits, see page 299.

Library of Congress Cataloging-in-Publication Data
Digitalis, Raven.
        Goth craft : the magickal side of dark culture / by Raven Digitalis.—1st ed.
              p. cm.
        Includes bibliographical references and index.
        ISBN 978-0-7387-1104-1
        1. Witchcraft. 2. Magic. 3. Goth culture (Subculture) I. Title.

    BF1566.D54 2007
    133.4'3—dc22   2007015992

Llewellyn Worldwide does not participate in, endorse, or have any authority or responsibility concerning private business transactions between our authors and the public.

All mail addressed to the author is forwarded but the publisher cannot, unless specifically instructed by the author, give out an address or phone number.

Any Internet references contained in this work are current at publication time, but the publisher cannot guarantee that a specific location will continue to be maintained. Please refer to the publisher's website for links to authors' websites and other sources.

Llewellyn Publications
A Division of Llewellyn Worldwide, Ltd.
2143 Wooddale Drive, Dept. 978-0-7387-1104-1
Woodbury, Minnesota 55125-2989, U.S.A.
www.llewellyn.com

Printed in the United States of America

Contents

Acknowledgments

Infinite thanks to my ever-accepting family for always encouraging personal growth and exploration in alternative paths, especially my parents, brother, and grandparents: Barb, Jeff, Justin, Bette, and Erwin. My life would be much different had you not blessed it.

Much gratitude to the publisher and everyone involved in the process of putting my words into form. Thanks for giving a new writer the opportunity of a lifetime.

To my two amazing Priestesses for teaching me so much along the way, and for being the most compassionate, trustworthy, and brutally honest guides a person could ever ask for: Esthamarelda McNevin and Zanoni Silverknife, as well as my "adopted Priest" and Brother of the Craft, Alan Wittenberg. Acknowledgments and well wishes to those involved in both the Inner and Outer Courts of my training system, Opus Aima Obscuræ.

Praises as well to my dear friends in the newly emerging Tië eldaliéva tradition! I also thank my professors at the University of Montana for telling me what's what about what, in particular G. G. Weix, Alan Sponberg (Saramati), and Paul A. Dietrich.

Humble thanks to my author friends who reassured me of my strengths: Christopher Penczak, Kala Trobe, Janet Farrar, Gavin Bone, Lon Milo Duquette, John Michael Greer, Michelle Belanger, T. Thorn Coyle, Raven Grimassi and Stephanie Taylor, Oberon and Morning Glory Zell-Ravenheart, Taylor Ellwood and Lupa, LaSara FireFox, Aaron Leitch, Kenaz Filan, Richard Metzger, Jason Louv, Rachel Haywire, Scott Treleaven, S. Rune Emerson, Roger Williamson, Ted Andrews, John J. Coughlin, Voltaire, Corvis Nocturnum, Sharron Rose, Donald Michael Kraig, Ellen Dugan, Dianne Sylvan, Fiona Horne, Shawn Mitzel, Catherine Wishart, Jonathan Goldman, Ann Moura, Timothy Roderick, Morwyn, Debra Magpie Earling, Justin Whitaker, Francesca Leader, Miranda Hewlett, Kadesh Nak Nahash, Ian Burton, Abel Gomez, Stacie Lomas, Calantirniel (AarTiana), Námovaryar (Ray), and my dearest Estha McNevin.

A special thanks to all my Gothy and alt-culture friends, as well as to all the friends who have expanded my spiritual sight by simply Being. I tried to make a list of all y'all, but it would have taken up a whole other book. You know exactly who you are, and I wish there were enough words to express the gratitude of friendship. I honor, love, and admire you more than I could ever say. Goodness begets Goodness; may your Paths be clear.

And finally, a tremendous thank-you to my forever f(r)iend and probably-forever web-master Michæl Vandenberg (mchl)!

Namasté, Blessed Be, and 93,
Raven Digitalis

www.ravendigitalis.com

Call to the Dark Mother

Behold!

She who holds the mysteries I seek under shroud of night.

Nocturnal Mistress, I fear thee not.

I call thee forth with love and humility.

Hail the Dark Mother; She who turns the Wheel,

She who is the Shadow Tide,

She whose mysteries are the blood;

She who is the moon eclipsed.

O Dark Mother, She who is known by many names:

Hecate, Persephone, Cerridwen, Rhiannon, Ereshkigal, Lilith,

Babalon, Hel, and Kali-Ma.

Descend upon me this dark eve, consume my fear and inhibitions.

Be at my side as I dare to see the unseen.

Let me know thine ways of nocturnal grace.

Surround my soul as I tread your infinite waters.

Accompany my rites this eve, in balance and in wisdom.

I call thee forth, my Mother, my Sister, my Matrix.

Hail and Welcome.

So Mote It Be.

Call to the Dark Father

Behold!

He who holds the mysteries I seek under shroud of night.

Nocturnal Master, I fear thee not.

I call thee forth with love and humility.

Hail the Dark Father; He who oversees the falling

of all things great and small.

He who is the shadow having come from sun's light;

He who is the sun eclipsed.

O Dark Father, He who is known by many names:

Osiris, Anubis, Hades, Pluto, Pan, Dionysus, Baphomet,

Cernnunos, and Mors.

Descend upon me this dark eve, devour my trepidations and fright.

Be at my side as I dare to feel the unfelt.

Let me know thine ways of dark enchantment.

Enter my world as I journey your endless terrain.

Accompany my rites this eve, in truth and in steadfast devotion.

I call thee forth, my Father, my Brother, my Patrix.

Hail and Welcome.

So Mote It Be.

This book is dedicated to all spiritual seekers worldwide who have devoted themselves to ushering in the new tide of consciousness by whatever means necessary.
This book is my Will, and it is my hope that its contents can contribute positively to your own.

Introduction

The twenty-first century is one of the most diverse times the world has ever seen. Numerous cultures are coming together; technology has ushered in new forms of communication and learning. People are, one by one, awakening to the diversity around them. Many people are choosing to live their lives away from the masses, increasingly disinterested in the ordinary and mundane. New cultures have arisen like phoenixes from the ashes of times past. History is rekindling itself, and the ethereal seeds of change planted by our ancestors are beginning to grow to fruition.

Interest in both the Gothic and Pagan lifestyles is increasing on a daily basis. Each person who becomes interested in these alternative paths has his or her own individual reason for doing so. Both cultures have a certain undeniable attractiveness about them. Many people these days, especially youth, feel a need to break the chains of the status quo. They adamantly refuse, or are emotionally unable, to spend their whole lives trying to conform to cultural expectations of how people should behave, look, and think. The Gothic and Pagan lifestyles take the *other* road—the one leading to personal empowerment and independent thought. Goths and Pagans simply cannot settle for the average, and certainly don't take the "just because" response as a legitimate answer to any question. We cannot just work, go to church, watch television, and do it all over again each and every day of our lives. Monotony is unsatisfactory for people of alternative paths, and life is much too grand an experience to waste. Of course, not fitting social expectations can often be just as difficult as it is rewarding for some, depending on one's circumstances.

Goth Craft is not a tradition or specific religion, and to my knowledge there is no Goth-exclusive form of magick. Rather, the title refers to the coming together of two ways of life: Goth culture and Paganism. A deep-seated interest in the mysteries of magick and mysticism, combined with a dedication to the Gothic subculture or other dark lifestyle, constitute a dark Witch or magician. The intersection of these two cultures will be explored in detail within this book. I shall look at the different elements of Paganism that Goths are naturally attracted to. Goth culture and Paganism are two separate entities and exist apart from one another, but they don't have to, and certainly don't always. There are plenty of similarities between the two cultures; indeed, there are reasons that innumerable people have an interest in both!

Dark does not mean evil. Nor does Goth. Nor does Witch. The media, and fundamentalists, would have us believe otherwise. You cannot be evil and truly be a Witch at the same time; that contradicts the whole of Paganism. This book is made for people who *understand* that, or at least honestly seek to know.

The word *dark* can, at times, allude to negative practices. In the case of this book, it rarely does. In my everyday conversation, I use the definitions of dark interchangeably when speaking to someone who understands that the aforesaid words are not indicative of evil. I may use a phrase like "s/he was in a dark place" to refer to a negative mindset, or "the house had dark energy" to indicate an uncomfortable or potentially negative situation. In that sense, yes, *dark* does allude to harmful energies. It must be understood that in the case of the teachings and ideas of this book, darkness most often refers to mysteriousness and is used to reference the beauty of dark culture.

There is an impressive amount of information out there aimed at "exposing the hidden dangers of Witchcraft and Goth culture." Most sources focus specifically on either dark culture or Paganism, but many like to equate the two to form an easily digestible pill of misinformation.

Dark Witches do not sacrifice children to Cthulhu, torment neighbors and dogs, or seek to convert children to devilry. Most of us do not listen to thrash metal or have a morbid fascination with death. In actuality, we're much more comfortable writing poetry by candlelight, taking long and introspective strolls, or reading and meditating alone in our rooms. We are not racist, sexist, or antiestablishment. In fact, we are some of the most accepting and even diverse people out there.

I assume that individuals who have purchased this book will be somewhat familiar with the Goth and Pagan cultures, at least enough to understand that their true intentions, philosophies, and motivations are not skewed or morbid. That's why I'll spend more time explaining what Goth culture and Paganism *are*, and exploring the similarities between them, instead of just explaining what they *are not*. I understand that all sorts of people, with different levels of understanding, will read this book, and therefore it is still necessary to include some information dispelling many stereotypes and misunderstandings, especially for those who seek understanding with an open heart and mind.

Most of my training and practices are in Witchcraft. For this reason, the Craft is the main emphasis of this book. I try to constantly research and integrate practices and philosophies of other esoteric and magickal traditions into my own personal ways, but at the end of the day, I am a Witch; I just happen to be very interested in other traditions as well and, like many, incorporate them into my own Craft beliefs and practices. Wicca itself is syncretistic in that it borrows from a variety of spiritual and magickal traditions as well as countryside folk practices, and is the most common form of Witchcraft practiced today. This book is not, however, limited to Wicca alone by any means. I also explore other Pagan and magickal paths and integrate philosophies from Eastern and Western traditions. The Craft is where the majority of my training lies, and it is from there that I can ground my ideas into one source, using it as a metaphysical and magickal springboard.

Much of the material herein is also appropriate to non-Goths, and even magickally or spiritually minded people who do not identify as Pagan. A great deal of this information may also be appealing to people who don't wish to use the labels Goth or Witch to describe themselves, but who have similar tendencies or curiosities nonetheless. Most Pagans who dress "differently" and have unique artistic tastes simply identify themselves as "alternative." Many alternative people have at least *some* interest in Goth music and culture, and will find elements with which to identify inside these pages.

I should forewarn the reader that "adult" material is discussed in this book, including sex magick, blood magick, death magick, and drugs. If you're a youth looking for cool and edgy ways to cast powerful and arcane spells, or for a forbidden, infernal tome of black magick, then this book is not for you. I present information and tips on practices that are designed for the progression of magickal and spiritual understanding, so that every experience in life has an opportunity to be seen for its spiritual potential. The Craft consists of much more than spells and incantations; it truly is a constantly evolving, living spiritual path. The ways of magick and spiritual awareness are in our bones, in our DNA, and at the core of our souls.

As I said before, you don't need to be Goth, or even necessarily Pagan, to get something out of this book. It is designed for people who honestly seek to know the ways of personal transformation and expression, magick, and healing. It is not an introductory book, and assumes the reader has some knowledge of Paganism, even if it's only the basics.

Goth Craft is meant to be more a guide and reference than a grimoire. For this reason, I've kept the number of spells to a minimum; there are only a couple that are fully explained, in addition to a variety of tips for creating your own. An old magickal law states that "the first thing magick changes is the self," and I hold to this idea when giving spells for the reader to practice. If personal transformation isn't achieved, then what use is magick in the first place?

This book also includes two full meditations that will assist you in gaining a deeper understanding of the mind and spirit. The first is "lighter" in nature, while the second is much "darker," for lack of better terms. Meditation is an invaluable practice for a Witch—or for any spiritual person, for that matter. I believe it is essential to meditate regularly, especially before any sort of ritual or spellcrafting is to take place. I say without qualm that meditation is an essential aspect of any spiritual quest, and I definitely agree with philosopher Hans Margolius when he states that "meditation allows us the opportunity to cultivate the ability of detaching from our thoughts, thus learning to distinguish mental drama from objective reality."

Thanks and many well wishes to you, the reader, for picking up this book. I truly hope that the material inspires you on your path to create positive change both in your life and in the lives of others.

I

Goth

Pagan practice and the Gothic lifestyle are different for everyone. Each person gets something out of each lifestyle that others may not. I can say only so much about each without generalizing about the whole. These lifestyles carry a different message for each person, and it would be foolish to generalize about a movement as diverse as Goth or Pagan culture. However, there are a few points that must be conveyed in order to more easily classify and recognize aspects of each movement.

What's a Goth?

Alternative culture is the result of similar energy patterns coming together, kinship being found, and the disassociated once again becoming united. One of these alternative neocultures is the dark art, or "darksider," community, many of whose members consider themselves to be part of the modern Goth subculture.

The terms *Goth* and *Gothic* have been in use only since the 1970s to describe people belonging to a particular subcultural faction. Goths can be described in a number of ways, but let's begin with the origins of the word itself.

Historical Goths

A tribe called the Goths originated in present-day Götland, Sweden, in the first century BCE and later made their way through Europe, all the way to Spain. By the third century BCE, they split off into the Ostrogoths (eastern Goths) and Visigoths (western Goths). I will use the spelling "Gothick" to distinguish the historical tribal Goths from the nineteenth-century Romantics and modern Goths.

One Germanic tribe or another seemed to be constantly invading Rome. Integration occurred between the Romans and the Germanic tribes over time. Though the two peoples were fighting, much of their cultures became intertwined through alliances, including the fostering of numerous sons and daughters. The Visigoths' infamous sacking of Rome occurred in 410 CE.

The Goths were originally uncivilized heathens, meaning they did not live in a city and they had a similar god structure to that of the Norse and other Germanic tribes. Before the rise of the Church, they saw no separation between their ways and those of others. The Goths were one of the last European tribes to want to remain nomadic (traveling) rather than become citizens of a political empire.

The majority of the tribes that wished not to become part of the greater Roman political structure saw the system itself as a violation of their freedom, as those in Roman rulership were believed to have the "mandate of the gods," particularly if a pure tribal bloodline was maintained. Every tribal culture that became a part of this political empire was absorbed, losing a great deal of its former culture. With the coming of each generation, more and more of the former tribal ways were lost, replaced by the greater government's unionized system. It is for this reason that so much animosity existed between the tribes and the city-states.

Nancy Kilpatrick, author of *The Goth Bible: A Compendium for the Darkly Inclined*, believes that modern Goth is facing a similar dilemma: the threat of absorption into the mainstream.

The Gothick people converted to Arian Christianity before being overtaken by the Græco-Roman Christians, even calling their way "Gothick Christianity." The Goths saw the Christ not as the world's one and only figure of salvation, but as a warrior, magician, and shaman.

Following a number of invasions and forced integrations by the Roman Catholics, Huns, and Muslims, the ancient cultures of the Goths became virtually extinguished.

The culture and its ideology survived only as an underground occult movement within persecuted and converted peoples, preserving the teachings of the Norse, the Gothick language (documented as early as 300 CE), and the adopted symbolism of the runes.

The Goths established secret traditions, greatly influencing nobility, but this underground movement largely remained exclusive to the lower classes. Further persecution of the Goths fluctuated over time; either they had legitimate political power with royalty and were left alone, or they were too underground and unnoticed to be targeted. This impact can be seen even now, considering the number of currently existing surnames that are Gothick in origin. Even members of Spanish nobility are called *gotos* ("Goths") today.

Though the ancient Gothick tribes virtually vanished upon the Muslim invasion in 711 CE, some of their culture survived all the way up to the Renaissance, when its spirit was restored in painting, sculpture, and architecture, becoming the Gothic Renaissance movement.

The architectural style of the time differed from the common Græco-Roman idea of proper form, gaining the title "Gothic." Because the art and architecture were unique and quite eerie—definitely against the grain at the time—the term Gothic was used in a derogatory fashion. At that time, the term was negatively associated with the barbaric, dark, and uncultured.

Gothic architecture is characterized by its towering vertical appearance, pointed arches, curved doorways, large spires and columns, ribbed vaults, stained glass, flying buttresses, and, of course, gargoyles!

European Romanticism was the origin of the literary use of the word *Gothic*, which evoked a particular lugubrious style of literature. Darkly themed stories around that time period began to be associated with the reawakened Goth movement. The Gothic literary style addressed the mechanisms of fear and sexuality within the human psyche. At the time of the Gothic Renaissance, fear and superstition were stereotyped as being representative of old Gothick belief.

Authors over time (if I may jump around in history) who might be said to have had an influence on the resurrection of the Gothic(k) spirit both in the Gothic Renaissance and the later nineteenth-century Romantic movement include Giordano Bruno, Morris Berman, Horace Walpole, William Shakespeare, Jean-Jacques Rousseau, Bram Stoker, Mary Shelley, William Blake, and Oscar Wilde, to name a few.

Also included is the Swiss author Hermann Hesse (1877–1962), known for his kinship with the Germanic peoples, having been born German and having an interest in Germanic mysticism. Hesse was a naturist (nudist), vegan, and earth-worshipper—definitely Pagan in many ways. His works, including *Siddhartha*, *Steppenwolf*, and *Demian*, influenced movements like the hippie counterculture.

Poets such as Edgar Allan Poe, Charles Baudelaire, and Sylvia Plath also reintroduced characteristically dark, foreboding writing to the people. The Victorian English poet Alfred Tennyson spent a lot of time in cemeteries, even lying on the cemetery ground for long periods of time. The turn-of-the-century poet Edith Sitwell insisted on wearing exclusively black for years, declaring herself to be "in mourning for the world." Many current writers, like Poppy Z. Brite, Anne Rice, Storm Constantine, Caitlin R. Kiernan, Kala Trobe, and Nancy A. Collins, are known for writing fiction in a "Gothic" manner, exploring cultural taboos and controversial issues in the confines of dark settings, atmospheres, and moods.

According to occult scholar Edred Thorsson, the word *Gauts*, which is the Germanic root word of *Goth*, means "divine progenitor" or "God." For one to be called Gothick meant to be a descendant of God or a "child of God," if you will. This concept came from the idea of a certain group of peoples having a holy bloodline.

"Books can be burned, religious leaders can be killed," writes Thorsson in his essay *The Secret of the Gothick God of Darkness*, "but the blood endures." This, he believes, is the way the knowledge of the Norse/Gothick god Odin (Woden) has survived, even into the current Goth movement.

Commenting on modern Goth culture, Thorsson writes: "This revival, or reawakening, of the Gothick spirit in many respects follows the characteristics of all the previous revivals."

There are plenty of similarities between present-day Goths, historical Goths, and the artistic movement of the Renaissance, though all three are separate entities. I've heard theories that modern-day Goths may be the reincarnation of the early Goths, now spread worldwide. I suppose this is possible, but that would bring up the unanswerable question "Who's Goth and who's not?" That aside, I do believe that people reincarnate in certain situations mirroring past-life experience; that is, souls come into alignment with other people and acute situations in life directly carried over from the vibrational patterns of incarnations past. Could it be that we reincarnated aside others from our past whose interactions with us carry similar lessons as before?

I agree that Gothic consciousness is not new to the earth plane. Well before the modern Goth movement, there were writers, painters, musicians, and other artists creating characteristically dark material. I would guess that writing poetry in solitude or walking about a burial ground contemplating life are not phenomena reserved for the modern age.

Going against the grain has been a common theme in human history. People have been "Goth" for aeons; it's only recently that labels for such dark artists have arisen.

Modern Goths

Back in 1970s England, when the street punks would pose for pictures with American travelers for beer and concert money, a new subcultural movement was being spawned. Punk was beginning to evolve and define itself as a real counterculture, appealing to youths of a different mindset, and was starting to branch out in a number of directions.

Members of the punk movement tended to take their anger and dissatisfaction with the world, society, and their personal lives, and express them through music, activism, and aesthetics. This provided a much-needed venue of expression and allowed a community of anti-normative youths to coalesce.

Some people in the early punk scene began to tire of the negative behavior and increasing apathy surrounding the lifestyle. They became more and more attracted to wispier, more melodic music and found more comfort in wearing darker shades of clothing and makeup, which was unique at the time. Eventually, the growing numbers of "dark punks" became known as Goths, further reawakening the spirit of the ancient Goths and the artistry of the Romantic period. In reviews and critiques, the media at the time also helped to push the label "Goth(ic)" onto post-punk bands of a darker flavor. The 1982 opening of London's first Goth club, the Batcave, helped define Goth's own individualistic subcultural identity. The movement in England spread around greater Europe, over to the Americas, and around the world.

Goths became known for taking their reaction to society to a place of sadness and reflection instead of anger and anarchy. While the punk movement could more easily be considered a counterculture or anti-culture, the Goth movement is more easily defined as a subculture (a smaller culture within the greater culture) or a *neo-tribe*.

I believe that Goths should still respect their cousin punk rockers and vice versa, understanding each other as having a similar drive for rebellion, and that both cultures should remember that originally they were nearly hand in hand. Many Goths and punks have similar outlooks on politics, corporatism, globalization, artistry, and human/animal rights. While there are variations in the ways each culture expresses its attitudes, both stand on common ground, and there is no need for anyone to look down on anyone else. We are all part of a new generation, and working for positive social change.

The most important thing to note about true Goth culture is that it is not simply a *style*, but a *lifestyle*. This is where many outsiders get confused on the topic and believe the culture to be less legitimate and solid than it actually is.

There is no set religion, attitude, or fashion that holds true for all Goths; there are no immutable criteria set in stone, and there is no Gothic mold that all adherents of dark culture must fit. What is seen as Gothic for one person may not be for another—nothing encompasses *all* Goth, and to believe so would be folly. Darkness is individualistic; it is each person's own personal experience, which is why it is so profound. Each person follows his or her own path, and Goth culture allows for absolute personal freedom, including religion or the absence thereof. There are common viewpoints many Goths share, but Goth culture is very diverse, even if it doesn't appear that way on the outside. Diversity, tolerance, and individuality add to the beauty of the culture.

There are common philosophical threads among Goths, but there is no constant singular viewpoint shared among all members. Most Goths are simply agnostic, believing in spirituality and acknowledging the possibility of the existence of God but subscribing to no religion in the end.

When Goths pursue religion and spirituality, many are drawn to earth-based and occult paths like Witchcraft and other magickal-spiritual systems. They are attracted by the nondogmatic appeal of these paths and the emphasis placed on personal development, power, and the mysterious. The Craft very well may be the path that vibes best with Goth culture, not only because of its mystic allure, but also because of its emphasis on nature, magick, and the self all being interlinked, as well as the interconnectedness of light and dark. Of course, *most* Witches are not Gothic, though many are.

Wearing giant dog collars and white contact lenses, hissing and barking at people downtown, and yelling obscenities at adversaries does not a Goth make. Wearing black bondage-strap pants and heavy, dark makeup with the intention of shocking and scaring bystanders does not earn Goth points. Nor does buying mass-manufactured "alternative" clothing from the mall, sewn by kids in Chinese and Taiwanese sweatshops, make someone "in the know" about the culture.

The fact of the matter is, Goth is much deeper than a look, and negative behavior only perpetuates the image that Goths are strange, bad, evil people who should be avoided at all costs. *Goth culture is not rooted in teenage angst.* It is rooted in alternative culture—in music, art, ideas, and fashion.

Goths are observers of life, and tend to be quite introspective. They are watchers, constantly analyzing everyone and everything. Some darksiders are very extroverted and enthusiastic, while the majority are more subdued, calm, and soft-spoken. Most are respectful and well-mannered in their speech and actions. Goths are often quiet and reserved, residing in the background and watching the dance of life go by, analyzing every bit of it. Sadness is most definitely permitted and often felt, but is not a constant or unchanged state of mind. Depression is *recognized* and becomes expressed and channeled through numerous forms of self-expression. Goths are also quite direct when speaking, usually having very genuine personalities.

Often, the quiet and contemplative demeanor is misunderstood. It doesn't mean that there are twisted thoughts going on inside their heads or that they're planning their next violent or magickal attack. There are no dangerous or threatening thoughts running through their minds; they are simply absorbing information and experience, processing it on various levels. Goths are, in fact, some of the kindest, most honest, and most open-minded people anyone will ever meet—darksiders are just a bit more willing to embrace depression and introspection.

Sometimes, Goths and other introverted people become more reserved because of society's reaction to their alternative appearance or mindset. The general public in smaller towns isn't as used to seeing a visually eccentric person as it is in large cities. Reactions will also differ in predominantly Christian areas versus liberal or artistic areas. When people are condescended to or discriminated against for their appearance, it can force them to become more withdrawn or antisocial, which can lead them to either dress up *more* or put a halt to decorating themselves altogether. Fear of oppression—even simply in the form of being stared at and judged—can be intense and saddening. It can lead to depression, insecurity, social anxiety, and various neuroses, depending on the person.

Many unfortunate things have become associated with the culture that are not, never were, and never will be part of modern Goth culture, like violent behavior, teenage delinquency, and devil worship. The idea of Goths as a sinister bunch most often comes from a place of fear. This has, unfortunately, been reflected in the media, and Goths have become the subject of blame for a number of horrid crimes in which the guilty are somehow wrongly associated with the culture. *Goths do not kill people!* They would much rather sit around thinking about killing themselves or watching actors be "killed" in B-rate horror flicks. Goth is simply not a violent culture; in fact, I would say it's the most passive of all subcultures. No wonder so many darksiders don't like to use "Goth" to describe themselves, considering the distortion the term has seen since it caught mainstream attention! In many cases, the media love to take such ideas and run with them, even if they're subjectively skewed. This, I hope, is changing with the times.

Many Goths purposefully do not refer to themselves as such. To quote my friend Ryan, "It seems that these days people are becoming less comfortable with the 'Goth' label. It has gotten to the point where bands that are obviously Goth are actively disassociating themselves from the label and claiming to be 'alternative' or industrial. They use the age-old argument of not wanting to be labeled or pinned down. This is especially interesting in that you don't ever see punk bands running away from the label 'punk!'"

I feel that the term Goth, at least for me, accurately conveys who I am. I find it to be very complimentary and inclusive of my lifestyle. I don't find it to be limiting or degrading in the least, as the term gives room for personal individuality. Many people with the Goth label or other labels like "Witch" or "Pagan" feel the same way about themselves, having an understanding that they are only pixels in the screen, representatives of a bigger picture.

To recite the most obvious observation of the scene, Goths prefer black; much comfort is found in darkness. At the same time, not all darksiders wear all black constantly; it's not a requirement by any means! Wearing dark colors is, for many, a subtle appreciation of the unknowable, the unseen. Goths are attracted to darker, more obscure things because of their mysterious and mystical qualities. Music, art, fashion, and the like are all forms of this expression. When darkness is expressed through these mediums, the internal is allowed forth on an external level for confrontation, acknowledgment, and healing. Fashion itself is one of the few *living* art forms.

Some Goths wear the color black for reasons of mourning, but what's being mourned is different for every person. For some, it's the fall of society; for others, it's the light that has died in so many people, rendering them empty and numb; others lament their childhoods. Goths know the injustices of the world and the torments of the mind—the weight of deep thoughts—and have been engulfed in sadness many times over; thus, the color black is very comforting. The color does not, however, have exclusive associations with sadness or mourning. Black means something different for everyone.

Goth is not about the way you dress. Sure, clothing is a factor, but it's ultimately a small one. Plenty of non-Goth people wear black and loads of makeup. I've noticed that a great many occultists, artists, and deep thinkers especially favor black clothing. Likewise, plenty of Goths do not "dress the part" but have inherently Goth characteristics. The clothing is but one venue of expression for the darkly inclined.

Goth culture is a way of life that is accepting and does not discriminate based on trivial issues like gender, religion, sexual preference, body size, disability, or ethnicity. Speaking of ethnicity, darksiders of non-European descent add color to a predominantly white scene and typically face no racial prejudice therein. Goth culture is not reserved solely for Caucasians in any way, shape, or form. Many Goths hold nonwhite individuals involved in the culture in high regard, as they provide physical diversification to a scene so commonly associated with only pale, ghostly-faced individuals.

Darksiders allow themselves the freedom to explore alternative practices and hold views on life that are indeed contrary to present-day mainstream ideology. If no harm is caused, and the self is being explored, then no remorse should be felt simply for being attracted to the arcane.

Goth, then, boils down to philosophy, to ideas expressed in numerous forms of art. To be Gothic is to think, feel, act, and behave as a dark artist—not because someone else told you to, and not to fit in, but because loving the darkness is simply your nature.

This philosophy embraces introspective sadness as a natural emotion and seeks to understand humanity and its motivations. Goths come from all walks of life, finding common ground with other dark artists. Goth will always remain considerably indefinable. Ambiguity is what makes it real—darkness is universal; shadow cannot be trapped.

In the end, and above all else, Goth is not something someone *does*. It is something someone *is*. We are the children of the night, and are *damn* proud of it!

Keep an eye out!

Watch for Gothism and Paganism portrayed in the media

Dark Pagan music:

Inkubus Sukkubus
Faith and the Muse
High Priestess
Unto Ashes
Qntal
Scott Helland & the Traveling
    Band of Gypsy Nomads
Wendy Rule
Faun

Goth-friendly cinema:

Gypsy 83
Beetlejuice
Preaching to the Perverted
Navy NCIS (television)
Big Wolf on Campus (television)
The Hunger
Elvira's Haunted Hills
The Crow

Pagan publications:

newWitch magazine
PanGaia
The Circle
Witchcraft and Wicca Magazine (UK)
The Cauldron (UK)

Gothic publications:

Gothic Beauty
Drop Dead Magazine
Asleep By Dawn
Propaganda
Blue Blood Magazine
The Ninth Gate
Orkus (Germany)

Pagan-friendly cinema:

The Wicker Man (the 1975 version, not the inaccurate remake!)
Practical Magic
The Craft
Book of Shadows: The Blair Witch Project II
Charmed (television)

Types of Goths

In a day and age when it's "beautiful" to be 87 pounds, wear diamonds, and sport $800 sunglasses with high-end designer socks, it becomes tempting to go against the grain. Alternative culture looks beyond image and into the reality of situations. Whereas getting facelifts and boob jobs are aesthetic desires to some, they can be seen as equally grotesque and flawed by others. There is a difference between dressing a certain way to *superficially fit in* and dressing a certain way as an artistic statement.

For people with "unusual" interests and modes of expression, there is no conforming to the rest of society; that idea was tossed out the window years ago. So instead of trying to fit in, Goths seek alternative expression as a form of separation. Why not revel in strangeness and embrace it for the rest of the world to see? Fashion is a great medium for this. It is a visible, living form of expression rich with art. Goths are fascinated by art and unconventional means of expression. It is beautiful and intriguing to appear different. The range of expression of feelings, emotions, and lifestyle through clothing as a medium can be absolutely profound. Fashion accentuates the inner self. This next section is designed to identify various visual expressions seen in the dark art community and to examine the interests, beliefs, and musical tastes that often accompany the specific styles.

One does not have to express the nature of the inner being on an external level (through clothing, makeup, and apparel) at all times. There is no strict clothing regimen to follow. Darksiders who are comfortable with all aspects of themselves and their identity have no problem with putting on some white sneakers to go for a jog, or wearing blue jeans for a hike or some tattered shorts for gardening—PVC and delicate mesh are just sometimes *not* the most ideal materials! Clothing accentuates one's personality, and the décor one immerses oneself in, as well as when and where one chooses to dress up, depend entirely upon the person and his or her own level of comfort in expression through appearance.

All alternative styles and substyles in the world have their own characteristic manner of dress. There also exist wide modifications of original styles within each grouping, nullifying generalization and cliché bit by bit. Each style within a subculture is formed largely by the individual's preference in music. Entire subcultures themselves are formed by music and its accompanying messages, and further groupings within each subculture are formed by variations of the original genre. By taking musical appreciation to an external level, styles of dress are naturally formed. Many punks prefer patches, buttons, boots, and crazy hair, all telling onlookers to question themselves and their placement in society. Many hippies like dreads, patchwork, and baggy clothes, which can visually encourage others to relax, be themselves, and find peace. Stereotypically, Goths are said to look like vampyres, Witches, zombies, ghosts, ghouls, and other dark creatures. That happens to be true a lot of the time, but in reality, each member of the scene is different.

Goths are generally believed to be somber, mopey, daydreamers, soft-spoken, serious, and depressive. While these behaviors are still very much a part of the scene's structure, all sorts of Goth and Gothesque types exist in the general darksider community. Many of these are listed in this chapter with descriptions of their personalities and interests and, of course, photographs to demonstrate their aesthetic tastes and stylistic tendencies. Some would argue that this visual appearance is self-segregating, just asking for negative reactions from outsiders. To a Goth, dressing differently—even within the greater subculture—feels only natural, a comfort that's worth potential finger-pointing. Then again, some people experience it on a level so painful that they save dress-up only for the club or at home.

Both Paganism and dark culture are focused on the internal over the external. As far as appearance, just do what feels comfortable, when it feels comfortable; there is no real Gothic "dress code," contrary to popular belief! There are, however, variations in style within the culture as a whole, which many individuals like to express.

This list touches on the better known dark subgenre varieties of Goths. I compiled this list before the 2004 release of Gothic singer/songwriter/artist/author Voltaire's comically kooky book *What Is Goth? Music, Makeup, Attitude, Apparel, Dance, and General Skullduggery* and was surprised to see so many similarities! For readers who are interested in further exploring these subdivisions and more, I recommend Voltaire's book without hesitation. For readers who are interested in understanding more about the Gothic phenomenon and its philosophies, I recommend both the aforementioned and the underground *The Autumn Cemetery Text*, written by a man called September. This seems to be available only on the Internet, and remains one of the deepest and most esoteric descriptions of dark culture I have ever encountered.

Some Goths feel comfortable adhering to a particular Gothic subtype, finding the music, art, and fashion perfectly appealing. Some strive not to be a part of any of these labels, while others are comfortable journeying between these subtypes based on how they feel at a particular moment in time. Most darksiders are drawn to a variety of Goth and Gothesque music, so many naturally favor experimentation among various darkly expressions.

More and more minor Gothic subgenres are surfacing on a regular basis, including the lesser known GypsyGoths, TribalGoths, EmoGoths, PirateGoths, HippieGoths, CowboyGoths, and "net.goths." The list is constantly expanding! I wonder if I could create a new Gothic subgenre if I wore a black vinyl space suit to a club and created a "dark moonwalk" dance. Perhaps it would be called the SpaceGoth or, more eloquently, CelestialGoth. You never know…

It's also interesting to note that in Europe, the birthplace of Goth culture, darksiders do not distinguish one another categorically as much their American counterparts do, focusing more on the similarities among members of the scene rather than the differences, however subtle.

The most prominent division among Goths is between "oldschoolers" (also called ElderGoths) and "newschoolers" (also called BabyBats or KinderGoths). Most newschoolers are teenagers. They are individuals who haven't been involved in Goth culture for an extended period of time and know little about it. They begin by experimenting in the scene and hanging out with more experienced Goths and darklings until they become more knowledgeable about Goth culture and what it represents. BabyBats are not poseurs per se, but they initially may have skewed ideas as to what the scene really is. This can be remedied with research and actual involvement with those who understand Goth culture, which works in turn to combat possible conformist pressure from school, parents, religion, and peers. If the internalization is not heartfelt, then the person may ditch dark culture altogether to get involved in something entirely different, letting that interest pass. It's true that teens are the largest age group attracted to Goth culture, because they are in need of some sort of grounding for the extreme amount of energy they have at that point in their lives. The Goth subculture provides an outlet for emotional intensity and a safe meeting ground for people of similar viewpoints and experience. For some teens, Goth culture is a fleeting interest. For others, they've found their place in a beautiful and serene culture that lets them be who they are for many years to come.

As a person of dark alternative persuasion ages, his or her "Gothiness" evolves. Such is the case with oldschoolers, those who have been involved in dark culture for a long period of time. Their state of mind, having been expressed externally through fashion and such, changes. Fashion begins to take a back seat to other forms of art and expression over the course of time. Goth aesthetics, having developed as an expression of the internal, tend to recede, lessening the need for so much visual stylistic flare. Goths allow their expression to internalize naturally over time as their experiences and philosophies evolve, and thus generally are content with their evolution of lifestyle. They probably will dress up now and again, but after a certain point in time, the need to decorate the body on a regular basis tends to wane. After all, expression is all about being comfortable and doing what feels right at any given point in time.

"Key to the Underworld" by OakRaven Photography. Model: Anna.

Babydolls

Babydolls prefer lots of makeup and big hair, and are sometimes seen cuddling dolls and sporting a pouty expression. Most wear comfortable clothing and short skirts. Lace and velvet often are preferred materials to accentuate this cute look, as are any childhood accessories like dolls and stuffed animals. Many people associate innocence with sexiness, and this more often than not holds true for the Babydoll.

Babydoll style and behavior are a sort of regression to a childhood mentality—not in a degrading or negative sense, but as an embracing of a portion of the self, the young self, that so many hide from or neglect to recognize. One may embrace this style to spiritually deal with and heal childhood trauma, or to simply play, indulging in youthfulness.

To have lightheartedness, playfulness, and humility at the same time as "grown-up" seriousness is to find a balance between two sides of life, integrating two elements into one. This brings to mind a quote from the *Tao Te Ching*: "The wise man, when abroad, impartial to the world, does not divide or judge… For wise men hear and see as little children do." This, in turn, reminds me of the Fool card of the Tarot, the first and highest card of them all.

Musical Tastes: *Switchblade Symphony, The Birthday Massacre, Emilie Autumn,* etc.

Nvwoti Atsasgili revels in infantilism by portraying the Babydoll style.

Jason doesn't need loads of makeup, vinyl, or spiked hair to live a Gothic lifestyle.

CasualGoths

Many CasualGoths are oldschoolers. They have been around through changes in music and fashion and tend to stick to the plain 'n' simple. Their aesthetic presentation isn't too "loud," like so many modern Goth styles, but remains considerably dark nonetheless. The guys tend to prefer basic black and have a fondness for band T-shirts and black jeans. The girls like similar clothes but might add a lacy glove, plain skirt, or poet's cap to the ensemble. With CasualGoths, neither males nor females are excessive with makeup and may choose to wear none at all, or simply just paint their fingernails.

CasualGoths embrace the darkness within and don't need to be boisterous about their personality. In the end, they usually know more about the subculture than do more eccentric Goths, having been exposed to the culture's evolution for a number of years. Simply wearing dark colors is enough of an expression to feel comfortable and subtly show the world their taste. They may dress up a bit more to go to a club, but tend to keep it minimal on a daily basis. CasualGoths demonstrate something very important: there is much more to dark culture than just an extreme style.

Musical Tastes: Depends entirely on the person.

CorporateGoths

CorporateGoths, also shortened to CorpGoths, must tone down their eccentric wardrobe for work. While it's true that Goths look fabulous, practicality cannot be forgotten! Sometimes it's necessary to alter one's appearance for another setting such as work, and there's nothing wrong with this. Some people have no choice but to work a nine-to-five job just to get by.

Karly wears a suit 'n' tie but still shows signs of a darker persuasion.

Male CorpGoths often wear a dress shirt and tie and mostly stick to as much basic black clothing as possible in order to feel comfortable. Women often wear the same but may add a skirt or dress shirt depending on preference. Some Goths don't mind visually conforming when need be, though it's undoubtedly detested to some degree internally. Personally, I see it as necessary partial suppression to get by in a world of conformity. Besides, it allows the person more time to build up energy to be expressed at a later time through the arts—dressing up to hit the clubs, venturing to a café, adorning oneself for the cemetery, or having a photo shoot.

Many CorpGoths incorporate subtly dark décor into their office space. Those with occult interests may also throw in some esoteric goodies if at all possible, or enchant their workspace as a sacred environment. Even the most meaningful water altar can be disguised as a simple bottle of spring water with a crystal in it!

The CorpGoth look is by no means restricted to the office space and is very much a nightclub staple. Even the band Covenant has pushed the CorpGoth look over the years, and the website www.corporategoth.net is becoming increasingly popular.

Musical Tastes: Depends entirely on the person.

Shannon dreams in digital.

CyberGoths

A relatively new addition to the school of Goth, the Cyber look is making its way into hearts and onto dance floors. CyberGoths, like Gravers, strongly identify with pulsing electronic music with Gothic vocals and overtones, including EBM (electronic body music), synthpop, futurepop, and powernoise.

CyberGoths are characterized by their futuristic look, complete with synthetic materials such as plastic, vinyl, and molded metal. They often are called NeoGoths because of their unique cyborg-esque fashion interests. Hair accessories are a must for the CyberKid, including big goggles (always worn on the head) and gigantic synthetic hair extensions. False hair extensions can be made of yarn, ribbon, vinyl, plastic tubing, rubber, metal piping, hardware, and other random materials to complete the digital style. No CyberGoth is complete without gigantic "stompy" platform boots and the optional toy ray gun. Some are even more anachronistic in that they incorporate old Renaissance and Victorian styles into their much-loved cyber wear.

CyberGoths force thoughtful viewers to question what's next for the human race in terms of evolutionary progression, both stylistically and psychologically.

Musical Tastes: *Combichrist, Neuroticfish, Ayria, Lights of Euphoria, Assemblage 23, Apoptygma Berzerk, VNV Nation, Icon of Coil, Imperative Reaction, Covenant, And One, Rotersand, Angels & Agony, Pride & Fall, Butterfly Messiah, Razed in Black, Funker Vogt, NamNam-Bulu, etc.*

Deathrockers

Ah yes, the dark punks and Deathrockers! These stylin' members of dark culture are the "Grimly Fiendishes" of the post-punk deathrock genre, and love to show it off. Deathrockers are not just punk, and not just Goth. They represent the middle ground between the two cousin genres. Their music and "fresh out of the coffin" look are intense, fun, and extravagant.

Deathrockers are characterized by layered clothing, ripped up fishnets, metal wear, patches, and an almost entirely DIY (do it yourself) wardrobe. They like to sew and create their own unique clothing and accessorize with any ookie-spooky props available. Generally, the makeup is extremely pale, with darkened eyes, lips, and cheeks, and is beautifully theatric—definitely a strange "corpsepaint" nod to old B-movie zombie horror flicks. They understand Goth culture *very* well and have no qualms about amplifying their love of dark art through style, even if it means looking ghoulish, exaggerated, and even humorously "evil."

Quite often, they sport the "deathhawk" hairstyle. The deathhawk is different from the Mohawk in that it's wider, less formed or gelled, and usually bigger and wilder than the Mo'. Fans of deathrock also like to shave portions of their head whenever possible, to accentuate the rest of the hair. This head-shaving draws, perhaps unconsciously, on tribal traditions, in which shaving the head was an initiatory way to separate the individual from much of society in a rite of passage.

Deathrockers like to get fancied up before getting liquored up at the club. The crossover of Goth and punk means they have a foot in both subcultural worlds: one rooted in introspection and one rooted in extroversion.

Musical Tastes: *Christian Death, 45 Grave, Specimen, Sex Gang Children, Tragic Black, Alien Sex Fiend, Skeletal Family, Cinema Strange, Scarlet's Remains, The Damned, All Gone Dead,* etc.

Ponyboy and RazorCandi: Goth, punk, or too fabulous for definition?

Wicked Mina embraces the subtle realms with the FaerieGoth style.

FaerieGoths

FaerieGoths are attracted to all things fae. They like to adorn themselves with décor characteristic of the realms of Faerie, like wings, glitter, and dark yet colorful clothing. Dressing in this way allows the FaerieGoth to maintain the energy of the ethereal planes alongside physical existence.

Because of their historical and metaphysical leanings, FaerieGoths often are drawn to Paganism. Paths that incorporate the mythology of the "wee folk" into their worldviews are of extreme interest to the FaerieGoth, for obvious reasons. FaerieGoths often frequent the public Pagan scene as well; certainly at least one can be spotted at any large Pagan festival—or was that just a flash of light in the periphery?

Musical Tastes: *The Mediæval Bæbes, Faun, Faith and the Muse, Loreena McKennitt, Collide, High Priestess, Tori Amos, Wendy Rule, Stevie Nicks,* etc.

Fetishists

Another aspect of dark culture that often gets intertwined with the greater Goth scene is the fetish and BDSM community. Every member of the fetish or bondage subculture is unique, having his or her own individual interests and sensual persuasions. Though the two are separate subcultures, many fetishists are drawn to Goth culture, finding it to be the only greater community that has the ability to integrate fetishistic tendencies both stylistically and philosophically.

Kitty makes us "learn the ropes" by demonstrating voluntary submission.

The fashion that accompanies interest in the fetish lifestyle varies for each person. Though some people carry the style into other aspects of their lives, most dress up in fetish wear only with their partner(s) in the comfort of their own home. For some, specific fetishes can be expressed through everyday clothing. For example, the Babydoll and vampyre looks can be considered fetishistic, even if they don't necessarily have sexual leanings. Others express their interest in fetishism through alternative clothing like vinyl, which is one of the most-used materials in fetish play, or other materials directly expressing their personal interests. I've seen a dominatrix wearing heels and carrying a whip for everyday activities; the expression of fetishism certainly is not restricted to the bedroom! Alternative sexual practices have long been taboo. This very misunderstood practice has gotten about as much negative publicity as Witchcraft, and, perhaps for that very reason, interest in alternative sexuality is increasing every day. Nearly all people involved in alternative sexuality report spiritual benefit from the sensual art forms that make up its practices.

Musical Tastes: *Lords of Acid, Bio-Tek, Die Form, The Genitorturers, Leæther Strip,* etc.

Covered in stardust, Diana may very well be one of the glamorous Spiders from Mars!

GlamGoths

Shortly before the time that punk was beginning to develop as a musical genre, rock 'n' roll was splintering into numerous factions, including glam rock. Artists like David Bowie, T-Rex, Roxy Music, New York Dolls, Johnny Thunders, and Iggy Pop showed the world that visual appearance can—and even *should*—accompany the music. Numerous artists of the glam rock niche dressed up with feather boas, heavy makeup, shiny synthetic materials, and loads of glitter—something that has carried over to this very day and, for aesthetic and musical reasons, has made its way into dark culture.

GlamGoths are the epitome of *fabulousness*. Their style reflects both their musical interests and their belief that looking glamorous is a very important part of life! GlamGoths integrate their affinity for Goth music with its punk and glam predecessors. A great number of modern Goth bands have been strongly influenced by glam bands. This fusion is now visually portrayed with extravagant clothing, which allows a person to find a balance between the colorful and the dark.

Musical Tastes: *David Bowie, Iggy Pop, The Voluptuous Horror of Karen Black*, etc.

Gothabillys

Gothabillys are fans of Goth music as well as the sub-genre of rockabilly called *psychobilly*, characterized by its blended influence of punk with traditional rockabilly style, with the addition of anarchistic and horror themes, usually portrayed in a fun and humorous light.

For men, the psychobilly clothing style consists of button-up lounge shirts, "bowling" shirts, and, of course, '50s-pin-up-girl shirts. Women also wear similar tops with the addition of frilly dresses and shirts, fancy shoes, and animal prints. Many modern rockabilly and Gothabilly clothes are printed with classic-looking logos complete with flames, dice, hot rods, gas pumps, kitty cats, skulls, and stars. Accessories include wallets with heavy chains, belt buckles, and bracelets. Rockabillys, psychobillys, and Gothabillys are also *big* fans of tattoos and fancy hair like the fluffed quiff coiffure.

To understand the Gothabilly style, take the aforementioned descriptions and add a dash of darkness. Gothabillys add makeup to the ensemble and stick to darker shades of clothing—like black!

Musical Tastes: *Nekromantix, The Cramps, Tiger Army, Horrorpops, Demented Are Go, The Coffinshakers, The Quakes, Koffin Kats,* etc.

Logan and Sandi strike a pose that seriously rocks our socks!

Gothic Lolitas

An international cousin of the Babydoll, the Gothic Lolita style is cute and girly but is not necessarily sexual. The word *Lolita* in Japanese culture is not synonymous with the common perception of the word in English. Unfortunately, the word Lolita (sometimes shortened to *Loli*) has gained negative associations, mostly through the pornography industry, referring to a sexually promiscuous and manipulative young female.

To combat the negative stereotypes, some members of the Lolita fashion community refer to their style simply as EGL (elegant Gothic Lolita) or another name referencing a similarly innocent look. Mana, from the dark Japanese rock (J-Rock) band Malice Mizer, created the EGL fashion with his clothing line Moi-même-Moitié. The EGL fashion and lifestyle gained momentum when Malice Mizer went public in the late '90s. Mana is now the lead guitar player in Moi dix Mois, whose members also embrace elegant Japanese Gothic styles; he also promotes EGL through his shop, Moi-même-Moitié, in Tokyo. The Lolita lifestyle is separate from the Gothic scene, though its variations present many overlapping qualities.

Some Lolitas lean more toward Victorian Lolita clothing, while others like more cyber and fetish wear, depending on what the style personally means to them. In Japan, there are even subsections of the subgenre, including Kurt (Black Lolita), Ama (Sweet Lolita), and Cos (Costumed Lolita). A further stylistic breakdown is this: Regular (traditional) Lolitas wear light, childlike colors and carry teddy bears, parasols, and stuffed animals, looking very much like porcelain Victorian dollies. Gothic Lolitas usually wear black or red with frills and lace, looking both

Kuro Bara shows her affinity for the Gothic Lolita lifestyle.

dark and innocent. They like black parasols, dainty top hats, and spooky-looking handbags. Elegant Gothic Lolitas have the same style, yet the dresses are longer and less skin is exposed. EGLs may also incorporate a greater amount of ribbons, frills, and lace. They look cutesy and girly, but from what I hear, they will rip apart your soul if you cross them!

Country (or Sweet) Lolitas prefer farm prints and the colors brown, red, and blue, and accessorize with straw hats or similar items, doing away with excessive makeup. Fruit (or Candy) Lolitas wear bright colors and rainbow accessories. Wa Lolitas wear poofed-out kimonos and traditional Japanese wear with a twist. Some refer to themselves as neo-Geishas, exhibiting stylistic characteristics of Japanese dancers balanced with vinyl, bondage straps, or caked-on makeup. Cosplay (costume playing) Lolitas dress like their favorite animé characters or musical idols. Punk Lolitas wear Lolita clothing with hints of punk and like to sew their own clothing as much as other Lolis. Elegant Gothic Aristocrats (EGAs) are separate from Lolitas, doing away with the frills and lace in favor of longer, straight dresses for women and Victorian-era clothing for men (also called Kodona), though both genders wear both male and female clothing.

While the Lolita styles are playful and childlike, the flip side is that some Japanese youths get jaded by it, wrapped up in the wonderland of it all, losing touch with reality through regressive escapism. Some take on alternative names, behaviors, and personalities to separate this part of themselves from their ordinary selves. There is often a thin borderline between play and consumption. With self-awareness, this fashion and exploration of the many sides of the self can be beneficial and fun.

It should be noted that Lolis almost exclusively *create* their own clothing by purchasing raw materials and sewing their outfits based on historical accuracy and personal flair. Because of the rising popularity of the Japanese Loli, Yankee, J-Rock, Cosplay, and Harajuku street styles, some non-Asian people have begun to see the style as only a fashion trend, having no problem with wearing only premade "Lolita" clothing instead of investing time, research, and creative effort into their chosen styles. This, above all things, upsets dedicated Lolita lifestylers, who shudder to think that their lifestyle and fashion could become corporatized.

Musical Tastes: *Malice Mizer, Moi dix Mois, Dir en Grey, D'espairsRay, Inugami Circus Dan, Cali≠Gari, X Japan, Buck-Tick, Gackt, Onmyo-Za, Psycho le Cému, Schwarz Stein, Deathgaze, Alice Nine, Kagerou,* etc.

The author sweeps the dance floor to some dark electro-beats, challenging Voltaire's statement that "fangs and glowsticks are never a good combination."

Gravers

Graver is a combination of the words *Goth* and *raver*. Gravers are basically dark candy ravers: big fans of electronic music and the healing ecstasy that comes about from that particular musical expression—and by *ecstasy* I mean "happiness"!

Gravers can be found both at Goth clubs and at raves. Because much of the rave scene has become equated with drug use and nothing else, laws have been passed and rave culture is now almost completely restricted to regular nightclubs and underground parties, at least in America. This is unfortunate for a scene rooted in the transcendental effects of music, but every positive subculture eventually attracts its opposite to one degree or another.

Gravers often are also CyberGoths but may not associate themselves with that title. Gravers can be seen with glowsticks, shiny plastic bracelets, big platform boots, vinyl clothes, intricate make-up, black visors, and even wide-legged "fat pants." Some, like their CyberGoth kin, like goggles and synthetic hair. They love to dance to any deep beat and may have unique dance moves synchronized to booming technological sounds. While they are still club kids, their musical taste isn't limited to dance-electronic genres (like progressive trance, psytrance, breaks, house, drum 'n' bass, etc.). It very much enters the realm of electro-industrial, powernoise, futurepop, and EBM, which tend to be the Graver's music of choice.

Musical Tastes: See CyberGoth musical tastes, as the two often overlap.

GutterGoths

GutterGoth style sprang out of the grunge and punk rock scene of the '80s. Also called TrashyGoths or GrungeGoths, GutterGoths have the ability to make a wardrobe out of material that anyone else would throw away. They are natural artists skilled in sewing and safety-pinning, who create totally unique fashions with a wide variety of materials. The style includes ripped fishnets, buckled boots, and shirts complete with endless rips, tears, re-pinning, and re-sewing. The Gutter-Goth fashion is comparable to a darker version of the gutterpunk style that frequents bars and street corners worldwide. It would be stereotypical to think that all "gutter" stylists are homeless, but it remains true that many indeed are, be it by choice or circumstance.

Who says that all darksiders have to look elegant? Countless fashionable items can be created upon a single trip to Goodwill or any secondhand clothing shop. GutterGoths like makeup as much as the rest; even the sloppiest-looking eyeshadow smear takes twenty minutes to perfect. It should also be said that GutterGoths' number one haunt is the cemetery!

Musical Tastes: Oldschool dark punk, deathrock, and grunge.

RazorCandi shows us that trashiness and fabulousness can mix quite nicely.

Sherri and Eddie give us the
MetalGoth scorn-of-death!

MetalGoths

Simply put, MetalGoths are people who are fans of
both Goth and metal music. MetalGoths' style shows
off this affinity, complete with metallic jewelry, spiked
collars, studded bracelets, and metal band T-shirts,
with images that range anywhere from classic heavy
metal to modern death or black metal. The amount of
makeup that each person wears is a personal preference, though there is definitely a leaning toward the
thick and heavy.

Most metalheads (fans of metal) are not Goth, and
this is where much confusion lies between the two
subcultures. Outsiders often confuse the "metal look"
with the Goth look. Metal is a musical genre of its
own, though many people are attracted to Goth music at the same time, and this is where the MetalGoth
comes into play.

Whereas metal provides a vigorous, loud sound expressing inner angst and the cries of the heart, Goth
music balances this with mournful, emotive tones,
calling the listener to look within before looking without. MetalGoths are very balanced, assuming they are
dedicated to both musical genres simultaneously and
understand the significance of each. Darksider culture
allows for a lot of variation and individual taste, which
is the reason that metal is but one of many additional
genres integrating itself with the classic sounds of traditional Goth.

Musical Tastes: *Black Sabbath, Tristania, Dimmu
Borgir, Type O Negative, Jucifer, Cradle of Filth, Therion,
URN, Within Temptation, Paradise Lost, Nightwish, Drain
STH, Hanzel Und Gretyl, Jack Off Jill, Otep, Xandria, La-
cuna Coil, Marilyn Manson, BlessidDoom, My Ruin,* etc.

MopeyGoths

Woe is the MopeyGoth, the most lugubrious of them all! Most BabyBats start out as MopeyGoths, being drawn to the culture for its embrace of sadness and the darker emotions. MopeyGoths are crestfallen, perceiving all life as a dismal pool of blackness. They long to be held and to be told that it's okay to cry, weep, and break down. Their mannerisms include looking down when being spoken to, mumbling, fiddling with their long hair, and spending hours alone in drifting thought. They are discontent with society, themselves, and everyone around them, knowing not where "the cure" for such sorrow lies. They choose to devote their time and energy to only select people, hoping that they won't be stabbed in the back as they may have been in the past. They seek to harm no one and pray for the day that others will pay them the same respect.

Raven mournfully reflects upon his shadow. Forlorn!

While some MopeyGoths actually do feel these emotions, some fake them just the same. In youth, it sometimes seems cool to be sad and misanthropic. MopeyGoths are readily accepted but tend to be the stereotypical Goth type that gets the most exposure to the mainstream. I fully believe that every Goth is a MopeyGoth somewhere deep inside. They represent a very real aspect of the scene, which is feelings of gloom, sadness, and uncertainty.

The accompanying style of dress is often casual and never excludes black. A trench coat is a MopeyGoth necessity, to be sure. Accessories are minimal but often include a plentiful amount of silver and pewter jewelry, band T-shirts, skirts, thick black eyeliner, and, of course, veils for the ladies.

Some people become drawn to the sadder aspects of Goth and revel in them for a while. MopeyGoths eventually begin to evolve in their subculture as the extreme melancholy is replaced with a more diversified outlook on life and the scene in general.

Musical Tastes: *The Cure, The Cure,* and *The Cure.*

Russ pokes fun at the kids by portraying a Mansonite.

NotGoths

NotGoth is a term for people who believe themselves to be dark and spooky but have no real knowledge of the subculture. Simply stated, they think they understand dark culture, but have probably never heard real Goth music in their lives! These are the types who give Goth a bad public image and are full of more rage and teenage angst than sadness. They are the "loudest" of the bunch, screaming for attention in every possible way. They usually are young and trying to find themselves, but rather than looking within, they express their social dissatisfaction externally, often without thinking things through. They sometimes are what can be called WangstyGoths, referring to the "whiny, sad, and angst-ridden" type who, instead of being Goths, are actually just rebellious (and often spoiled) teenagers. WangstyGoths are characteristically self-absorbed and will disrespect their parents, their elders, and the law, even if these authorities actually *do* have good intentions. They generally are fans of ultragory horror flicks and pretend to be morbidly sinister by trivializing violence and suicide. Sadly, the general public frequently labels these individuals "Goth," pinning negative associations on anyone who is truly involved in the subculture. People dedicated to and knowledgeable about alternative culture call them "poseurs." So why are NotGoths on this list? As a fair warning!

Let's start with the Mansonite. The word refers to someone who is obsessed with Marilyn Manson. While a handful of Manson fans are Goth, and a handful of Goths are Manson fans, most are not. Marilyn

Manson plays metal music rather than Goth music, though a few of the songs have characteristically Goth lyrics. Mansonites are not necessarily bad, but they give Goth a warped image when outsiders label them as such. For most Mansonites, Goth is only a phase, and their fashion and outlook on life change alongside Marilyn Manson's.

Another group of people, who usually overlap with the former, are called NINnies. They are the obsessive fans of Nine Inch Nails (NIN) who are in love with Trent Reznor's industrial-esque music and devilishly good looks. While the Mansonite style can be called pseudo-Goth, the NINnie style can be called pseudo-industrial. NINnies usually aren't as rabid or overtly angry as Mansonites, but often have just as skewed a view of Goth culture. Then again, some NINnies actually *are* involved in the Goth-industrial culture and just happen to like Nine Inch Nails quite a bit!

Last on this three-part list is the MallGoth. MallGoths are young in age, spending the majority of their time after school at the mall. They are not, however, ordinary mallrats. They are addicted to certain "alternative" stores in the mall, wearing Goth like a fashion accessory. MallGoths dress differently to seem "in the know," when, in actuality, they have no clue what Goth culture really is. To them, Goth is a fashion statement and nothing more. When one person wears a studded bracelet or fishnet shirt to school, others tend to copycat in hordes! To the dismay of many, they call themselves "Goth" without liking music aside from nu-metal bands like Slipknot, Korn, ICP, and Mudvayne—in other words, bands that are not Goth in the least! They may, however, throw around some band names like "Bow's House," "Sushi and the Banshees," and "Christine's Death"!

If exposed to the right influences and given accurate advice on the reality of dark culture, so-called NotGoths *can* eventually become actual members of the scene should their effort be from the heart.

Musical Tastes: See above.

PerkyGoths

PerkyGoths are tired of the old Goth cliché of gloom and doom. They prove that, yes, Goths do have facial muscles and are perfectly comfortable smiling and feeling good about life! They are akin to Gravers and CyberGoths and usually consider themselves a member of one of these two subgenres as well. PerkyGoths can also be called Rainbow-Goths, GlitterGoths, or even CandyGoths, depending on their specific style and artistic/musical taste. Members of the multifold PerkyGoth subgenres prefer "sparklies" over "darklies."

PerkyGoths, or "PerkyGoffs!," often create their style from a combination of Goth culture and their personal tastes, like glitter, rainbows, sparkles, and neon makeup. Some are into animé or performance art and incorporate into their wardrobes the beauty they see in these forms of expression. Their speech is usually colorful and enthusiastic, such as "Ooh, ooh, I really really likies sparklies and fabulousness colorfulness! Yay, yay, yay! Woot!"

PerkyGoths do a lot more for the Goth scene than they are given credit for. They have the ability to get people who take life too seriously to lighten up...their joyous smiles are indeed contagious! If you are feeling forlorn in a club and someone runs up to give you a bouncy, happy hug at random, know that you've just been blessed by a Perky! While the more conservative ÜberGoths consider Perky-Goths to be anything but Gothic, people in the scene who understand the necessity of positive emotions believe them to play an important and even emotionally spiritual role.

Musical Tastes: *Voltaire, Alice in Videoland, Placebo, Goldfrapp, Shiny Toy Guns, The Faint, Ladytron, Mindless Self Indulgence,* anything upbeat and optimistic.

Miss Rip Redrum "perks" our interest!

Rivetheads

Rivetheads, or "rivets," are fans of both industrial and Goth music. Visually, they are fans of leather, pleather, chains, hardware, and other wonderfully strange materials of the sort.

Timo likes all things grindy, clanky, noisy, and metallic.

Industrial music is Goth music's close cousin. The two genres have always overlapped, and each style includes elements of the other. Industrial music is said to be the antithesis of the hippie culture's "peace and love" mentality. Originally, industrial music spoke to modern people who were surrounded by the concrete jungle. Bands like Throbbing Gristle, NON, Coil, Einstürzende Neubauten, Cabaret Voltaire, and Clock DVA were main influences for the rise of industrial culture in Europe. Goth and industrial are separate movements, though the Goth and industrial subcultures have merged to a great degree at this point, largely due to the influence of the band Skinny Puppy in the 80s. Whereas Goth is more melancholy, spooky, and emotional, industrial is more angry, experimental, and noisy. Both have branched into numerous subgenres, many of which now flirt with one another's vibes. Modern industrial music subgenres and fusion-genres include EBM, futurepop, powernoise, aggrotech (terror-EBM), coldwave, elektro, dark-electro, and industrial-metal. Yes, it can be quite confusing.

The "rivet" in the rivethead title comes from the metal bolts of the same name, which are used in the industrial construction of architecture. The "head" in rivethead just means "fan." Rivetheads prefer army surplus military garb, like flight jackets, pins, patches, and combat boots. Though rivets love angry German electronics, they are never to be equated with or related to Nazism.

Musical Tastes: *Skinny Puppy, Nitzer Ebb, Front 242, :wumpscut:, Frontline Assembly, My Life with the Thrill Kill Kult, E-Craft, Amduscia, Nine Inch Nails, Evils Toy, Grendel, Leæther Strip, Hocico, Xyla, Zombie Girl, Ministry, Psyclon Nine, Tactical Sekt, Experiment Haywire, Velvet Acid Christ, Mentallo and the Fixer, yelworC, X-Marks the Pedwalk, SPK, Decoded Feedback, Fractured, Soman, Distorted Memory, Reaper, The Us Electric, Aslan Faction,* etc.

RomantiGoths

Analisa was born in the sixteenth century.

Perhaps the best known of all the types, the RomantiGoth is the most "Gothique" of the bunch. RomantiGoths can also be called Renaissance-Goths, preferring a pre-Victorian style and attitude. Some types of RomantiGoths are also often referred to as EtherGoths. They have the demeanor of a mystical ghost or a dreary somnambulist, recognizable by their porcelain skin, thick makeup, and radiant beauty.

RomantiGoth clothing is dark and mystical. Parasols, hoop skirts, large dresses, button-up frocks, and lace are all smiled upon fondly. Styled hair, flowing shawls, and Gothic cross jewelry pieces are always a plus! Napoleon said, "The corset is the murderer of the human race." If this is to be believed, then RomantiGoths are proud to be the first to perish!

RomantiGoths tend to take life seriously (well, usually) and are always searching for love and emotional kinship among peers. They are poets, artists, and musicians, and love to put their feelings into form. They enjoy walking in the rain and visiting cemeteries for midnight strolls, and quite often can be caught reading a book, listening to darkwave/ethereal tunes, writing poetry, or sipping tea at a local café. Members of this Goth type are particularly fond of Gothic architecture and literature, and definitely do a great job of evoking the style of the Gothic Renaissance movement.

Pre-Raphaelite avant-garde painters and writers undoubtedly have some influence on RomantiGoth style and ideology as well.

RomantiGoths are into all things lovely and the "greyscale" aesthetic. Many have a French or English accent regardless of whether they actually were born in Europe! Many RomantiGoths frequent Renaissance fairs, reveling in nostalgic European history. They may ponder whether they have lived past lives in Europe and feel a kinship with people of eras past.

Musical Tastes: *Rasputina, Dead Can Dance, Andalusia, Cocteau Twins, Paul Mercer, Black Tape for a Blue Girl, Unto Ashes, Raison d'être, Delerium, Dream Aria, Evanescence, Sigur Rós,* etc.

SkimpyGoths

SkimpyGoths show a lot more skin than your every-day black-clad individual. They are big fans of lingerie, adoring the beauty of a sensual appearance. One misunderstanding about ladies who dress this way is the presumption that they are overtly sexual. Some are, yes, but most SkimpyGoths embrace *sensuality* instead of promiscuity. They are akin to the RomantiGoths, just with fewer clothes. Their attitudes are sharp and exotic. They know their bodies, understanding the exquisite art of eroticism as an accent to the corporeal.

Some so-called SkimpyGoths like to wear dark '50s pin-up-girl-style clothing, adoring the fashions demonstrated by Bettie Page and her taboo fetish girls. Wear includes high heels, corsets, stockings, and short skirts. The amount of clothing each lady sports is dependent entirely on personal choice, and is usually based on her mood at any given time.

Musical Tastes: Depends entirely on the person.

Jamie the Metal Goddess shows us that sometimes "nothing" is everything!

SophistiGoths

Also known as IntellectualGoths, SophistiGoths are commonplace in the Goth world. Because so much of dark culture is based in art, it's only natural that many darksiders live their lives devoted to the art of creation. This includes writing, reading, painting, sketching, sculpting, and photographing, to name but a few venues of expression. Numerous artists are drawn to the color black, regardless of whether or not they identify with the "Gothic" label. It makes sense that artists, as creators, are drawn to the darker shades. Black represents the darkness, the blank slate from which all things spring forth into creation.

Karen contemplates all things gloomy and macabre.

As a result of deep thinking, study, and examination of the world around them, SophistiGoths see life in a way that many do not. These folks are partial to knowledge, including the workings of the mind, pondering human nature and all of its attributes. It makes sense that most SophistiGoths are deep, spiritual thinkers.

Many Goths of sophisticated leanings are highly educated, often having done specialized study of ancient or classical world histories. Understanding and identifying with prior periods in history determines much of the Sophisti Goth's tastes. As a downside, some take their knowledge into the realm of self-assurance and even arrogance, earning some members of this "class" more degrading titles like AristoGoth or RichGoth. This touches on the ÜberGoth category discussed later in this chapter.

Everyone has an intellectual side. The SophistiGoth is but an embodiment of the artistic side of Goth culture—which is a *huge* part of the culture! To create is to manifest and induce change, and is one of the most important aspects of any subcultural movement. If it weren't for the deep thinkers and philosophers, paths like our own would never come to fruition in the first place.

Musical Tastes: Anything with deep emotion and intellect.

Gashley prefers spiderwebs, coffins, bats, and pointy shoes.

TraditionalGoths

Also called ClassicGoth or TradGoth, this style developed as another step in Gothic expressionism and served to identify Goth as its own individual movement: separate, but not too distant, from its original punk roots. Spiked hair, leather jackets, and studded collars took a backseat to lace, flowing clothes, capes, and coats for those delving into Gothic uniqueness, wishing to define themselves as separate from their punk brethren. In TraditionalGoth, the women tend to take on a more Morticia Addams/Lily Munster appearance...and the guys aren't too far behind!

Apropos to their style, TradGoths are mainly into early Goth music. Many of the artists below and others of similar ilk can be called the "staples" of Goth music because they helped define Goth rock as a genre of its own.

TradGoth is similar to CasualGoth, just with a bit more ornamentation. The TradGoth style draws on the earlier apparel of artists belonging to avant-garde art movements, who had already found comfort in being clad in black. Taking that look another step, TradGoths added Halloween accessories to the mix. The fashions and musical interests associated with TraditionalGoths are called *traditional* because, other than the basic black clothing, they were virtually unknown until Goth developed into a subculture of its own.

Musical Tastes: *Bauhaus, Gary Numan, Souxsie and the Banshees, The Sisters of Mercy, Love and Rockets, Mephisto Walz, The March Violets, Corpus Delicti, Depeche Mode, Ikon, Fields of the Nephilim, Tones on Tail, Joy Division, Rosetta Stone, Nosferatu,* etc.

ÜberGoths

The terms ÜberGoth and UltraGoth refer to those who believe themselves to be quite "hardcore" in the Goth movement. The term is more humorously deprecating than an actual statement about the individual's hierarchical Goth role. It's usually used as a silly insult to refer to people who take themselves, and life, a bit too seriously. No one actually refers to themselves as an ÜberGoth, lest it be in jest. Goths often call themselves or each other *über*, a German word meaning "super" or "ultimate," if they're acting highly melodramatic or stereotypically "Goth." Luckily, most Goths have a tendency to poke fun at themselves! The term is always used humorously, and is additionally used to refer to those unfortunate members of the scene who see themselves as being superior and "Gother than thou." This mentality is condescending to others involved in the scene, and is reflected by their constantly conde-

Anna mockingly teaches us how to be ÜberGothique!

scending attitude. Said ÜberGoths gossip, insult, manipulate, and belittle others in the subculture. They also tend to talk behind other people's backs (usually insulting their clothing), recite obscure band names to give themselves validity, and pay little attention to those they deem unworthy of their time. Paradoxically, their ÜberGothiness is solidified by the fact that the last thing they would want to do is label themselves as Gothic, even though they wear black, wear dark makeup, go to Goth clubs, and listen to Goth music. However, they tend to be all about the "product" rather than the practice, the image over the being.

Sadly, ÜberGoths play a big role in the potential disintegration of Goth as a positive and accepting outlet for self-expression. Many have been involved in the scene for so many years that the original reason they were drawn to it in the first place is lost and convoluted because of a superiority complex.

Musical Tastes: Whatever is popular in the underground, as to seem more "in the know."

Eden appropriately bears her fangs.

Vampyres

Needless to say, many Goths are interested in vampyre culture. Goth culture and vampyrism go together like wormwood and vodka! Because of the copious amount of romantic associations with the image of the vampyre, it's only natural that this energy would be incorporated with the Goth movement. Vampyres represent the enigmatic and unknown sexual aspects of human nature, which dark culture on the whole actively delves into through style, music, and other art forms.

Many portray their love for vampyrism by dressing the part. Vampyres' clothing of choice is Renaissance and Victorian garb, including laced cuffs, crushed velvet, long jackets, frocks, and, of course, fangs. Those who are deep into modern vampyre culture go beyond plastic- and porcelain-fanged inserts and actually get their canines professionally filed to points.

Many individuals in Goth culture adore the dark mysticism surrounding these creatures of the night. Some do, in fact, claim to be actual vampyres, though most either say quite the opposite or refrain from commenting on the issue. For information on vampyrism and modern vampyre culture, please see the "Empire of the Vampyre" section in the last chapter of the book.

Musical Tastes: Usually metal or industrial music, and anything with a vampyre theme.

VictorianGoths

VictorianGoths are the scene's Transylvanian concubines. The women adore petticoats, hoop skirts, corsets, large hats, and waist cinchers. The men fancy frocks, button-up shirts, dress shoes, canes, and top hats. Both like their style to be perfected down to the last frill, and certainly dress to depress—er, *impress*!

VictorianGoths wish for all things to be prim and proper, including makeup, clothing, and attitude. They are eloquent, elegant, and well-spoken. Their words and movements flow like water, and they often are well versed in history, particularly nineteenth-century European history.

VictorianGoths also venture into the realm of the RomantiGoth, being attracted to poetry and whimsical expression. Many darksiders combine the aesthetic imagery of the Renaissance, baroque, and Victorian eras into their wardrobe, not always distinguishing among the three because of the many visual crossovers.

Musical Tastes: See RomantiGoth musical tastes, as the two often overlap.

Melissa the Doll Maker smiles and nods to the nineteenth century.

VintageGoths

Close cousins of the VictorianGoths, VintageGoths have a style slightly more modern than the former. The majority of their wardrobe comes from thrift stores, and they are always on the lookout for creepily fabulous old clothing. Their look can be out of any era of the 1900s and may change from day to day. As long as it's not new, it's fit to wear. Their musical tastes range from classical symphonic, to '70s underground, to modern apocalyptic folk.

Stephaña shows us how classy VintageGoth really is.

Fashion styles became more individually defined in the twentieth century. Fashions evolved many times over and branched out into subsections based on alternative interests. Each decade of the twentieth century built upon the fashion of the previous one. Vintage-Goths have a special affinity for these gone but not forgotten styles and now have the freedom to choose their favored decade of the past, in terms of clothing.

Beyond physical appearance, VintageGoths also fancy vintage furniture, accessories, and décor, having a special fondness for phonographs, concertinas, fancy lamps, and classic telephones. They adore the work of long-deceased artists, and collect art from their favorite age. They are fans of music both Goth and otherwise, and favor dark noir films like *Nosferatu*, *Metropolis*, *The Golem*, and *The Cabinet of Dr. Caligari*—and, of course, old Bela Lugosi flicks! Some VintageGoths adore burlesque fashion, vaudeville, and cabaret. Others like the common styles of the 1910s and '20s, while yet others are into the retro garb of the '60s and '70s. A number of Goth types are drawn to various periods in time and actively embrace anachronistic living, which is one reason a number of people with an affinity for the 1900s find their place in the dark art community. Luckily, and like many darksiders, most VintageGoths are aware of the state of the world. As far as fashion is concerned, those who wear fur almost exclusively choose to wear only antique, used fur rather than supporting the horrifying and torturous modern animal-skin industry.

Musical Tastes: *Nick Cave and the Bad Seeds, Leonard Cohen, Tom Waits, Johnny Cash, Amy Winehouse, Warren Jackson Hearne and the Merrie Murdre of Gloomadeers, Reverend Glasseye & His Wooden Legs, The Dresden Dolls, Audra, Jill Tracy, Creature Feature,* classical music.

Lady Datura demonstrates duality with the WhiteGoth look.

WhiteGoths

Also known as AlbinoGoths, individuals in this rare Goth sub-section tend to wear almost exclusively white clothing, balanced with either dark or light makeup. The WhiteGoth expression most likely originated in Asia, either China or Japan, and is recognized as being influenced by geisha aesthetics.

Many Asian Goths would (and still do) bleach their dark hair to shades of either blonde or platinum as an expressive contrast to their naturally dark features. Many wear pale whiteface make-up to match the hair, and follow with clothing of the same color. This practice has spread to alternative culture in the West, but to a lesser degree.

Is black the combination of all colors or the absence thereof? When all colors (excluding black and white) are mixed properly in paint or with physical color pixels, the resulting color is black. At the same time, when true light (scientifically termed "white light") is refracted, colors appear. Though black and white appear to be opposites, they really are one and the same, and this duality is what the WhiteGoth represents.

Musical Tastes: Depends entirely on the person.

II
Craft

There is so much information when it comes to spirituality and magick that deciding what to discuss in an overview proved to be an almost never-ending process! I aim to cover some of the most important aspects of our life's chosen path, that of magick, spirituality, and mysticism, without going *too* deep into any one point and at the same time not brushing over anything.

What's a Witch?

There is a special allure about the magickal arts. Many of us are drawn to esoteric paths that seek connection with the earth. We may have had ideas and practices in our early years that ended up, upon discovery, to be aligned with metaphysical principles. This is the hand of the universe showing us our destiny, our place of power, from an early age.

Magick itself is uniquely intriguing. It presents the idea that we actually have power in structuring our lives and modifying our own existence for the betterment of all beings. It stresses healing and peace, clarity, and wisdom. Magick, according to anthropologist George Peter Murdock, is culturally universal. That is, the practice of magick is recognized in *all* cultures across the globe, and has been since the earliest times.

The full-bodied Venus of Willendorf sculpture, found in modern-day Austria, is anthropologically dated to the Upper Paleolithic era, around 30,000 BCE. It was sculpted of limestone and stained with red ocher, and is believed to be evidence of fertility magick and early praising of the female form (Goddess worship).

Magick has existed as long as humankind has. It is believed that sympathetic magick was performed even in the Stone Age. Tribal members would ceremonially dress in animal skins while the tribe's huntsmen would metaphorically stalk and "spear" the animal represented. This would energetically and psychologically encourage the fruition of the hunt.

Dancing, chanting, singing, and celebrating have always been a part of tribal culture, as has healing with plants and energy. Members of ancient tribes across the globe would engage in rites of trance and meditation. They knew of the spirits, the soul, and the importance of the cycles of nature. Ancient tribal cultures saw the physical and spiritual planes as overlapping. It is only recently, in the grand scheme of things, that we would call such views "Pagan" and such practices "Witchcraft."

Magick is as old as humanity itself and is very much embedded in our culture. All humans have the power to be magicians—it is only a matter of how much accountability we wish to take for our lives, our emotions, and the world that we create for ourselves moment by moment. The magickal arts are one way we are remembering our roots and natural abilities.

The word *Witch* comes from the Old English *wicce* (feminine) and *wicca* (masculine), referring to European diviners and spellcasters. The later Middle English form was *wicche*, combining the masculine and feminine into a singular phrase.

Gerald Gardner, one of the founders of the now-widespread Wiccan movement, resurrected the Old English spelling and applied it to his tradition of modern Witchcraft, which combined various elements of many pre-Christian traditions, including ancient European Pagan religions and folk magick.

Witches and Wiccans are considered Pagan, while practitioners of Western esoteric ceremonial magick may consider themselves Hermeticists or occultists. The word *Pagan* is rooted in the Latin *paganus*, meaning "rural civilian" or "country dweller." It is used predominantly to refer to people practicing the ways of earth-centered polytheistic spiritualism. The word also extends to practitioners of tribal traditions and is sometimes used to refer to those of any religion unrelated to the monotheistic beliefs of Islam and Judeo-Christianity.

Witches are holistic thinkers, recognizing the presence of Spirit in all things, knowing that the divine is all around us in different forms. Witches communicate with Spirit both throughout the day and in magick ritual. We do not require another person to be the intermediary between humans and God, as we are all channels of the divine to our own degree. This is not to say that we are above seeking advice from other Witches or spiritual folks, but rather that we recognize our innate ability to align our energy to the higher source and receive needed guidance one-on-one. This is a modern form of mysticism. As the Witch is a nature mystic, he or she is also a healer.

Witches make use of herbs, stones, astrological configurations, and an array of other tools that help deepen a connection to the natural world. From this connection comes the ability to heal—the process of restoring balance. The Witch is a healer on a multitude of levels. The connection between mind, body, and spirit is understood. It is through this connection that energetic currents flow—each energy body affects the others. Witches try to remain as balanced as possible and seek to help others find their own balance. Witches are counselors, spiritualists, shamans, diviners, guides, and ritual specialists.

Witches have not, are not, and never will be evil people. There is no Satan in Witchcraft (he is a Christian deity) and no grand evil force that we worship in secret. I've been told numerous times that we "accidentally worship" Satan, as he wears the disguise of nature and deceives us by making us think we're doing the world good by practicing Witchery.

As hard as I try, I cannot grasp the concept that Satan, who is a relatively new deity in his current form, is underhandedly controlling the entirety of our lifestyles without us even realizing it. This view comes from a place of fear. If healing people on various levels, loving the land, and working for peace on earth are reasons to be condemned to Hell at a later time, then bring it on! I'd much rather build an honest life of helping people on this plane without being distracted by what's next. I'd rather go about my life in peace in the present moment without the fear of a god's vengeance—one god of the many hundreds of thousands of deities currently recognized in the world. Fear tactics are not part of the Craft.

Witches are generally quite aware of their influence on others and strive to understand when they cause harm, knowing the unavoidable repercussions. Instead of relying on a book to tell us what is sacred and what is profane, we recognize our own ability to discern our actions and understand if we are helping or harming ourselves and the people around us. Books, teachers, and other people definitely help point the way for us all, but the true answers lie within.

The Witch finds spirituality by embracing truth in all religions worldwide. No religion is negated or entirely discredited, yet none is exclusively subscribed to. In this sense, the Witch is universal, understanding that spirituality permeates all paths to one degree or another. The ways of the Witch transcend religion by embracing *spirituality* as attuned to the earth, the body, and the mind. The essence of Paganism and Witchery is paying homage to ourselves, one another, and the world around us, gaining limitless wisdom the whole way through.

Witchcraft is both monotheistic and polytheistic. God, or Spirit, is not viewed as having only one face or a singular, unchanging personality. There is no one face and no one truth; Witches find God for themselves, still relying on others to help point the way. Instead of holding a limited, individualistic view of divinity, Witches see Spirit as being both masculine and feminine, though Spirit is, at the same time, neither male nor female.

Witchcraft does, however, divide Spirit into more easily recognizable and workable forms. The Craft acknowledges and honors the divine, which is seen in three ways.

First, Spirit is recognized as an element. Spirit encompasses all spirituality—all of reality. Nothing is apart from Spirit. Spirit is all, and is the very essence of our being. It is the grand force that connects humans to nature and indeed all life. Spirit has gone by a multiplicity of names through the evolution of time. Spirit transcends any and all associations, yet encompasses all ideas. Spirit is the infinite nature of reality, of which humans only see one piece at a time. Spirit cannot be singularly defined or rationalized, but instead encompasses all definitions. Because Spirit has no exact, acute, precise personality and no set of behaviors, judgments, or norms, the Witch is free to decide which faces of the divine he or she will pay homage to. Witchcraft gives the freedom of spiritual choice through self-empowerment over dogma.

Second, Witchcraft honors the forces called the Father and Mother, often called the God and Goddess or Lord and Lady. They are faceless, yet can appear in any way, shape, or form. They are the division of Spirit into two polarities—*yin* and *yang,* as some would say. As there are males and females of every species, Spirit is divided into the same polarities. This solidifies the idea that the natural world is a direct reflection of the spiritual. The God and Goddess represent the grand cosmic balance. Instead of being enthroned in the clouds, pointing fingers and casting judgment, they are seen as permeating every aspect of being, not separate from this world or *ourselves.* Similarly, ancient spiritualists have long recognized the Earth Mother and Sky Father; the divisions of Spirit are put into appropriately representative physical form.

Finally, the Craft divides the Great God and Great Goddess into multiple forms. There is no set pantheon of deities for all Pagans or Witches. This, in modern Witchcraft, is where great personal freedom lies. Some Witches don't even follow a pantheon, choosing to work with the Mother and Father forces alone. Neither way is less valid or less respectable. Wide arrays of deities appear in all polytheistic religions worldwide, all acting as personifications of the forces of nature and aspects of the human psyche. Witches can choose the system they deem most appropriate to their own beliefs. Some of the most common in the West are Celtic, Græco-Roman, Egyptian, Norse, and Native American. From these traditions and others, countless traditions and subtraditions have been created. There are many flavors of the Witch, but they all are naturally interconnected.

Most Witches don't worship deities as though they are unreachable or invisible people who must be groveled to. Instead, direct and personal connections with the gods are emphasized in the Craft, as this assists to elevate a person to mystical states of consciousness and bring the world of humans and the realm of the Mighty Ones closer together. Both gods and humans alike have perfections and flaws, and both are capable of interacting with one another on an equal level (though this also depends on the deity's view and expectations).

If a Witch finds him- or herself in a state of utter despair or deep contemplation, which does happen to everyone now and then, he or she can turn to the elements: Earth, Air, Fire, Water, and Spirit. They surround and permeate every aspect of our physical existence and are there to listen and heal when no one else may. The elements are comforts; nature holds many unspoken answers.

The Witch also pays close attention to the cycles of the moon, sun, and stars. Astrology is certainly one of the Witch's sciences, and allows the Witch to play a role of dictation to the masses. The most noticeable astrological occurrences are the solar and lunar cycles—their influences can be immediately observed by stepping outside and looking at the earth and sky. Nature is the Witch's best friend, and the Witch knows that we are not separate from it whatsoever.

Because of the connection with the natural world, the Witch is an environmentalist at heart, recycling as much as possible and using as few materials as absolutely necessary. He or she does not take for granted the gifts the earth has given, always treating them with respect and admiration. Recycling allows nature's cycles to regenerate and continue flowing. The reuse of bottles, cans, and paper allows for numerous products to be created without the usual effects of environmental devastation. Even this book itself is a product of the recycling process!

The Witch is additionally aware of what he or she consumes, be it food, drink, or other substances. Every act of consuming material the earth provides is a spiritual communion with nature. The Witch pays strict attention to nature and his or her effect on its well-being.

Most Witches try to eat as natural a diet as possible, eliminating toxins like fast food, additives, preservatives, and genetically modified "food" as much as possible. Keeping the physical body in shape by consuming organic, holistic products sustains the body as the spiritual vehicle it is. Witches are conscious of the earth and conscious of their own minds and bodies. Having awareness in all these realms is a foundation for living a progressive spiritual life.

Because many Witches, magicians, and spiritual people are both health-conscious and environmentally aware, many likewise are aware of human and animal welfare. A great number of magickal folk work for political and environmental causes. Many also choose a vegetarian or vegan diet, understanding the unnatural living conditions and unnecessary cruelty inflicted on factory-farmed animals for the sole purpose of economic gain. People who are vegetarian or vegan or who choose to consume only ethically farmed meat and dairy actively strive to decrease the suffering of other beings simply by being mindful of their choice of food. Vegetarianism and veganism can also be extremely healthy and thus spiritually conducive.

The Witch constantly has one foot in this world and one in the other. He or she functions in the mundane world but is ever aware of other planes existing simultaneously. The Witch understands that physicality and spirituality are not separate, but are

entirely interlinked. He or she understands physical reality as a series of patterns, signs, and symbols that directly reflect the unseen planes of thought, energy, and ether.

The Witch is a watcher—one who observes and seeks to comprehend the patterns of reality, from the larger spirals, like the sun and moon cycles, to smaller ones, like the growth of plants and trees. Similarly, the Witch pays attention to psychological and energetic spirals, like long-term personal habits and past-life predispositions, as well as the smaller ones, like meaningful coincidences and synchronicities, through signs and omens in everyday life.

Most Pagans experience what is called "coming home syndrome" upon discovery of magickal living. After years of believing and practicing certain things that seemed very natural, they eventually discover that these things are part of the Pagan path. For example, I remember picking up stones and rubbing negative feelings into them when I was young. I would then throw them behind me or into running water, having no idea that this was a miniature spell. I always believed in the interconnectedness of all life, animate and inanimate, and that one thing influenced the next. It wasn't until later that I discovered that this was a timeless esoteric and occult philosophy. I had no idea that these things were accepted or natural, much less magickal. Paganism showed me that, yes, I was on to something! This experience is widespread and speaks to almost every Witch not initially raised in the arts. A great number of Witches and Pagans come to similar realizations, recognizing their natural inclinations as inherently spiritual practices.

Simply reading a book on the Craft, casting a few spells, and attending a couple of public gatherings does not make someone a Witch, any more than going to church and praying now and then makes someone a Christian. Buying a bunch of herbs and candles, creating a "grandmother story" about genetic Witchery, and wearing a million pentacles does not make one a Witch either. Unfortunately, these types of things occur in the Craft scene far more often than they should.

There is no ultimate degree of magickal attainment after which there is no further progression. There is no almighty king or queen of all Witches, no High Priest or Priestess more advanced than the rest, and no title to work toward that will teach you everything there is to know. To think so would be entirely opposite the premise of Witchcraft, which recognizes the reality of change and the cyclical nature of all things.

The Craft requires study, experimentation, and mindfulness. It requires contemplation, meditation, reflection, humility, and dedication. Witches understand that we must be devoted to our art in order to develop a fuller understanding. If we choose to advance in the ways of the Witch, we must have absolute awareness of our effects on others and ourselves. We must have full accountability for our actions, and we must be willing to face the depths of our souls, even if portions are dark, tainted, or broken.

Witchcraft was never meant to be just *practiced*, but was meant to be *lived*. The path is 24/7. Witchcraft is not a hobby, nor is it a meaningless interest. It is absolutely real and constant. It applies directly to our lives and it weaves itself into every moment. Our ethics, lifestyle choices, and self-awareness play directly into our lives as spiritualists. Every choice we make and everything we do is spiritual, simply because existence *itself* is spiritual. We are reflections of our ways.

To venture outside and take a deep inhalation of pristine oxygen is to feel the essence of true magick. To be taken aback by the profundity of the trees, the stars, and the setting sun is to feel the breath of the gods. To stand in humility and absolute awe under the full moon is to invoke the mysteries of old. To feel bliss when a snowflake or drop of rain falls on our lips is to connect our energy to the cyclical nature of existence. To examine the amazing, intricate structures of the natural world and to contemplate the big, unanswerable question *Why?* is to immerse ourselves in the essence of the Craft. The road of knowledge is infinite; the learning never ends, and Witchcraft is but one way of remembering who we are.

Types of Witches and Magicians

In this section, I will give a brief description of various types of Witches, Pagans, and magicians. The list is actually quite small and covers only a few of the many thousands of magickal traditions and subtraditions in existence. The ones listed here tend to be either the best known or those that serve as the roots for numerous additional offshoot traditions. Some of the traditions mentioned here may or may not be associated directly with Witchcraft per se, but are magick-working spiritual traditions nonetheless and deserve a mention.

The magickal arts of non-Witch magicians generally do not follow the patterns of the seasons or the moon cycles, though many work heavily with astrology and metaphysical science. Some don't mind the word Pagan attached to their religion or practices, while others try to avoid it. Most of these are ceremonial traditions whose orders are Hermetic in nature. Others are shamanic or indigenous tribal traditions. I include descriptions of some of these paths, understanding that many occultists are drawn to them in addition to Witchcraft.

While many groups of practitioners may belong to a different tradition, it must not be forgotten that *all traditions are interlinked*. Each tradition has its own way of doing things, but that does not make them all entirely different from one another. Instead, it makes them uniquely connected on an energetic level, as they each have their own means to accomplish similar ends. Some choose to be more traditional in their activities, adhering to a sound structure that has been maintained for many years. Others are more adaptive in nature, adjusting to the times and choosing to be more eclectic.

If you read about a path that resonates with you, or have been feeling a calling to a particular tradition for some time now, then I encourage you to research it more. It doesn't mean you have to join the tradition—but odds are that if you're feeling the "pull," there's something important to learn there!

The books referenced at the end of many of these entries will give you suggestions for where to begin your search. It would be next to impossible to include a mention of every tradition within the Craft, much less of every magickal tradition in existence. There are literally several thousands of traditions and branch traditions; new ones are being formed constantly by like-minded people coming together and creating their own structure of training and celebration based on previously founded paths. I will give examples of some of the most common traditions being practiced today, providing the most accurate short overview I can for each.

Alexandrian Wicca

One of the most influential and now widespread branches of European Witchcraft, Alexandrian Wicca was founded in England by Alex Sanders. Sanders was initiated into a coven of Gardnerian Wiccans in 1960 prior to starting his own branch of British Traditional Witchcraft (BTW).

Alexandrian Wicca follows similar ethical precepts and observes the same holidays (Sabbats) as the Gardnerian tradition. It is also based on the three-degree system of initiation, requiring dedication and study by all neophytes and initiates. Though Sanders claimed to have copied his tradition's original Book of Shadows from his grandmother, it was later revealed that much of his book was, in fact, copied from Gardnerian material, which erupted in quite a scandal at the time.

Because of Sanders' willingness to bring the Craft into the public eye through the media, he and his covens were the targets of much intrigue and scrutiny. A number of people were attracted to his newfound tradition of Witchcraft and worked up to initiation directly through the founder. Currently one can find a great number of directly descended traditional Alexandrian covens worldwide.

Ásatrú/Teutonic/Germanic

Ásatrú is an Old Norse term for the *troth*, or loyalty, of the gods. This tradition originated in the long-lived practices of the northern European Teutons. "Teutonic" actually is synonymous with "Germanic" nowadays. The term with which one identifies is up to the practitioner him- or herself. Old Germanic culture had its own unique worldview, cosmology, and magickal system. The name of the system is Ásatrú, which means "belief in the Æsir" or "religion of the gods." Most practitioners of this magickal system do not claim to be Witches, though some do. Ásatrú, however, is a separate practice from the Craft, and many of the practitioners choose not to identify with Wicca, as the majority of its practices are derived from other European areas. Many prefer the term *heathen* to Neopagan. The word *heathenry* is often used to distinguish it from other Pagan paths. With the rise of the Church, negative connotations were attached to the words heathen and Pagan, both referring to people who refused to accept the ways of the Church and stayed close to their old religious roots. Some practitioners refer to themselves simply as Odinists—adherents of the god Odin (or Woden) and usually his goddess counterpart Freyja. While there certainly are some differences between the terms for the followers of this pantheon and the precise magickal applications the practitioners undergo, they are naturally interconnected and follow similar codes of conduct.

Ásatrúars have nine noble virtues by which they are dedicated to live: courage, truth, honor, fidelity, hospitality, discipline, industriousness, self-reliance, and perseverance. They believe that these virtues must be practiced at all times to strengthen the community and their dedication to one another and the gods.

Ásatrúars recognize a number of deities, as well as the Valkyries, who they believe carry them after death. The creation myth is one of fire and ice, in which two worlds collided to form the world and universe we live in now—Muspelheim (the world of fire) and Nefilim (the world of ice). They see the universe as being made up of many layers, as revealed in Yggdrasil, or the "World Tree." This is different from the Qabalistic Tree of Life in that it represents nine planes of reality existing simultaneously, both in this universe and the astral Otherworlds.

In Norse mythology, Odin hanged himself by a foot from an actual Yggdrasil tree for nine nights. This image is reflected in the Hanged Man card of the Tarot. In Odin's days of suspension, the secrets of the runes were shown to him in vision. Divination with and reflection on the runic system are common practices among followers of the Norse ways. Some rune casters call upon Odin to magickally charge their runes, as Odin is seen as the keeper of the runic mysteries because of his contact with Yggdrasil. Runes are said to embody all of consciousness, and this is the reason they make such ideal divinatory tools.

The three races of deities in the Norse pantheon are also recognized. They are the Æsir (the gods of order), the Jotnar (the giants of chaos), and the Vanir (the deities associated with the tides of nature and fertility of the land). The Æsir and Jotnar are constantly warring with one another, maintaining the balance of order and chaos to sustain equilibrium. Existing within these clans and races are the gods of the Norse, including Odin (Woden), Frey, Freyja (Freya), Thor, Frigg, and Ostara, as well as other "lesser deities" like Hel, Loki, Balder, Tyr, and Ægir.

Further reading: For more information on Norse mythology and magick, I recommend the works of Edred Thorsson, Kvelduf Gundarsson, and Ed Fitch.

Chaos Magick

The unique path of chaos magick is impossible to strictly define, generalize, or rationalize. To do so would go entirely against the premise of chaos magick itself! The system (or perhaps, more appropriately, *approach* or *movement*) is best described as a retaliation against traditional, uptight magickal orders. Belief systems are seen as useful tools but not ultimate truths. If chaos magick could be considered to have any sort of a rede, it might be "nothing is true; everything is permitted." Responsibility, intelligence, and active dedication to magick and spirituality as one personally understands and utilizes them are of utmost necessity when practicing chaos magick.

This system emphasizes personal empowerment through actual, solid experience. It is very much opposed to blind belief and dogmatism, seeking to know truth above fiction. I see chaos magick as the antithesis of structural reality. The system's emphasis on the exploration of the paradigms of existence, and the paradoxical reality of all things, makes it nontraditional and highly individualistic. Chaos magicians focus much of their energy on studying a number of occult systems, and integrate a variety of cultural teachings to form their own practices—eclecticism to the extreme! Psychology and the workings of the mind are of utmost intrigue to chaos magicians. In the end, the methodologies of each chaos magician are different. Chaos magick is founded on a "do it yourself" and "as long as it works" ideology. Chaos magicians do away with the perceived extraneous elements of ritual magick by seeking the rawness of simplicity, letting intuition guide instead of rules.

Practitioners of chaos magick are very experimental and utilize life's strongest experiences, like sex, drugs, exhaustion, sound, music, and pain, to project magickal energy and shape the planes. These activities are seen as inherently magickal, especially when performed ritualistically. The goal of engaging in extreme experience is to experience *gnosis*, or conscious unity with Spirit. This state is achieved through direct exercises aimed at dissolving the ego and ridding oneself of attachments of any kind. Chaos magicians believe that chaos is the root of magick and life itself, and it is this power that is drawn forth. Practitioners regularly perform individualistically tailored ritual magick to center themselves in the middle of the Chaosphere, the spirals of life stemming from chaos.

There are many influential figures in chaos magick. The first and most notable is Austin Osman Spare, who often is referred to as the grandfather of chaos magick. He was a London-born artist who was trained by a hereditary Witch (named Mrs. Paterson) in the arts of visualization and evocation. Spare was also, for a short time, a member of the A∴A∴ (Argenteum Astrum), a magickal order founded by Aleister Crowley.

The modern occult author Robert Anton Wilson, often associated with chaos magick, taught readers to question life and everything in it by dissecting the brain and human psychological behavior. Wilson's writings, especially the *Illuminatus! Trilogy*, co-written with Robert Shea in the 1970s, draw heavily on the Discordian movement, the followers of which praise Eris, the Greek goddess of chaos and discord. Wilson understood the interrelatedness of psychology, philosophy, and magick. By integrating physics with metaphysics, Wilson's writing makes the readers rethink reality as they know it.

On January 11, 2007, I had just purchased and was watching one of Wilson's DVDs when a friend text-messaged my mobile with the news that Wilson had passed away. I walked outside to get some air, and it was then that the largest shooting star I'd ever seen swept across the sky, illuminating even the snowy ground. There he went. When I came inside, the clock read 11:11, and an e-mail regarding the profundity of Wilson's writings showed up in my inbox from a different friend who had not yet heard the news of his death. Magick and synchronicity in every way, just as Bob would have it. May he be free!

Another influential writer is Grant Morrison, who has been called the "new William S. Burroughs." Morrison is known for popularizing chaos magick through the stories and characters in his comic series *The Invisibles*. The characters in the comic are countercultural heroes and heroines who fight the world's lies and oppression by way of anarchistic occultism. Morrison has written and illustrated a number of other comics, many of which have earned him awards and worldwide acclaim. Each story line incorporates covert or overt aspects of occultism, often revealing spells and magickal truths through the story line as a medium.

Perhaps the most influential modern artist associated with the rise of chaos magick is none other than the infamous Genesis P-Orridge. Orridge's music is eccentric, chaotic, and psychoactive in and of itself, and xyr (*sic*) live performances are ritualistic in the sense that the beats, movements, and visuals all are performed with coded magickal intent. Orridge is known for bizarre visual art and music, especially in the form of xyr bands Psychic TV, Throbbing Gristle, and Thee Majesty. Orridge is the founder of Thee Temple ov Psychick Youth, a magickal and occultural "organization." Orridge's music ranges from experimental electronic, acid house, noise, and industrial to punk, psychedelic rock, and even pop. Orridge xemself (*sic*) actually coined the genre term *industrial* when xe (*sic*) cofounded Industrial Records in England in 1976. Orridge's music is crafted with magickal intent in mind, designed to change the listeners' consciousness on a multitude of levels.

Despite unfounded negative British press and the controversy surrounding Orridge's unique art, philosophy, and pandrogynous appearance, xyr music has made a profound impact on the alternative scene, experimental industrial music, and "occulture" as we know it today. It should also be noted that the term *pandrogyny* was coined by Orridge and xyr partner Lady Jaye. Indeed true to the spirit of chaos magick, Psychic TV's MySpace site says, "Pandrogyny is art, more specifically, it is a concept/project of Lady Jaye and Genesis that attempts to analyze the future of evolution as it pertains to the human body and gender, with the goal of illuminating the very real possibilities provided by modern technology to alter our bodies, thereby altering our minds and our societies." Other bands that were influenced by the work of Orridge include Current 93, Coil, and Nurse With Wound, all of which most certainly embrace occult spirituality and the chaos current.

All of the aforementioned figures express chaos through modern art. Technology and pop culture are the perfect venues for weaving chaos magick by bringing people out of their ordinary states of waking consciousness in order to question reality altogether.

Further reading:

Generation Hex edited by Jason Louv (Disinformation Press, 2006)

Liber Null & Psychonaut by Peter J. Carroll (Weiser, 1987)

Condensed Chaos: An Introduction to Chaos Magic by Phil Hine (New Falcon, 1995)

Prometheus Rising by Robert Anton Wilson (Falcon Press, 1983)

Druidry

Druidry is one of the two main branches of traditional British Paganism. The Druids most likely were more systematic in their magickal practice than the common Celtic Pagans were. Next to nothing is known about the ancient Druids, considering that written records were rarely kept, for reasons of secrecy. We do know, however, that they were on the upper end of the Celtic caste system.

Greek and Roman writers talk about three classes of Druids. The first class was the Ovates, whose primary role was to study the cycles of nature and practice divination. The second was the Bards, whose sole job it was to preserve the legends of the Celts through song and written word. The third and highest class was the Druid Propers, whose role it was to teach magick and the spiritual mysteries to neophytes and the community at large.

Druidic bloodlines are among the few Western clans still honored for their historical role in the rise of political Britain. Many efforts have been made to reconstruct the ways of the ancient Druids. Gerald Gardner raised the possibility that the Druids and Celtic Witches were of the same family. There now exist a number of "Druid Wiccans," those who integrate the known teachings of both systems into one syncretistic unit. Members see this as a positive integration of two sects that may have been united at one time. There also are Druid reconstructionists, who believe enough evidence exists to reconstruct the pre-Christian Celtic religion. There also exist the vastly differing Druid revivalists, who practice a nature-based spirituality that is only somewhat connected to the practices of historical Druids. The latter came about as a result of eighteenth- and nineteenth-century European visionaries, and thrives through organizations such as the Order of Bards, Ovates, and Druids (OBOD). The first modern group, called the Ancient Druid Order, was founded in 1717.

Further reading:

The Druidry Handbook: Spiritual Practice Rooted in the Living Earth by John Michael Greer (Weiser, 2006)

A Brief History of the Druids by Peter Berresford Ellis (Carroll & Graf, 2002)

The Druids: Celtic Priests of Nature by Jean Markale (Inner Traditions, 1999)

The Druids: A History by Ronald Hutton (Hambledon & London, 2007)

Enochian

John Dee was the court astrologer for Queen Elizabeth I of England. While working with scryer Edward Kelly, Dee was communicated to by a number of angelic beings claiming to be the same entities to have communicated with Enoch (Cain's son in the Bible), who was said to eventually have reached a state of oneness with God before death. There is debate as to whether these beings were actually angels, other beings, or manifestations of the men's unconscious minds or higher selves.

r	Z	i	l	a	f	A	y	t	l	P	a
a	r	d	Z	a	i	d	P	a	L	a	m
c	z	o	n	s	a	r	o	Y	a	v	b
T	o	i	T	t	z	o	P	a	c	o	C
S?	i	g	a	s	o	m	r	b	z	n	h
f	m	o	n	d	a	T	d	i	a	r	i
o	r	o	i	b	A	h	a	o	z	P	i
t	N	a	b	r	V	i	x	g	a	s	d
O	i	i	i	t	T	P	a	l	O	a	i
A	b	a	m	o	o	o	a	C	v	c	a
N	a	o	c	O	T	t	n	P	r	n	T
o	c	a	n	m	a	g	o	t	r	o	i
S	h	i	a	l	r	a	P	m	z	o	x

The Enochian beings communicated a large amount of material to the magicians, most of which was extremely arcane and difficult to interpret. Much of the decipherable information has to do with humankind, the cosmos, human consciousness, and complex magickal application. This included a list of 48 Keys, words said to open gates of various levels of angelic consciousness throughout the world, that is, ethereal planes of existence accessible to magicians. Musings of spiritual hierarchy, including divisions of angels and demons, were transcribed—as was a detailed system of magick. Another important channeling was the Enochian (or Angelic) alphabet. Additionally, tablets representing the essence of the four Watchtowers were transcribed. It is from this channeling that modern Witches get the system of Watchtowers as invoked in the magick circle. The Watchtowers are the metaphorical residences of the four base elements: Earth, Air, Fire, and Water. When scrying in his crystal ball, Edward Kelly perceived four Watchtowers, each representing a different cardinal direction and thus an elemental association.

The Enochian system of magick remained underground for some time, until it resurfaced with the advent of the Hermetic Order of the Golden Dawn, which used a section of it along with other Western occult systems. Surprisingly, Dee and Kelly never actually practiced the magick, but left it as is after it was received; the first person historically recorded to have practiced the full Enochian calls was Aleister Crowley. Some modern Pagans utilize the Enochian magickal system to a degree, especially when writing scripts for spells, and the invocations to the Watchtowers are also commonplace in ritual Witchcraft.

Further reading:

Enochian Magic for Beginners: The Original System of Angel Magic by Donald Tyson
(Llewellyn, 1997)

Look into this ↓

Feri Witchcraft

Victor and Cora Anderson started the Feri tradition of Witchcraft in the mid-1900s. The Feri tradition's focus lies more in the realm of the evolution of each individual practitioner's soul than in Sabbatical or seasonal celebrations. Practitioners of Feri Witchcraft feel that true spiritual work begins in the heart of the seeker, and that is the point that must be focused on first and foremost before full balance can come about.

Feri is influenced by a number of previous traditions, including British Traditional Wicca, Ozark folk and root magick, Vodou, Huna (Hawaiian spiritualism), and various forms of shamanism. Victor Anderson chose to use the name Feri for their tradition because of his affinity with the "little folk" around the world. Beyond the obvious connection with the faerie realm, Anderson was intrigued and influenced by the shamanic practices of the physical kin of fae like the Picts and Aboriginals, who are known for coexisting in both the physical and ethereal realms.

Feri is active, determined, poetic, passionate, sensual, and ecstatic. Self-expression and personal soul-searching are at the heart of the teachings. The tradition honors the Goddess and God in their nature guises, particularly the Star Goddess. As in Wicca, the lunar and solar tides are celebrated. At the same time, Feri has its own ritual tools, practices, and methodologies distinct from those of other Wiccan traditions. For example, a person's energetic field is divided into three bodies, which, when aligned, balance the whole of the soul and put the practitioner in a state of total equilibrium.

The Feri tradition strongly emphasizes humanity's connection to the natural world, including the realms of the gods, faeries, guardians, and ancestors. It should be not-

ed that the Feri tradition, which often is considered one of the only American-born branches of the Craft, is separate from the exclusively Welsh Faerie tradition of Witchcraft. The spelling used, more often than not, is "Feri," in order to differentiate the two; it is the spelling introduced by the founder.

Victor Anderson initiated world-renowned Pagan author Starhawk prior to her starting an offshoot tradition of her own in the late '70s, called Reclaiming. The Reclaiming tradition is akin to Feri, though the focus is predominantly on political activism, ecology, environmentalism, and anarcho-feminism, all tied to Mother Earth and her peoples. Because politics shape so much of the world's policies and general psychology, the Reclaiming tradition seeks to work magick on the physical plane through activism and protest, as well as on the spiritual plane through strong energy-focusing global magick. Both the Feri and Reclaiming traditions know that communication is a key to personal and universal evolution, and that there is much to be done with our time on earth.

Further reading:

Etheric Anatomy: The Three Selves and Astral Travel by Victor and Cora Anderson (Acorn Guild Press, 2004)

Evolutionary Witchcraft by T. Thorn Coyle (Penguin, 2004)

The Spiral Dance: A Rebirth of the Ancient Religion of the Great Goddess by Starhawk (Reclaiming tradition) (HarperCollins, 1979)

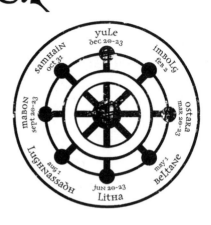

Gardnerian Wicca

Gardnerian Wicca was founded in England by Gerald Gardner. Often called the "grandfather of Wicca," Gardner was one of many European occultists devoted to reclaiming the Old Ways.

Through research into classical mythologies, Hermetic magick, and Indo-European folk traditions, Gardner constructed his own syncretistic/revivalist tradition of modern Witchcraft.

Gardner worked with a number of influential magicians, occultists, and historians of the time, including Aleister Crowley, Margaret Murray, and Doreen Valiente. Valiente, his initiate and High Priestess, contributed to Gardner's tradition by collaborating on much of Gardner's Book of Shadows material and by writing, compiling, and editing various spiritually charged poems. Witches of many flavors use the popular "Charge of the Goddess." In many ways, Gardner built the framework for this new "Witch cult," while Valiente provided much of the interior substance.

Gardnerian Wicca consists of a three-degree initiatory system, Sabbatical and Esbatical observations, and traditional male-to-female initiations. The Gardnerian tradition influenced numerous additional branch-off traditions and covens and provides the framework for countless aspects of modern Witchcraft both philosophically and ritualistically.

Gardner was the first to resurrect the word Wicca (*wica* or *wicce* at the time) into a modern context. Wicca wouldn't exist as it does today had it not been for Gardner's influence. It is difficult to decipher fact from fiction in Gardner's constant inconsistencies and high claims, including his possible initiation into ancient hereditary Witchcraft through one of Old George Pickingill's nine covens, one of which was said to have also initiated Crowley.

Though many occultists believe the Gardnerian tradition was founded mostly on imagination, and though much confusion surrounds the tradition's precise origins, it nonetheless remains true that the Gardnerian tradition of Wicca was one of the most influential magickal movements to come about in the twentieth century.

Golden Dawn

The Hermetic Order of the Golden Dawn was founded in London in 1888 as a magickal society, referred to at the time as the Esoteric Order of the Golden Dawn. A group of occultists merged to form this new system based on teachings of Qabalah, Rosicrucianism, alchemy, Theosophy, Egyptian magick, and Freemasonry, to name a few. Founders of the Golden Dawn included Samuel Liddell MacGregor Mathers and Dr. William Wynn Westcott, who sought to ground a variety of occult techniques into a singular unit to provide a unified system of progression for neophytes and practitioners. The teachings, because they were not restricted to one order alone, allowed the student many forms of study both in magick and occult philosophy. Initiations from one level to the next required the practitioner to commit various aspects of occultism to memory and prove dedication to the material through rigorous practice. By the turn of the century, many temples were in place throughout Western Europe. Various offshoots of the original order emerged soon after the founding of the original tradition. Arthur Edward Waite founded the Holy Order of the Golden Dawn, Dion Fortune founded the Society of the Inner Light, Aleister Crowley founded the A∴A∴, and so on.

At a time when the Golden Dawn seemed to be faced with the possibility of failure, Israel Regardie (Crowley's secretary) decided to make public much of the once-secret texts of the Golden Dawn, publishing a great amount of the order's material in four volumes, released between 1937 and 1940. Needless to say, this angered many of its founders and students who had worked so hard to dedicate themselves to the teachings. Prior to Regardie's release of this material, Aleister Crowley and Dion Fortune had released bits of the Golden Dawn's inner secrets to preserve interest in the path and keep it from becoming totally lost. However, the material that they had previously presented was nothing in comparison to Regardie's massive publications.

The Golden Dawn has influenced virtually all orders of Western occultism, including modern Witchcraft. Some Wiccan and Neopagan groups have adopted elements of Golden Dawn ritualism, particularly rituals for protection. Golden Dawn traditions are still practiced today by many orders and organizations.

Further reading:

The Essential Golden Dawn: An Introduction to High Magic by Chic Cicero and Sandra Tabatha Cicero (Llewellyn, 2003)

Women of the Golden Dawn: Rebels and Priestesses by Mary K. Greer (Park Street Press, 1994)

The works of Israel Regardie.

Green (Wild) Witchcraft

Green Witchcraft, which is also called Wild Witchcraft or *Seidhr* in Teutonic, may be the form of the Craft truest to the sense of the word Witch. The words *cunning man/ woman*, *hedge Witch*, and even *kitchen Witch* are associated with these earth-based practices. Countryside practitioners in days of old made use of the magickal and medicinal qualities of plants, herbs, stones, and other natural substances. Green Witches work to attune themselves to the cycles of nature, including astrological cycles, especially for purposes of gardening. They create potions, brews, and natural elixirs that heal and transform a person on many levels. The Green Witch crafts charms, amulets, and spells for a variety of purposes. The patterns of the earth are carefully mapped, and the influence of earth changes is recognized as affecting human consciousness both on a global and a personal level. Green Witches pay particular attention to the Sabbats and lunar cycles, and are aware of the environment and its effects on the spirit.

Additionally, many individuals who identify as genetic or hereditary Witches were trained by one or more family members in old folkloric methods of magick and spell-crafting now associated with Green Witchery. Most of these practical magicks have been preserved since Pagan times in the culture of the Witch's lineage. Because folk-loric beliefs and spellcrafting influenced the development of Wicca and other Neopagan paths, a great number of these methods are now utilized by Witches and magicians both hereditary and otherwise.

Green Witches work with the faerie realm and spirits of nature. These include the elemental spirits—gnomes (Earth), sylphs (Air), salamanders (Fire), and undines (Water)—the specific divisions of which were recognized in Hermeticism and incorporated into Neopaganism. Each of these spirits embodies its associated element. Green Witches work with the elements to initiate positive change. They work for themselves, clients, friends, family, and the global community. They often see "through the veil" between the astral/ethereal planes, perceiving more than the average person, working with beings and energies unknown to the common senses. They communicate with otherworldly spirits and beings and work to unravel the mysteries of the natural world.

The biggest difference between Green Witches and modern Wiccans is that Green Witches use little formal ceremonialism in ritual. The focus is the earth, her tides and cycles, and has little to do with common forms of Western magickal practice. Many Green Witches are of a Celtic leaning—drawn to practices directly from the lands of greenery! Green Witches work with the gods of the green earth, particularly those of harvest and fertility, and the ebb and flow of nature's cycles. The primary deities of Celtic Green Witchery are the God and Goddess in their nature guises as the Horned God and the Earth Mother.

Further reading:

Green Witchcraft series by Ann Moura (Aoumiel) (Llewellyn)

Craft of the Wild Witch: Green Spirituality & Natural Enchantment by Poppy Palin (Llewellyn, 2004)

Wild Witchcraft: A Guide to Natural, Herbal and Earth Magic by Marian Green (Thorsons, 2002)

Qabalah (Kabbalah, Cabala)

The Qabalah is a Jewish mystical tradition whose teachings have been absorbed and worked with by many modern Witches and Pagans. It was introduced to modern Witchcraft by way of Alex Sanders, founder of the Alexandrian tradition of Wicca. Most of its early writings (c. thirteenth century) were in Hebrew or Aramaic, and were based on the scriptural teachings of the Torah and a later massive volume of commentary called the *Zohar*. While the system is Judaic in nature, its modern teachings are rarely dogmatic, but are very much esoteric and based in both research and experience. The word Qabalah can be spelled at least two dozen different ways, which is mostly a direct result of translating the word itself into English.

Qabalah encourages a direct and personal connection with the divine. The symbol of the Qabalah is the Tree of Life, which is said to be a map of all existence, assessing every layer of human experience. The Tree consists of ten main sephiroth, or spheres, which can be understood as layers of reality or emanations of God. Each sephira has its own personality, sacred name, and specific associations. The Qabalah is a very intense and complete system that can be magickally utilized and philosophically understood to find the keys to healing and spiritual transformation. The Tree also includes twenty-two "paths" that connect the spheres to their neighboring spheres. Each path additionally corresponds to one of the twenty-two letters of the Hebrew alphabet. The sephiroth and paths are reflected in the major and minor arcana of the Tarot. French occultist Eliphas Lévi studied the correlations between the two systems and speculated that the Tarot cards actually had developmental origins in the Qabalah.

The word Qabalah comes from the ancient world *qibel*, meaning "that which is received," basically alluding to the Qabalah as a transmission from God. The map of the Tree of Life was first revealed in the ancient *Sepher Yetzirah*, also called the Book of Formation or the Book of Creation. This book was written with heavy Greek and Hellenistic influences and was the framework for the development of Qabalistic theosophy and theurgy. The Qabalah remains a living system that is utilized by a wide range of spiri-

tualists. Qabalists strongly believe that every action has an influence on the spiritual plane and that we must act in accordance with the laws of balance.

Further reading:

The Mystical Qabalah by Dion Fortune (Weiser, 1984)

Magic of Qabalah: Visions of the Tree of Life by Kala Trobe (Llewellyn, 2001)

Paths of Wisdom: Principles and Practice of the Magical Cabala in the Western Tradition, by John Michael Greer (Llewellyn, 1996)

Satanism

Satanism is another religion entirely, quite divorced from the Pagan path. A number of people are drawn to Satanism by the belief that it is one of the paths of Witchcraft. It simply is *not*. However, there are plenty of Goth types who like the philosophies of this religion and become involved in it because it speaks to them personally, not just because it seems evil or antinormative. The belief in Satan as the Witches' God is rooted in the persecution by the Christian Church during a period of unmentionable horror and torture that modern Pagans refer to as the Burning Times. It was during this time that the Celtic Pagans' image of Pan (equated also with Herne, Cernnunos, etc.), the horned and goat-footed god of the forest, became synonymous with the image of the Devil to the Church.

Satanists do not worship Satan as a being from the Christian pantheon, but as a *concept* or an energetic current. Satanism is not devil worship in the common use of the term. If you were to ask Satanists who they worship, their first answer would be "myself." Yes, Satanism is a selfish path, and for this reason it usually doesn't appeal to Pagans and followers of earth-based religions. Satanism is indulgent in life's experiences, resenting the common view of sinfulness and people's subservience to dogmatic structure. Satanists practice their own forms of magick and ritual, which are most often used for personal gain.

While Anton Szandor LaVey, High Priest of the Church of Satan, made associations between Witchcraft and Satanism, the truth is that the two are separate entities. Nevertheless, some Satanists refer to themselves as Witches, not because of an interest in the Pagan path but because of the use of the word *Witch* as a reference to an outsider of society.

Satanists do not condone animal or human sacrifice, but actually speak against it. They see this as unjust and therefore not something to be incorporated into their practices. They believe in kindness when someone is deserving of it, but also believe in taking vengeance if wronged. Satanism is not evil, but is very much uninhibited. It emphasizes personal gratification, though many practitioners take this too far and let this ego recognition become delusions of grandeur. The path recognizes nine sins that practitioners must not commit: stupidity, pretentiousness, solipsism, self-deceit, herd conformity, lack of perspective, forgetfulness of past orthodoxies, counterproductive pride, and lack of aesthetics. Because of the noted sin "stupidity," Satanists tend to be well-read, stern, and opinionated.

Further reading:

The Satanic Bible by Anton Szandor LaVey (Avon Books, 1969)

The Satanic Life: Living the Left Hand Path by Corvis Nocturnum (Diabolic Publications, 2007)

The Encyclopedic Sourcebook of Satanism edited by James R. Lewis and Jesper A. Petersen (Prometheus Books, 2006)

Shamanism

Witchcraft and other magickal paths are rooted in shamanism. The word *shamanism* actually originates from the Tungus people of Siberia. Anthropologically, the word was further applied to other cultures with similar tribal associations. Shamanism has become a broad term, unrestricted to any one tribe or group of indigenous people.

Shamanism has been practiced since the beginning of human culture in varying yet similar forms, and can be traced back to the Paleolithic era. In pre-religious times, people relied on shamans for insight and healing. Shamans were the medicine men and women who utilized elements of the natural world for healing and spiritual discovery. They were the spiritualists of old who helped members of the community maintain their spiritual roots. While the rest of the community had their specific duties to provide the culture's

mundane necessities like food and shelter, the shamans were the maintainers of the tribe's spiritual connection.

In many ancient cases, shamans were ousted from society and were either left to their own devices or trained by others experienced in the ways. Many of them were unable to function in the mundane world due to physical disabilities, psychological uniqueness, or social inabilities, and as a result, they moved away from the greater society and began to communicate with people only for spiritual matters. Because of this, they are considered to be *ritual specialists* in terms of their community interaction and social role. Individuals from the greater society would seek the shamans for their specific services. They worked through trade: the shaman's assistance was traded for physical necessities.

Shamanism does not refer to any one religion, but represents similar practices among visionaries of many cultures. What is practiced in the West is different from what is practiced in, say, Southeast Asia. Anthropologically, a shaman usually refers to a man or woman who is in direct contact with the spirit world through a trance state, and may have personal spirits or beings attached to him or her that carry out his or her wishes. Shamanistic practices can be seen in neo-tribal cultures, Native American spiritual communities, and some forms of modern Paganism. There are few ascribed medicine people throughout present cultural structures because of modernity and expectations of normality, specifically in the Americas. Vision quests, sweat lodges, and ritualistic psychedelic voyages are not what they once were, but they still exist as modern shamanic practices.

The recognition of a "World Tree," versions of which are seen in the Druidic, Qabalistic, and Norse systems, is also part of the worldview of the shaman. Shamans have the ability to journey to alternate planes of reality and may consume psychoactive substances to aid in this journeying. The planes are usually seen as the Upperworld (the realm of the gods), the Middleworld (the realm of humans), and the Underworld (the realm of the chthonic spirits). This worldview dates back to ancient times and has carried over to the present day. Shamans take voyages to these planes to uncover secrets of the world. They may meet their spirit animal guides and other personal guides, and receive messages and visions that strengthen their knowledge of the healing arts. They also perform divinations both in trance and in "waking life," using various natural items as divinatory tools. They act as conduits between the world of the living and the world of the dead and have provided spiritual comfort and rite-of-passage ceremonies for people going through intense life changes. Within this notion of spiritualism, when someone fell sick, the person was believed to have lost a portion of his or her soul. Shamans have always been healers, who work with their patients to retrieve portions of their spirits in the case of illness.

Shamans work with their hearts, not their heads. They do not follow exact ritualistic instruction, but form their practices through experiences like naturopathic magick and ecstatic, visionary trance. Shamanism is experiential, the methodology of which used to be passed from generation to generation (and still is in many cultures). The elder could not teach his or her neophytes all things shamanic through words alone. The trainees had to learn how to access other realms of consciousness on their own, sometimes through the influence of natural drugs, self-deprivation, or asceticism (including self-mortification).

Further reading:

The Way of the Shaman: A Guide to Power and Healing by Michael Harner (Harper & Row, 1980)

Shamanism: Archaic Techniques of Ecstasy by Mircea Eliade (Princeton University Press, 1964)

The Temple of Shamanic Witchcraft: Shadows, Spirits and the Healing Journey by Christopher Penczak (Llewellyn, 2005)

In the Shadow of the Shaman: Connecting with Self, Nature & Spirit by Amber Wolfe (Llewellyn, 1988)

Thelema

The word Thelema is Greek for "will." Shortly after the turn of the century, the ubiquitous British magician Aleister Crowley met the sister of his friend Gerald Kelly, named Rose Edith. The two married and then honeymooned in Cairo in 1904, during which Crowley decided to introduce his wife to the magickal arts, as she had no previous knowledge of esoteric philosophy. While following a set of rituals, the couple successfully (and unintentionally) invoked the god Thoth. It was then that Rose's abilities as an oracle were revealed, elevating her to the title "Ouarda the Seer," Crowley's first Scarlet Woman. Rose soon began working with her abilities more in depth. She would enter a trance and channel various messages to Crowley, all of which had spiritual significance.

Rose channeled a great amount of pertinent information concerning the dawn of the Age of Horus ("the crowned and conquering child"), the aeon to replace the 2,000-year-old Age of Osiris, beginning that year. Rose also transmitted that it was Aleister Crowley's job to rekindle the ancient fire by preserving sacred traditions.

Perhaps the most surprising moment was when the beings speaking through Rose mentioned an untranslated funerary stèle existing in the Boulaq Museum with the catalog number 666, a pre-Christian solar number (not associated with Satanism) to which Crowley felt a particular connection. This "Stèle of Revealing" depicted Horus and was a confirmation of the validity of Rose's abilities.

Crowley himself later received a book of channelings from a being called Aiwass, Crowley's Holy Guardian Angel. This book became known as *Liber AL vel Legis* (*Liber CCXX*), or *The Book of the Law*. Within its messages were codes of enlightenment concerning the gods, humans, the cycles of life, and cosmic destiny; it became the cornerstone of Thelema.

Followers of Thelema are called Thelemites. Practitioners can belong to structured lodges that revolve around these teachings, though formal dedication to a particular tradition is not required to simply walk the path. A number of magickal orders and lodge systems have spawned from Crowley's teachings of Thelema, including the Argenteum Astrum (Order of the Silver Star, or A∴A∴) and the Ecclesia Gnostica Catholica (EGC). However, the order that has been most responsible for preserving and carrying on Thelema has been the Ordo Templi Orientis (OTO).

Freemasons Carl Kellner and Theodor Reuss originally ran the OTO. Following Kellner's death in 1905, Reuss began working heavily on the rituals and structure of this new magickal system. In 1912, Reuss met Aleister Crowley and elevated him to the Rex Supremus position, the tenth and highest rank in the order. Shortly thereafter, Crowley revised and reorganized the order's degree system, as well as many of the rituals, to more closely align with the principles of Thelema. Surprisingly, the OTO and its branches were relatively unsuccessful until much later in the twentieth century.

From the time of Crowley's death in 1947 until the late 1960s, the OTO and all its branches were almost entirely lost due to disinterest and disputes among members. In 1969, Grady McMurtry, an American who interacted with Crowley in his dying years,

resurrected the order and spread its influence. The OTO is now one of the largest occult orders in the world and continues to spread the message of Thelema to those who seek its wisdom.

Further reading:

The Book of the Law by Aleister Crowley (many of the most recent editions have been released by Weiser)

The Magick of Aleister Crowley: A Handbook of the Rituals of Thelema by Lon Milo Duquette (Weiser, 2003)

New Aeon Magick: Thelema Without Tears by Gerald del Campo (Llewellyn, 1994)

Vodou (Vodoun, Voodoo)

Despite common misconceptions, Vodou is a religion that focuses on personal growth, spiritual connection, and community. The path is separate from European esoteric traditions, including Witchcraft, though its practices include magick and spiritual communion and it is in many ways similar to other forms of magick and mysticism. Its roots are African, the most recent sects being in Haiti. The largest populations of American practitioners are in New Orleans and other parts of Louisiana. This is due to the tremendous amount of slavery that was prevalent in these areas.

Vodou is one of many Afro-Caribbean spiritual pantheons. Others include Santería (Lukumí or Regla de Ocha), Ifa, Condomblé, and Obeah, many of which originate in the religion of the West African Yoruban people. Anthropologists believe the religion to be older than 10,000 years, rooted in primitive shamanic practice. "Voodoo," like Witchcraft, has gained an incredibly inaccurate reputation throughout time. This seems mostly due to Hollywood's exaggeration of misunderstood elements within the religion that perpetuates an inaccurate ideology. Images of pinpricked dolls and bizarre rituals come to mind for the uneducated observer; a more correct perception might be of rites filled with dancing and drumming. While these concepts have at least partial validity, the majority of negative perceptions that the film industry and mass media have built upon come from practices misunderstood by Caucasian slave masters during the period of slavery.

The slaves had no way of making their voices heard or changing the political system at the time. Instead, they drew on religion and magick rooted in indigenous tribal practices. The slaves were "ruled" by Christian peoples, but most were not permitted to pray to the Christian God, much less their own ancestral deities and spirits (called lwa or loa). Nonetheless, the majority of slaves claimed to be Christian so as to appease their masters. Eventually, the ideology had shifted from believing the slaves should not be permitted to practice religion of any sort to understanding that the slaves could be kept under control if allowed to practice Catholicism. Slaves began masking their practices by associating Catholic saints with their own lwa, thus avoiding persecution by appearing to convert to Catholicism. Practitioners recognized the self-protective necessity of this and understood it to be approved by their gods. Rituals, magick, and celebrations were performed in the wee hours of the night when the slave owners were asleep, presumably around midnight, "the Witching hour."

Hoodoo spells certainly played their part in the movement; "gris-gris bags," bottled concoctions, and Vodou dolls were used in a process of *comparative* or *sympathetic magick*. Certain herbs were understood to have inherent magickal properties. Combinations of these herbs, along with items representing the intent of the spell, created powerful energy, which was then sent through intention. Even if one did not believe in the power of magick, the psychological effects alone were profound. If slave owners found a doll or herbal concoction (often complete with hair, nail clippings, feathers, and written petitions) in their yard or home, they would believe themselves to be cursed. This might cause them not only to have a nervous breakdown but also to analyze their actions and the possible consequences from them. Many of the "cursed" individuals changed the way they treated their slaves, fearing their powers and abilities. Some, on the other hand, became enraged and sought to viciously punish anyone possibly responsible for such spells, with the help of their Church.

Luckily, practitioners of Vodou are gaining recognition for the validity of their spiritual path by the greater community worldwide. Many are published authors, shop owners, teachers, businesspeople, or celebrity figures. They practice the same rituals, ceremonies, divinations, ancestral invocations, and spirit possessions that their ancestors did.

Further reading:

The Haitian Vodou Handbook: Protocols for Riding with the Lwa by Kenaz Filan (Destiny Books, 2006)

The Book of Vodou: Charms and Rituals to Empower Your Life by Leah Gordon (Quarto Books, 2000)

Vodou Shaman: The Haitian Way of Healing and Power by Ross Heaven (Destiny Books, 2003)

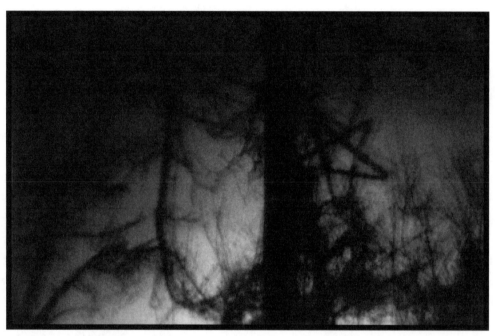

"Formatron" by OakRaven Photography. Location: Greenough Park, Missoula, MT.

III

Philosophies
of the
Dark Witch

This chapter discusses some of the philosophies of the dark Witch, including general observations on commonalities among members of the path, as well as the necessity of spiritual balance and the importance of the emotional realm.

As previously mentioned, there are no absolute views held by all Goths, Pagans, or dark Pagans. Each person undergoes individual experiences and has his or her own take on what each path means on a personal level. This having been said, friction can exist among members regarding what is correct and what is not. This chapter is designed to give the dark Witch or magician a clearer picture of his or her path and provide information that will help along the way.

Shadow to Light

In recent times, the Craft has resurfaced and both *Goth* and *Pagan* have practically become household words. Both ways seek to ride the wave of the future, integrating themselves in the minds of people unsatisfied with obsolete ideas.

Is darkness associated with Witchery because of the obvious stereotypical "dark = evil = Witch" connection, or is there a deeper meaning behind the association? In a 2004 interview in *newWitch* magazine (issue #6), John J. Coughlin, the author of *Out of the Shadows: An Exploration of Dark Paganism and Magick*, stated, "[In television and movies] the Witch is usually portrayed as being somewhat Goth and that has made an impact on the latest generation of Pagans."

Indeed. I would additionally say that Goths are often portrayed as a little bit Witchy in the media, perpetuating a sort of apparent synthesis between the two lifestyles.

I believe it safe to say that Witchcraft *is* characteristically Gothic, or "dark," in many ways. Witchcraft is *not* all love and light, though much of it certainly is. The Craft is *balanced*. Witchcraft is rooted in tribal shamanism, which often seeks to uncover and understand the dark part of the self through directed practice like meditation, trance, and vision quests. Shamanism is the original nondogmatic Witchcraft and earth-based spiritual path. The shaman has the ability to journey to the astral Upperworld, the Middleworld, and the Underworld. The Underworld is the plane where the shadow self is said to be located. This part of the self must be recognized and identified just as much as the light part of the self in order for there to be actual balance. Shamans are known for making intense inner journeys to the Underworld to meet the face of darkness and death itself. They return to a balanced state with a higher attainment of knowledge each time. The true way of the Witch is that of discovering both the higher self and the lower self in order to form balance and awareness, thus strengthening the Craft and understanding the extremes of both lightness and darkness.

Because Paganism itself is very much centered in balance, working with darker aspects of the psyche and the world around us helps restore this to a path that seemingly has the potential to lose its footing in diluted or "fluffy" ideas of what the Craft ought to be—much of which has come about as a result of society's religious conditioning, the impending fear of damnation always lingering in the back of the mind. This fear can inhibit a great deal of personal growth, spawning uncertainty, not to mention the possible reliance on the fantasy of a one-sided spirituality as opposed to the reality of our dual nature. We cannot accurately walk the path toward enlightenment without recognizing and working with our own darkness. We cannot evolve without the humility to face that which we have pushed aside.

Nature itself is light and dark, creative and destructive. If we ignore this in our own practice, delusion becomes kin. Spirituality focused solely on the "light," acting as if internal darkness doesn't exist or can forever be vanquished with the wave of a crystal, is superficial and idealistic, and lacks the depth required for progression. More and more Pagans understand this simple truth every day.

To the dismay of many who follow the Old Ways, the Craft has lost much of its potency by becoming virtually mainstream. As Paganism became better known, especially in America, its balanced focus on the light *and* dark began to sway to the light alone: the light side needed to be publicly presented to dispel negative connotations about the Craft. Now that many Pagans around the world have understood this development, we are allowed to once again simultaneously practice the darker aspects without nearly as much fear of persecution as when Witchcraft (specifically Wicca) initially caught the public eye. At the same time, we mustn't become immersed in the dark to the point that the lighter aspects of our practices (and there are plenty) go unseen.

Humans have both a light and dark side; overemphasis on one side or the other simply causes imbalance, making the person overwhelmed and ungrounded. To practice dark Witchcraft is to walk a light path in a dark skin, balancing lightness with darkness for the sake of balance.

Most dark Pagans do not walk a Left-Hand Path (LHP). Sure, some do, but most do not, especially considering that Witchcraft itself is not Left Hand. The Left-Hand Path is amoral; that is, it does not make a distinction between the moral and immoral, refusing to recognize it altogether. Dark Witches don't exclusively practice what is often termed "black magick." We do, however, understand that everything has its time and place, and therefore don't dismiss the possible need to practice negative magick should the gravity of a situation be intensely enough imbalanced to call for it, and should it be necessary to bring about the greater good in a situation.

Dark Witches generally practice what can be termed *grey magick*, if a distinction is to be made. This is the magick of the Middle Path, the balanced path between light and dark. Though this does include intense, sometimes unpleasant magickal workings, the dark Witch's magick is not considered "black," which (in common terms) tends to have connotations of causing unnecessary harm and senseless suffering. To believe that any Witch works with negative magick alone is simply false. To do so would be to shut out light completely, rendering the caster imbalanced rather than adept.

The dark Witch summons the limitless energy of the night in most magickal workings, using what is called *shadow magick*. The "shadow" refers to anything obscured, either internally or externally. I believe that even things like divination, deep meditation, astral projection, and introspective emotional magick—things that all Witches do—can constitute shadow magick because they reach into the subtle layers of the self or one's environment.

Dark Witchcraft has nothing to do with evil, self-serving, or sinister motivations. The goal of shadow magick isn't to attain godhead or control over others; it is to know all sides of the self and become the master of one's *own* existence—not everybody else's. It carries the same ethical principles as other forms of Witchcraft but doesn't sugarcoat magickal motivations or ignore the shadow self and its importance. Inner darkness is simply not feared on the dark Witch's path—and if it is, then it's worked with. Our dark side is allowed to exist in order to be healed, for we can ultimately begin to know our true selves by examining our own darkness, in turn letting us have power over our own shadow rather than becoming disempowered by it.

When our own dark side is brought into awareness, when we accept our faults, shortcomings, and the nature of our human tendencies, we begin to develop more fully. Our inner darkness is recognized, explored, and *channeled* instead of ignored, repressed, and given the chance to run amok via unconscious, unexpected explosions of chaotic emotions. Illusion is shattered when we are forced to ultimately face ourselves. We must truly see ourselves for who we are and keep our darker side in check every single day. Through shadow magick and the necessary self-exploration that accompanies it, we enter a process of knowing all aspects of ourselves, shadow *and* light, giving us a more complete sense of self and a willingness to pursue our own paths, uninhibited by pent-up guilt and shame.

Dark Witches practice intense forms of Pagan magick that can seem threatening or be easily misinterpreted, and everybody has a different method and focus of practice. To practice darker elements of Paganism ritualistically, the practitioner must allow him- or herself to become totally immersed in the energy being raised, dropping all inhibitions and doubts. This is why wordy, dull, or monotonous rituals generally are unappealing to the dark Witch. The energy raised in ritual is meant to be intense and highly transformative, belonging only to the practitioner(s) and divinity. Dark Witches understand that the night holds a limitless amount of power, and that it is from this divine darkness that all things, including life itself, manifest.

From the empty darkness, light can come into being—any energy can be harnessed to bloom into manifestation. The infinite nature of emptiness is what makes the darkness such a powerful force, capable of being utilized for spiritual means.

The dark Witch walks a lunar path, illuminated by the ambience of the moon's light, and aspires to see every single moment of life as a spiritual experience, keeping him- or herself constantly in check on as many levels as possible.

The nighttime takes up about a third of the daily cycle. Its energy is infinite. What differentiates dark energy from light energy is that the darkness is unseen, unilluminated, and vacant. Darkness is the unconscious mind, calling us to search deep within and without for the answers we seek so desperately. First and foremost, dark Witches more often than not look internally, rather than outside the self, for answers. This promotes self-responsibility instead of perpetuating endless cycles of victimization, reminding us that *we* construct our own reality and have the potential to change our lives for the better.

Both lightness and darkness are profoundly powerful, but it's the darkness that we are drawn to, and that is what we must utilize; it's our job by default. Nocturnal energy is all around, is always present, and will never cease. The dark Witch works mostly at night when energies are subdued, knowing the time to be especially conductive to magickal intent in order to instigate change on multiple planes. The shadow is the unseen, the hidden, and aligns with the Witch's search for answers on the esoteric spiritual path.

The dark Witch reaches into darkness to uncover the light, and is unafraid of the potential repercussions of doing so. Oftentimes, the path leading to a greater understanding of Spirit, the self, and reality requires the seeker to "die" inside, to face the inner darkness and return with greater awareness. In this sense, the path of the dark Witch is similar to the path of the shaman. It requires us to focus on that which we'd rather not, forcing our consciousness to really know the fullness of our experience. The amount of humility and courage this requires is profound, and it is not an easy task for anyone. Additionally, everyone's method of shadow magick is different.

The dark Witch is like a shadow put into form…moving through life, walking the Middle Path between life's polarities, often remaining quiet and curiously observing, thinking, and dreaming, having the semblance of an apparition. Artistic expression of any kind is the dark Witch's release. Magick and self-awareness are the keys to understanding.

Many people drawn to Paganism and Goth culture in this life are indeed old souls—those who have traversed the planes and learned the mysteries many lives over, here or elsewhere. Many are conscious in ways others are not, further putting an apparent barrier between the self and the outside world. Why are we this way, and is it okay? A plethora of reasons could be put forth, but the fact remains that we are different, we are strange, and we are drawn to the darkness. We must use this truth to empower ourselves on our path, which is that of change and transformation that constantly influences others *and* ourselves.

Discipline and Traditionalism

There are so many spiritual paths that it's nearly impossible to know them all. Ancient traditions have come and gone; some have resurfaced as much as possible, and others have taken on new skin. Most traditions have their own unique spiritual viewpoints, cosmology, and means to achieve metaphysical awareness. Often, surrounding environmental and political influences at the time of a system's birth play the largest role in determining the uniqueness of each path; ideology shifts in cultures due to location and social structure. At the same time, esoteric traditions from every culture have numerous commonalities and correspondences. Most commonalities have to do with paths holding similar roots in ancient traditions, thus having similar base ideas, practices, and spiritual symbolism.

Every spiritual tradition has its own form of magick, be it prayer, meditation, ritualistic devotion, or spellcraft. Each emphasizes the practice of magick/prayer to its own degree, seeing it in its own light. Traditions of the occult are unique from many other spiritual paths in that they stress personal empowerment, teaching that each of us is in control of our own life and destiny. Instead of placing the hands of fate entirely outside of ourselves, magickal traditions emphasize that *we* are the creators of our world and our reality, both individually and globally.

A person's dedication, diligence, and endless curiosity cultivate spiritual awakening. We must ask ourselves what the best avenue is for our own spiritual growth. What are the outlets and what wisdom is out there waiting to be understood? This brings us to the contents of this section.

In modern times, spiritual discipline is lacking—something that lends credence to the fact that many spiritual seekers drift in and out of the magickal arts. Strict adherence to spiritual beliefs and magickal systems was commonplace "back in the day." Now, nearly everything is in print. It's only a matter of seeking out the information and choosing a path…or letting the path choose you.

Many inner-court secrets that esoteric schools once guarded are now widely published, just waiting on bookshelves to be discovered. Few texts remain unpublished and even fewer contain brand-new information applicable to modern times. High magick formulas and invocations once reserved for exclusive bloodlines are now available at any New Age bookstore, ancient scrolls have been translated, once-underground folk traditions have been revived (or reconstructed), archaeologists have unearthed items pointing to the true nature of ancient occult philosophies…the word is out and the tools are there. Some traditionalists view this as an unfortunate development and believe their ways have become diluted, diffused, and misunderstood. Secrets, magickal methods, and spiritual realizations have been revealed to the masses, and this understandably upsets people who have held on to these things through years of secretive study and practice. Traditions have long trained and initiated their students in secret rites designed to trigger spiritual awakening in a specific process that is inaccessible without formal training.

Fortunately, few people actually use printed esoteric information for negative purposes. For most, the plethora of information available provides countless venues for further research to a spiritual seeker. This is why eclecticism is so prevalent in modern Paganism. People feel comfortable researching numerous paths and applying portions to their own practices and philosophies. This creates a syncretistic unit—a personalized path of sorts. I believe this is all part of the evolution of spiritual understanding and the integration of cultures. Perhaps this intermingling is a blessing, so long as the ones studying are serious and absolutely respectful of the information they immerse themselves in.

One big problem with nontraditionalism (which some traditionalists are quick to point out) is that the seekers often remain undisciplined in their studies. A number of practitioners pick and choose whichever concepts work for them, regardless of origin, and let that be the extent of it, remaining relatively stagnant without pursuing further studies. Witchcraft and other spiritual systems actually are much deeper than they may seem at first. In order to undergo honest spiritual transformation, the seeker must look within and see which lessons are waiting to be understood on the internal level—personal lessons that no book in the world can teach. Seekers must take the initiative to transform on many levels and be prepared for the will of the universe to align with their own. I believe that nontraditionalists have the inherent requirement to develop spiritual discipline and actualize their dedication to the path they've chosen, however eclectic. Simply practicing a variety of methods may be beneficial in the short term, but this choice must be grounded with a recognition of personal strengths and shortcomings. Self-discipline alongside constant spiritual study aids us immensely in our evolutionary path.

Some traditions actually *require* the student to research and study other traditions before completely declaring one path over the others. Each tradition can provide a different aspect of esoteric study, leading to a more holistic view of magick and spiritualism. Paths of discipline are in place to act as complete guide systems. They are designed to provide precise training methodologies as steppingstones to spiritual progression. I agree with this systemized approach, but at the same time believe that these metaphorical steppingstones are present in all spiritual systems in one form or another, and can be utilized properly if approached with awareness.

For example, Buddhism may teach seekers various methods of meditation and finding inner peace. Tantric systems may teach them about the chakras and human energy system to strengthen knowledge about energetic anatomy to practice the healing arts. Shamanism may teach them how to contact astral guides and spirit animals. Green Witchcraft may show them how to use herbs, plants, and the tools of the earth to manifest intent. Druidic teachings may reveal the Wheel of the Year to strengthen their connection to the natural cycles. Ceremonial magick systems may explain concepts of the planes and proper methods for calling spirits. Each system provides its own piece of the puzzle, and it is possible for someone to gain spiritual understanding by working with one tradition alone or with a combination of many. However, if one system appeals to a person over another, then hard and fast dedication may be the next appropriate step.

This is not to say other systems should be disregarded, but that undergoing the steps of a particular devotional system could in fact be just the key a person needs to unlock his or her own awakening.

There are many, many paths to Spirit, regardless of what fundamentalists might say. A person who has bad experiences in one religion or another will probably naturally work his or her way out of it in due time. Negative experiences can happen in even the most appealing religions (and subcultures). If someone's experience is solid, real, and satisfactory, he or she is likely to stay with the path for the rest of his or her life. In the end, no one person or experience can represent the whole of a path; the best way to uncover its truth is through active research and reflection by the seeker.

The tradition I follow is a form of "disciplined eclectic" Neopagan occultism called Opus Aima Obscuræ. Every year and a day following a person's initiation, the seeker undertakes various forms of sacrifice and sacrament to further spiritually progress and bring about a greater understanding of life in a metaphysical sense. These ordeals (including tonsures, fastings, and devotions) are never easy because they necessarily require intensive study, dedication, and self-realization through personal sacrifice. This and other similar systems are examples of how ancient energies and disciplines are resurfacing in unexpected forms.

My first Priestess was Zanoni Silverknife of the Georgian tradition of Wicca. In training, she stressed that traditionalism is like a skeleton: it is a framework serving as a foundation for further development and personal pursuits. To stick to the skeletal system alone is to practice the same rituals, say the same words of power, and train and initiate using the exact same method. This has the tendency to become rigid and monotonous if "flesh" is not added to the frame. The flesh consists of anything that isn't part of the strict traditionalism, including new ideas, prayers, chants, mantras, lore, spells, and magickal methods. A person should not, however, negate his or her past traditional teachings (if the person has them) but rather *add on to them* based on personal callings. More and more former traditionalists have been turning to this method, expanding their original skeletal structure into a more extensive and diverse system.

If someone chooses nontraditionalism, he or she must maintain the utmost respect for traditionalists and the systems they follow. Spiritual seekers should not become full of themselves or think their ways to be more diverse and open-minded than those practiced by conservative traditionalists. At the same time, those living according to traditional systems should not believe their ways to be more grounded, realistic, and ancient than the practices of "those delusional New Age Pagans." Each person must do what is right for him or her, remembering that *everybody is different*. Generalizations are useful sometimes, but can limit a person from seeing very real anomalies.

People who are not based in a particular tradition and feel that certain teachings are not appropriate to their own spiritual journey must know that they *do* have the option in this day and age to blend ideas and practices from various paths into what works best for them individually. This blending of traditions has become a hot topic in the Pagan community. There is no sense in arguing traditionalism versus nontraditionalism as a superior style; every practitioner must decide which path is best suited to him or her. Each way of practice is unique and beneficial in its own way. We are all working for a common cause. Each tradition shares the goal of honoring and healing the earth and her people, weaving magick in the world and celebrating times of change. If mutual respect is present between traditionalists and nontraditionalists and they seek to learn from one another, then there is no reason to fight beyond a constructive sharing of ideas. We are all in this together.

When one is open—sincerely open—to the universe's teachings and is willing to endure the painful process of shedding one's ego, realizations *will* tumble into view, regardless of whether one is trained in a particular mystery school or tradition. The Craft is a living, experiential religion. Lessons come to you as you open yourself to them; the universe is an never-ending open book waiting to be read. The amount of actual knowledge a spiritual seeker learns is ultimately up to the seeker. Books, teachers, and guides can point the way, but it's up to the seeker to either apply the information to life or let it go in one ear and out the other! Both traditions and nontraditions offer systems to help you discover your purpose on earth.

If you are seeking the ways of magickal spirituality and do not have a teacher (that is, a *reliable* teacher) to help you train, then get all the books you can and research your way to understanding as much as possible, even if it be without the structure of a coven or training system. As spiritual beings, we have the right to educate ourselves and advance to our destination of clarity.

Attitude and Personality

Dark Pagans embody a social double whammy: not only are we practicing and learning commonly misunderstood occult philosophies, but we also choose to express our ideologies on an external level through our appearance. For onlookers, it can be scary to see such strange-looking beings as ourselves, as it may open mental/spiritual doors in their minds they likely have never considered before. Of course, this can spawn a variety of reactions, from interest to slander. These and many other factors in turn influence our reactions and attitudes toward life. What is your general attitude about things? With what attitude do you observe life, and how does it influence your reaction to experiences? These are questions we must constantly ask ourselves, keeping our egos in check to step into a greater level of awareness.

Looking different and having alternative interests are actually extremely beneficial socially. They serve as a natural filtration process against people who would end up causing harm in the long run. If people are shallow enough to cast harsh judgment against you for alternative living, especially because of something as trivial as looking different, listening to strange music, or having nonmainstream spiritual views, then they are not worth befriending in the first place, and you should hardly internalize their judgment.

One key to looking different is *being nice*. How you interact with others shows not only your personal ethics but also your spiritual worth. Painful experiences must be integrated in order to let light once again manifest itself, so that pain or sadness don't resurface in everyday situations, including in interactions with others who may pass harsh judgment.

If, for example, someone hits you with a scowl or pointed laugh from a nearby car after seeing how you look (if you look out of the ordinary), how do you react? If you yell profanities or make obscene gestures back, it only perpetuates a negative image on behalf of all "freaks." A negative reaction confirms the other person's preconceived notions, giving the person the idea that, yes, all different-looking people are angst-filled baddies. This idealism is precisely what we don't want when trying to gain acceptance for behavior that is out of the norm. I, for one, get upset when I see alternative kids shooting insults right back at judgmental people; it creates a chaotic spiral of separation between the two parties, regardless of their originally defined differences. Try returning someone's middle-finger gesture with a peace sign instead ... it really makes them think.

The simple act of smiling at people is a good thing, even if they react negatively toward you. If you dress differently, you will be stared at. That's just how it goes! Stares and sideways glances come with the territory of looking different. One can't blame people for trying to make sense of the strange sight in front of them if they're not used to such a thing. It's an unavoidable side effect of eccentricity and must be accepted as part of the bargain. C'est la vie!

Don't let joy become secondary to anything in your life; don't allow yourself to suppress this happiness. Goths and Pagans are emotional people and like to express their feelings in many different ways, including the positive ones. Give hugs to your friends and family; tell them how much you love and appreciate them and why. Odds are, they'll do the same, even if it takes time. This positive expression encourages a soul connection between two parties and naturally gives rise to personal happiness and well-being.

Witches must see with absolute clarity as much as is humanly possible. It's part of our job. We must keep both ourselves and one another in check. How do we react to our surroundings and day-to-day experiences? Are we seeing things objectively or subjectively? It's very easy to see things subjectively; existentialist philosophers would probably add that it's impossible not to. Subjective sight is seeing things as you believe or want them to be, not as they actually are. For example, if you believe someone to have ill intentions toward you, when in actuality the person does not, then your subjective mind might perceive anything that individual does as a personal attack.

The world must be seen as it unfolds around the self with as few emotional attachments put on the external environment as possible. If someone puts his or her own twist on occurrences and blows things out of proportion, it can only add emotional baggage to the situation, digging the hole of misunderstanding even deeper. It separates the person from the reality of the situation, lessening comprehension of the energy at hand and thus stunting spiritual growth.

Objectivity is crucial. It allows us to see personal patterns occurring in life—spiritual lessons replaying themselves so that we can learn from them. If we look around, patterns are constantly being repeated on a smaller level. Lessons may recur through small things like the people we associate with, lovers, jobs, or situations that we seem to repeatedly find ourselves in. Sometimes it takes a "cosmic two-by-four" to make sure we're listening. Extreme issues come to the forefront in an intense rush that may create changes all at once. This can be wounding, but we mustn't attach ourselves to the negative feelings of these experiences.

It's so easy to become jaded with life and turn to pessimism, judgment, and emotional attachment. The world isn't all love and light. Not all the time. It's easy to become so wounded from the moral corruption of the world that we shut down, pushing everyone and everything aside. Life doesn't have to be lived in bitterness. There is still hope; there is always balance of the negative and positive. As magicians and spiritual seekers, we are the bringers of great change, a great shift of spiritual awakening, leading eventually to worldwide unity and compassion. Ours is the challenge of a lifetime; let's be the first to initiate it as a magickal experience.

Dissension Among Us

Both Pagans and Goths seem to be harboring a similar internal conflict: members of the scenes are frequently fighting among one another. *This is ridiculous!* We are all members of a unique subculture; we are all unified even if we don't always approve of each other wholeheartedly. A hundred years ago, being openly Pagan and/or otherwise "spooky" were basically unheard of. As members of alternative paths, we must stick together no matter what the cost. Indeed, as spiritualists, we must have absolute respect for one another in the alternative scene: Goth, Pagan, or otherwise. Both lifestyles currently face dissension, due in part to judgment, arrogance, manipulation, and self-righteousness. Sadly, a number of both Goths and Pagans believe their way is the right way, the only way, for everyone—but when we believe ourselves to have reached the top, we stop learning.

Dissension is very real but is something many people look past. Even the most rewarding of lifestyles face the same problems as any other, though it may be to a lesser degree. If we feel impassioned about something, we must express it before it builds. Drama, gossip, and egotism don't help Pagans and Goths build solid structures, but lead to their downfalls bit by bit. Each one of us helps form the greater community; we are equally important to the whole. Until we stop bickering about the accuracy of our lifestyles to other people (be they within or outside of our communities), the issues must be addressed in order to be vanquished.

Surprisingly, a large number of people haven't caught on to the simple truth of human unity: we are all one people. This is a universal spiritual truth. Individuals like us have taken it in our own hands to spread diversity and freedom to the masses, even in the face of judgment. Despite minor discrepancies between us, we are all working for the same cause. We are the people of the New Tide and must make the best of our experience, not only for ourselves but for everyone else.

I agree with one quote from a Native American that I heard, the gist of which is: "There is no tree so foolish that its branches fight among themselves." One can surmise that the tree's trunk represents consciousness and the branches are its children: all people, all animals, and all beings. This quote is simple, appropriate, and wise. Think about it...

Utilizing Emotional Energy

So what do emotions have to do with spirituality and magick? Everything! Change is triggered by magick, magick is triggered by intention, intention is triggered by thought, and thought is so often triggered by emotion. Spellcasting itself requires emotions. The caster must project emotion to manifest will. Without emotions, the spell is just as mundane and insignificant as any other activity, and very little power is focused into the working. Emotions are our guide. Emotions connect us to the spiritual realms. They conduct our lives, making our experiences *real*. They keep us interested in the world and give us a sense of fullness in the human experience. Humans have the unique ability to experience emotions and thus have the opportunity to embrace them fully as internal spiritual vehicles.

Ancient teachings, most notably those of Buddhism and other Eastern mystic paths, teach us not to get attached to our emotions when feeling them. This means monitoring yourself and your reactions to what's going on around you. Become aware of yourself as a soul in a human frame, feeling what you are as a reaction to stimuli in your surrounding environment. It is not the whole of your being feeling these sensations, but your human emotional body. This is a significant part of you, but is not the whole. Increasing self-awareness leads to a greater understanding of how you function and brings about self-acceptance.

If one is not emotionally stable, studying the more intense aspects of the magickal arts is like gripping a lit firecracker. This is especially the case when studying or practicing shadow magick. Being in a state of psychological/emotional balance with utmost self-awareness is essential when practicing deep or complex magick, as the forces being worked with can be overwhelming and even scary if one's feet are not planted on stable ground. Once this state of groundedness is reached through self-reflection, therapy, and basic methods of magick, a greater understanding of the mind can be had, and certain esoteric information and practices become more attainable and feasible to immerse oneself in.

It is not easy to perceive multiple realities when the most important one is little understood. To understand the emotions, one must constantly be aware of one's emotional state. "I feel this way right now for what reasons?" is a key question you should ask yourself throughout the day. Emotions surface as reactions to stimuli. Follow up this question by asking, "Do I like feeling this way or not, and what can I do to change my current state?" Constantly becoming aware of and working on the emotional body will help spiritual seekers understand their motivations and personalities, gradually leading to the deconstruction of negative mental states. I have no qualms about saying that emotional work is the foundation of spiritual and magickal progression.

Contrary to popular belief, doom and gloom do not penetrate every aspect of Goth culture. We're actually pretty ordinary people who experience just as many emotions as the rest of the human race. However, we are more than willing to face reality and embrace all parts of the emotional spectrum. The same can be said for dark Witches, those who utilize the darker emotions for means of spiritual progression. The importance of such emotions *must* be understood. A very, very small handful of people have truly mastered the fullness of their emotional bodies…and Goddess knows I'm not one of them! To truly know all aspects of the self takes lifetimes to achieve—so let's begin now!

Everything we do influences the next moment. Every little thing. This spiritual fact of life is easily recognizable when looking at emotional spirals: if an individual is overtaken by emotion, be it happiness, depression, nervousness, or anything else in the sphere of experience, the aftershocks can be felt for quite some time. Emotionally sensitive people, including many Witches and magicians, naturally tend to internalize personal experience, dwelling on it for quite some time. These feelings must be worked with for metaphysical awareness to grow.

Emotions affect one's internal reality, thus weaving their way into external reality. If you feel sad, you look at life through a "sad filter." Likewise, if you are optimistic, positivity seems to exist in abundance in your environment. I call this *emotional filtration*. This simple but very real psychological occurrence is in accordance with the magickal law of attraction, which states that "like attracts like." If a person's aura is emanating a particular vibratory pattern, similar energies are drawn toward it, creating a spiral of experience.

Being in a perpetual state of happiness is just as detrimental to someone as being in a perpetual state of sadness. Both emotions in and of themselves are natural in moderation, but have the potential to become psychological disorders if they supplant all others.

According to Chinese traditional medicine, there are seven emotions in the human experience: joy, concentration, grief, anger, fear, anxiety, and fright. Additionally, Vajrayana (Tantric) Buddhism recognizes six basic emotional "afflictions" that hinder our spiritual development: anger, craving (desire/attachment), lack of awareness (ignorance), pride, doubt (uncertainty), and afflicted view (clinging to views of the self). Many are similar in nature and are derived from one another. A healthy balance of positive and negative emotions is necessary for the fully functioning spiritual person.

The Downward Spiral: Sadness

"Art thou willing to suffer to learn?" These are key words in the first-degree initiation of traditional Gardnerian Wicca. They are not to be taken lightly. Life is a process of learning, and oftentimes pain is our greatest teacher. Many Witches understand the fact that spiritual initiation is not limited to ritual training. Life has the grandest of lessons to teach, and if we overcome the pain and torment of various stages of being, then we ascend to higher levels of learning, facing new challenges at every step. If Spirit permeates every aspect of our lives, then it's only right to believe that lessons come to us through turmoil, because ultimately we need them to do so.

It's okay to feel sadness. We all have to be depressed at times. It's okay to feel as though your life is falling apart. To feel absolute misery, wishing nothing more than to escape this reality and all things in it. To feel dead inside, rendered powerless by a constant stream of tears, finding it nearly impossible to even wake up in the morning. To be numbed by the world and feel worthless in it all... Seriously, it's *okay*. Deep sadness and lamentation are very much a natural part of experience, and, well, Goths and dark artists often are more prone to feeling these things than those who repress their emotions.

Feelings of grief and desolation are nothing to be ashamed of and are in fact *necessary* at times. If nervous breakdowns didn't happen, there would be no real growth in the spiritual realms. If you suppress tears and don't allow yourself to feel pain and embrace absolute sorrow, then life is incomplete. If your emotional centers aren't allowed to flourish, then you are not progressing on your spiritual path.

In many ways, sadness can be comforting. The lulling uncertainty it brings makes a person feel alive. To experience strong emotions is to feel the experience of life at its fullest. It's only when a person gets stuck in a rut of habitually entering a state of melancholy that it becomes a problem. As Pagans, we must strive for full recognition of our emotions and how we utilize them.

Many psychologists say that the ego only likes to suffer if its identity is formed as a result of the suffering. That is, if we identify ourselves by our suffering, then we become attached to the sensation and our ego begins to identify itself strictly with the feeling. Over time, the association between the self and the suffering can become almost inseparable.

Though the Craft does not require perpetual happiness, it does require magickal practitioners to be accountable for the lessons in their lives and realize their own influence in the creation of emotional states. Magicians must not only learn from the lessons that life is continually teaching—which is not always an easy process—but also move on to higher planes, discovering the means to lead a more sentient life. Feeling depressed presents two options: we can either fall victim to sad emotions, letting them consume us, or we can choose to accept them and learn by facing them head-on, that is, by becoming proactive in coping with and healing from such experiences.

Sadness doesn't always need to have a direct reason to surface any more than happiness or simple contentedness does. Emotions often force you to experience them because you need to know them at the time, even if external influences are not immediately apparent. Then again, more often than not, reasons *are* apparent for feeling sadness. Sometimes it just takes the pressure of one more negative occurrence to cause a number of pent-up emotions to explode.

The world is filled with many, many evils. This can be observed by reading the news, or with any exposure to the public. Evil exists both locally and globally and is very difficult to avoid. Just knowing the impurities around us, not to mention experiencing them firsthand, is enough to tempt us to shut off our emotional centers and make us apathetic toward life. Repressing emotions is easy to do but extremely dangerous. The risks associated with emotional repression are numerous and should be taken into consideration. If you suppress negative emotions for an extended period of time, the pressure naturally will build and may eventually explode. This can be a worse experience than simply dealing with the emotions in the first place. Mood swings are a part of life. The Craft does not require its adherents to be joyous and happy all the time. The world, at least right now, is not a pure and untainted place. People are cruel, life's a bitch, and it's okay to realize these things and express them in a positive and therapeutic manner.

Some people who embrace the Gothic lifestyle get caught in the hang-ups of development, drawing inward and rarely coming out. Rather than coming to terms with the shadow, some get trapped in the sadness of it all and embrace negative emotions to an unhealthy degree. Depression leads to tunnel vision; sadness is all that is focused on. When sadness gets to this point, the person either gets so comforted by sadness that it serves as a tool of attention-getting and emotional codependence, or the person honestly feels that there is no hope in life. Both views are so easy to take because we are emotional beings, but both views also keep a person imprisoned in what Buddhists call the vicious Wheel of Samsara: suffering. But these feelings are only as real as we make them. We control our actions and reactions and ultimately our life path. We can create anything we wish, and this includes emotional balance.

In times of sadness, we shift our energies from external to internal. We face our shadow and deconstruct our ego. We question what is real and what is illusory. Everyone has a different way of dealing with this most intense of emotions. Some bottle up their sadness and try not to express it on the surface, while others are boisterous about their dissatisfaction and look to others for help. Still others isolate themselves from the rest of the world for a period of time out of an instinctual need to look within, not without.

When overcome with depression, it can be easy to throw this negative emotion outward, shifting blame onto others. This is a form of *negative projection*. In doing this, the person feels momentary comfort by placing the pain externally, usually onto someone else. Naturally, this manifests as anger. Such anger is rarely justified and serves as a mask for sadness and internal pain. This reaction is drawn from the ego and is a form of instinctual self-preservation. Pointing the finger outside the self rarely solves problems. Rather, it perpetuates the blame game and harmful interactions. This downward spiral is difficult to unwind, but it is possible to do so with *constant* awareness. Everyone projects their pain in a different manner. When we project internal pain onto others, it comes back to us in the end.

I am not proposing that anger be avoided at all costs. At times, feeling anger is entirely reasonable. In fact, it is extremely beneficial to experience any form of emotion so long as you maintain control over the emotion—and not allow the emotion to control you. You must realize who has dominance in any given situation: you or the emotion itself. Getting lost in emotions is a problem for spiritual people. Many of us are aware of various states of reality existing simultaneously, and this can be overwhelming. The emotional plane is one of these and is so easy to get overly wrapped up in because of its presence.

Pagans perceive a multitude of patterns in the fabric of reality that others don't. It only follows that such extrasensory perception leads to a feeling of alienation. Goths, especially spiritual Goths, are evolved thinkers, contemplating numerous things simultaneously and investing a lot of time in discovering the eternal Self and its place in the cosmos. Sometimes it can be all too overwhelming and usher in feelings of isolation, not to mention the fact that if extrasensory perception isn't honed, channeled, and grounded properly, it can lead to a mental breakdown.

Psychic awareness is very, very real, and to be swept away by acute perception is reason enough to feel as though you're losing your mind. Spirituality and occultism require that we work with these abilities and remain grounded, so that particular emotions don't turn out ultimately to be consuming. This is mastering our destiny.

All things pass and are constantly subject to change. Change is the only constant. Depression is a *stage* of being, not a *state* of being.

Wounds and Scars

Many people are drawn to alternative cultures because of emotional wounds. Eccentric ways of life are attractive because they draw people of similar experience and belief together to share their lives in what is often sacred communion. Just as human interaction can be the most wounding of experiences, so can it also be the most healing.

The deepest emotional wounds can stem from childhood experiences. This is why a loving childhood is one of the best gifts a person can receive (and give). So often, parents project their own emotional wounds onto their children, perpetuating a negative cycle through multiple generations. It's up to people like us to break these cycles, not to fuel the fire. It is said that "the abused often becomes the abuser." This link can be broken with awareness and acceptance, and the cultivation of love for others as well as the self.

I find it impossible to comprehend the treatment that many children endure, and the shame, insecurity, and extreme pain caused by such abuse. Through shadow magick and innermost examination, we can pull these demons out from the recesses of our unconscious and, through humility and dedication, invite in the healing forces necessary to overcome traumatic events.

Being rejected, crossed, wounded, and abused, whether in childhood or later in life, leaves emotional scars that take a very long time to heal. Personal wounds leave us in a dark, cold place in many aspects of our lives. We then constantly question our worth and our placement in life and may end up seeing things unclearly as a result, simply because we cannot answer the question "Why did this happen to me?" Perhaps it has to do with past-life karmic cycles playing out. Perhaps it's because the lessons to be learned could not have manifested in any other way. Perhaps it happened so that the recipients of the abuse eventually can come to help others in similar situations. The answers to these most painful of questions can come to light only when the utmost attention is paid to the wound. The wound must be taken care of and (ad)dressed before it has the opportunity to become infected. The first step in doing this is to accept the painful experience or experiences, knowing that this came into your life for some reason. Instead of playing the blame game, take absolute responsibility for your current state of being and really determine the best route of healing. Only then can the role of victim be released and the greater aspects of things come to be realized. We must learn to "own" our experience by facing painful emotions that surface but have never fully healed. We must get to know them and eventually master them.

Witches understand that action equals effect and that every single thing builds on the next. If you are raising children, then be the best parent you can be. Be a guide, teacher, and mentor. Educate your children about other ways of life. Don't hurt or repress them in any way for their unavoidable transgressions, but rather give them uninhibited, unconditional love through and through so as to not allow wounds to perpetuate. If you are a friend or romantic partner to someone, settle for nothing less than Perfect Love and Perfect Trust. That includes being honest at all times, addressing issues when they arise, and keeping your emotional receptors and projectors in check *constantly*. Be a good friend or partner, and expect the same in return. When emotions are repressed or reactions are based in fleeting, momentary feelings, actual balance is difficult to achieve and truth is difficult to see. Life is just too short.

"White Widow: A Memory; The Psyche" by OakRaven Photography. Model: Sasha

Dark Night of the Soul

When we are emotionally hurt, a certain numbness takes over. Feelings of hopelessness and misery override logical thinking, and insecurities tumble into the forefront. In the times of our deepest misery, all the demons we have hidden away break their chains to face us head-on. Life seems altogether meaningless, and reality seems to crumble on all sides—nothing seems real…nothing *is* real. All is lulled, nulled, and bleak. Only hopelessness exists—a sense of dread and emptiness. While no words can fully convey the intensity of the experience, this process is called the Dark Night of the Soul. The Christian mystic St. John of the Cross was the first to use the term in the sixteenth century, recognizing the experience as the feeling of the loss of God and the absence of any mystical experience.

My dear friend and fellow dark Witch author Kala Trobe once gave a speech at London's Witchfest in 2004, describing the Dark Night of the Soul: "All you know is that you suffer—and not even 'to learn.' In some systems it's described as the Trance of Sorrow and relates to the experience of Binah on the [Qabalistic] Tree of Life. You question the validity of your entire existence. Your magickal truth becomes hypocrisy, your hopes a sham, vanity merely. Panic attacks and suicidal impulses ensue."

All occultists, magicians, and progressing spiritualists must endure spiritual desolation at various points throughout their lives. The experience should be recognized as part of the natural process of metaphysical growth. Just knowing this can add a bit of padding to the pain, making the experience a bit more endurable. The Dark Night of the Soul is not a trivial experience, for it reaches to the innermost depths of the soul, forcing it to be pulled inside out for examination. Every bit of the self is drawn into question, and everything one knows as truth is disbelieved. Everything is stilled at this crossroads, which forces the practitioner to choose between giving up or trekking on.

Periods of despondency are signs of spiritual growth. If magick, spirituality, and life itself are never questioned—even doubted—then the path will be followed only blindly. During the Dark Night's process, a psychological death takes place. It can be a frightening and uncertain experience, but the dying must take place in order for rebirth to occur. We must go *below* before we can rise *above*.

Upon returning from the depths of sorrow, one is more aware. Disorientation *leads* to self-awareness. Pieces of the formerly unseen begin to make themselves visible in the blurry whirlpool of lamentation. Once the negative has been examined and deciphered, the positive makes itself clearer. Happiness and sadness are two sides of the same coin; once one side is understood, the other is more perceivable as well. We must know both sides of the self to see the bigger picture.

The world is filled with much evil and apathy; it's often very difficult to understand where those on the path of ushering in higher consciousness really fit in, if anywhere. In many cases, all we can do is trust in Spirit, believing that everything is in place, unfolding as it is naturally meant to. When that trust is shattered, all we can do is pick up the pieces, breathe, and try to make sense of our own experience. Does everything hold a blatant or obscured lesson? Indeed. Is it always easy to see what it is? Not by any means.

We must break before we can truly find the path we are to follow. In many ways, pain is our ultimate initiator. It is one of our greatest teachers and is an experience we must honor as a guide. We mustn't get trapped in our emotional states; we can't let any emotion rule us. Dark Nights deconstruct our spirits to give us the opportunity to reconstruct our path…and slowly…eventually…we rebuild, becoming all the stronger because of it.

Suicide

It's tempting to feel so fed up with living that escaping it altogether seems the only way to really change circumstances. It's not. This is an illusion of hopelessness that the moment of desolation presents. When we feel absolutely devastated, we see life with shadowed vision, overlooking the positive and beautiful aspects of life.

If you find yourself in a state of extreme or seemingly uncontrollable sadness, understand this: the bottom of the downward spiral is death. If you allow death to take you before your time, then you are giving in and giving up. Life is a very intense experience—it's serious, it's hilarious, and everything in between. In the end, it's just a game. It's a game of learning, of facing the darkness and returning with the light: the skills of the shaman, the way of the Witch. We walk our paths because we are chosen to, and each moment is precisely in place for us to learn from. This is easy to say but not always easy to see.

No matter how deeply you think you're drowning, no matter how bleak and hopeless it all seems, the seemingly endless downward spiral *will* pick you back up. Life will turn around if you go with the flow and let experience take you higher. It wants to. The gods thirst to bring you to higher states of awareness, even if it means facing absolute despair to gain an accurate perspective.

With magick and meditation, deep, honest sadness can be soothed and alleviated. For any and every wish there exists a spell. More than likely, this will not be found in a book. Instead, allow books to be the guides and framework for self-created rituals targeted at the source of agony. And as for tools, there is always at least one herb, one stone, one color, one prayer, one mantra, one *something*, that can assist in energetic focus, strengthening a very specific process of healing and change.

To kill oneself is to give in to a tide of life that is absolutely temporary, even if it doesn't seem like it at the time. Life is in a constant state of flux. We must tread on, knowing there will be change. Present circumstances will change if you take the initiative to change them. If your will is strong, then all else will follow in suit. *Life will change* as pain and repeating cycles come more clearly into view. It will change because you will take the necessary steps to make it so. You will be led out of the darkness; all ailments will pass with time. Let this become your goal and spiritual will. The inevitable nature of existence is change. Breathe, calm yourself, center, and relax; help release your pain through intuitive magick, and wait for the sun to rise again. It always does.

Suicide is not something to take lightly. It's not cool or glamorous to have slash marks across your wrists. A lot of people "fake" suicide attempts as a cry for either attention or actual help. They may think they are trying to take their own lives, when in actuality a large part of themselves is afraid of dying and facing the inevitable unknown. The rational mind knows that death is not the solution, but the emotional mind doesn't always agree. Suicide is not glamorous and is not admirable, and it certainly doesn't make someone more Goth, emo, or what have you. The tragedy of it mustn't be trivialized.

Suicide is not even a way out; it's not a true escape. More often than not, the soul of a person who has committed suicide *remains* in that vibratory state. That is, the soul becomes an "earthbound disincarnate," or ghost, trapped in that energetic state of suffering, thus constantly reliving the misery with no awareness beyond that state of being. Suicide may seem like an escape, but it is actually spiritual entrapment. The misery is being experienced for a reason and must be conquered with time.

Suicide not only damages the individual soul's developmental cycle, but it also rips apart a piece of the soul of anyone else who cares. And trust me, somebody cares. If it doesn't seem like it, believe you me, somebody *will* care given time—let the first be yourself. If you truly are in a state of perpetual hopelessness and feel that suicide is a viable option, then you *must* find the road leading away from this darkness before it consumes you. It's there. It's always there.

Channeling Dark Emotionalism

Spiritual paths are healing mechanisms: devices to be utilized for purposes of inner healing and personal awareness. The question is, how much are you willing to invest? How much time and energy are you willing to dedicate to ways of life that can heal you from the core of your being if used properly? To what extent do you use your magick?

Magick is at our fingertips to utilize. We decide our fate every day of our lives—every minute and every second. Each thought we have, each action we undertake, affects the rest of our lives. We are in control of everything that happens to us—*everything*. This is not to be taken lightly nor brushed aside as New Age fluffiness. Ancient spiritual truth states that we create our own reality. Applying this to emotionalism, we understand that everything we feel is self-created and has a purpose greater than we may know moment to moment. The energy that comes about with the fusion of emotion and magick must

Effigies as Emotional Channels

If you cry regularly, it's a good idea to keep a channel for your pain. For example, you could make a poppet or effigy to represent the pain, giving it a form. In this case, the doll or symbol does not represent any particular person, but rather the emotion as a whole. If you make a doll, the best color of cloth to use is black (for banishing), and it would be best to fill it with herbs for banishing and releasing. Use your intuition. Smear tears on the effigy, and grip it in your hands as you weep, seeing the pain flowing into the item. Smear the effigy with your tears and snot, scream at it, and just...release. Dig very deep within yourself and pull out old, painful memories. Allow them to surface and be banished as much as possible; this is internal shadow magick. If you keep performing this magick, you may wish to imbue it over a period of time, like from a full moon to a dark moon or during the waning half of the solar year. When you're through, ceremonially burn, bury, or sink the effigy. Keep in mind that performing this magick doesn't mean you'll never feel sadness again—that would be even more reason to worry! It means you are actively going about finding the way out of emotional trauma in order to reclaim your power.

be utilized. This powerful force is transformative if channeled properly. In the case of sadness, the most appropriate form of magick to do is to work on the self by banishing.

Tears are healing. To cry without reservation is to surrender to the will of the gods. We cry to release and to banish the misery held inside us. Crying opens all our centers, allowing the ego to dissolve through a process of emotional channeling. Tears are water, and water is emotion. As tears exit the eyes—the only windows to the soul—they can shed deep-seated pain if intentionally directed.

When you cry, try channeling this intense rush of energy into something constructive. Not cutting yourself, not breaking things, not clawing your face or pulling out hair. Use the magick within you like it's never been used before; command the pain to depart from your sphere. Direct it into the earth or the ether, and shield yourself from its return. There is an endless number of things we can do to combat emotional instability through magick. Part of the joy of any magickal path is that we can create our own rituals, prayers, and activities based on our unique situations.

Though wearing black can be a therapeutic and spiritual act to be sure, sometimes it just isn't enough to cope with strong feelings of sadness. As dark artists, artistic creation comes naturally to us. Find your own niche to express yourself beyond external appearance, be it painting, sketching, gardening, sewing, performing, photographing, writing, creating music, or any other "out." When we have channels for our pain, the intense energetic states we experience are allowed to cycle outward, beyond the body and into external sources to provide a release of some kind.

When doing magick concerning emotions, bathing is essential. Water is the element of emotion and change. Immersing ourselves in a cleansing bath aids in bringing us to a more complete level of emotional awareness while cleansing the body of energetic debris at the same time. To not use magick, prayer, and meditation for personal transformation and to cultivate satisfaction in life would be folly. Magick is all around for us to utilize, acting as an escort to bring us out of the abyss of darkness, if we choose to use it as such.

Finally, therapy is a viable option—don't disregard it. Speaking with a psychotherapist or psychologist can be extremely beneficial, depending on the therapist's or counselor's empathic receptivity to the patient's distress. Sometimes all it takes is for us to get our worries off our chests and allow someone—anyone—to reassure us that there is always hope, no matter what. When we feel like shit, it's not easy to see objectively, which is why another person's suggestions can be more than helpful. If you wish to pursue counseling, I *highly* recommend calling a number of therapists and giving them an overview of your mental state, personal interests, and life's path. See how much experience they have in the area for which you are seeking them out, and see how nonjudgmental they seem to be. Gauge each person's reactions by your own intuition, throw some Tarot cards or runes, and decide who would be the best fit. It's also a good idea to get recommendations of therapists from friends and family members who report success in their counseling sessions.

If you are at the point of honestly contemplating suicide, you *must* talk to someone, even if it's an anonymous person contacted on a 1-800 helpline. *This* is the lifetime to overcome chaos; don't let it drag on, and don't wait for the next lifetime.

To end on a cross-cultural note, I'll make mention of the people of the Polynesian islands of Samoa. Because of extreme expectations of how to properly go about life, the Samoans understand the reason and necessity of "letting it all out." When life becomes too intense, a person has a nervous breakdown and temporarily withdraws from society. Samoans are allowed a period of time to halt their family and employment obligations and center their focus only on themselves and their own mental state. The person's relatives or friends will pick up where they left off and take over the person's responsibilities. Friends and family also will deliver food to persons going through the experience and will monitor them regularly while they have their meltdown, and slowly gather themselves to re-enter society.

The feeling of shame attached to sadness is not prevalent in every society. As Witches, we must know the ways of our ancestors, many of which are still reflected in indigenous cultures around the globe. When sadness is recognized, and the person is allowed time to come to terms with it—through magick, meditation, reflection, or therapy—it will allow the whole of the person to come clearly into view. Allow yourself time to heal and experience what you do. Find a channel and learn from the extreme emotions. In the end, emotions are our ultimate guide.

Self-Acceptance

Goths and Witches are not like most people. We don't fit in with the rest of society, plain and simple. Undoubtedly, this is reason enough to feel social discomfort, especially if you are ostracized for being unique. If this dissatisfaction is perpetuated enough, it can lead to extreme social anxiety. The remedy for this is self-acceptance.

It may sound easy, but becoming truly self-accepting takes time. We must begin by understanding that, frankly, we are freaks. This may sound more self-deprecating than accepting, but the fact of the matter is that people with our sorts of interests and practices are, for the most part, socially unaccepted. This is gradually changing, and others are beginning to feel less threatened by our obvious weirdness, but for now, fully fitting in is *not* an option, nor a desirable one. To the masses, we are freaks. We must be proud—people of the subcultural movement, regardless of the form it takes, dare to be different and truly think for themselves. Thinking differently is a gift, and though it often renders us cold and mournful, it is a blessing greater than any shallow experience could ever be.

As Goths and Pagans, we are a minority—okay, a *double* minority at that! While it may not always be this way, it is at the present time. This, too, is something we must accept and adapt to. Unless we have good enough "cloaking" skills or are lucky enough to find friends, occupations, and the like that are totally accepting of our type of diversity, it will be a longtime challenge to meld with society at large. So many people are afraid of ideas and people who are different or foreign (a fear called *xenophobia*), and this is just an unfortunate fact of life.

People, especially Americans, generally have little exposure to other cultures, much less alternative lifestyles within our *own* culture. This makes it exceedingly difficult to have people understand that we are here, we are real, and we are part of the same society they are. Media, money, and television have taken the place of the ancient gods and ancestors. Being a Goth or Witch or anything of a positive path separate from the mainstream is, even unconsciously, the act of reclaiming an ancient tribal structure and introducing a much-needed energy to the earth plane at this time. Good luck trying to explain that to the next person who would rather fear and condemn us than make an attempt at understanding! Truth be told, more people understand our lifestyles now than ever before, but we still have to wait for others to catch up, even if it's a painful process. Given these circumstances, we must work on ourselves first.

The most important form of acceptance is self-acceptance, regardless of how many people do or do not seem to appreciate you for who you are. It's very enlightening to make a list of personal strengths and weaknesses. To know one's own strengths and weaknesses is to cultivate knowledge of self. When doing this, it's essential to be as honest and objective as possible. There should be a balance between positive and negative traits; if the list leans too far to one side, then bring your focus to the other and meditate on how the opposing side of the list can be elongated.

Another method of cultivating self-knowledge is to perform a meditation by staring in the mirror. Take a few deep breaths and gaze at yourself (wearing no makeup) in the mirror for a few minutes. Examine your skin, your face and, most importantly, your eyes. When self-doubt arises, and it will, release the thought like a cloud dissipating in the sky. Acknowledge your beauty, both physical and otherwise, knowing that you were put in this physical form for very specific reasons. If you look at yourself long enough, especially in the eyes, your face seemingly will begin to shapeshift. For many people, this meditation reveals visions of past lives, of ancestors and spirit guides, especially if done in a ritual setting in candlelight. If you practice this meditation regularly, your self-acceptance will bloom and just as many questions will come about as will be answered.

Magick's effectiveness largely depends on one's internal state of being. If one is uncomfortable with oneself, it puts limits on the possibility of manifesting change. Absolute acceptance must enter the soul of the magician—acceptance of the past, present, and future. You must begin to accept yourself for who you are, for your past experiences, and for your future role in life, which you are to create. If you are unhappy with your past choices, then find the best way to mend the present situations that came about from those choices, and change the course of your life in accordance with your regrets—start on new feet today. Accepting and trusting in yourself, as well in as your abilities and gifts, is the foundation for effective magick.

The most powerful and magickal force in all the world is love, and you must first love yourself—every bit of you—before others can fully love you in return. If self-love is uncultivated, difficulty will present itself in receiving love from anyone else. Love is the ultimate force that permeates all things. Many spiritual traditions are built around this key principle. Witchcraft stresses Perfect Love and Perfect Trust as the "keys of entrance" into the traditional magick circle. Love is essential. Of all other emotions or experiences, love is transcendent. To love one another, the land, and life itself is to truly live our existence to the fullest. To honestly accept others and oneself is to embrace love.

Cultivating Love and Compassion (Meditation)

I have a special affinity for Buddhism, finding its ideas to integrate superbly with Pagan spirituality. Because of its emphasis on the emotional body, I find it appropriate to discuss some of its ideas here. A number of Witches I know, myself included, have benefited from the *dharma* (the teachings and wisdom of the Buddha) and have been able to successfully incorporate the teachings into the Witch's way. The Buddhist path is one of peace and compassion for all beings. It's difficult to feel compassion for everyone, especially those who don't have our best interests at heart. Compassion does not, however, mean that you must overextend yourself or become subservient to someone else's will. It means that despite unavoidable differences, everyone deserves the opportunity to heal and cultivate the light of peace. Of course, everyone has mixed feelings about how the vilest and most perverted members of society should be treated, and this is certainly a spiritual dilemma worth pondering.

The meditation that follows is called a *Metta Bhavana* meditation. The word *metta* is Pali for "loving-kindness." *Bhavana* basically means "to develop into being" or simply "spiritual practice" in the broadest sense. Pali is an ancient Indian language similar to Sanskrit, and is nearly identical to the language spoken in the time of the Buddha Siddhartha Gautama (c. 500 BCE), called Magadhi. Metta is akin to compassion in that its essence is all-encompassing and freely given. The world would be a much better place if more people could cultivate uninhibited loving-kindness, and that is the goal of this meditation.

My Buddhist teacher, Saramati, taught me this meditation for cultivating metta. It is designed to help bring about acceptance of yourself and others and bring more loving-kindness, compassion, acceptance, and love to your daily routine. If this meditation or something similar is practiced enough, you may find it increasingly difficult to feel unpleasant emotions toward certain other people on a regular basis.

In this meditation, you will focus on four different people (including yourself) whose influences evoke varied reactions in you. The people you think about in the meditation can be different each time you practice this (aside from yourself, of course), or you can focus on the same individuals each time until you feel ready to change. It's best if you choose people who are living, but if there are unresolved issues with a person who has passed or has simply left your sphere of interaction, there's no reason not to include the individual in the visualizations.

Many Buddhists practice this meditation daily in addition to other exercises aimed at improving their well-being, as it's one of the most comprehensible and direct forms of meditation. Metta Bhavana is a form of *samata* (or *samatha*) meditation, which involves focusing on the breath to raise consciousness and increasing self-awareness by calming the body. This ancient Hindu method of concentration meditation is mentioned in the sacred Upanishads. I have slightly modified the original method, adding a bit here and there yet still maintaining the essence of the traditional exercise.

You may prerecord the meditation or have a friend read it to you in a soft, slow, monotone voice, inserting a pause between each step. You can also memorize the meditation by reading it many times over or jot short notes to glance at throughout, assuming this won't snap you out of the meditative state.

---

1. Enter your temple room or ritual space, if you have one. If you feel comfortable meditating where you know there will be no distractions, then find your place there. Any form of light will do as long as it's not fluorescent or overpowering artificial light, as these distract from the focal energy at hand. Some practitioners prefer to work with sunlight or moderate backlighting, but the readers of this book most likely will prefer subtle candlelight, moonlight, or pitch blackness.

2. In your sacred space, find a comfortable posture that aligns your energy and allows your mind the clarity of focus. After grounding and centering, become aware of your physical body. Look at your hands, wiggle your toes, feel your hair: this is the body you're in and is the shell that maintains your spiritual progression, centering your mind and your senses on this plane. Become aware of your six sensory faculties: touch, smell, taste, sight, hearing, and mental process. These are the functions that serve as filters for spiritual experience. Observe your physical body even more deeply by seeing beneath your skin. In your mind's eye, see your organs, muscles, and skeletal system, and try to understand their roles in your daily life. Mentally examine your body and all its parts.

3. Having become aware of your physical frame, close your eyes and enter the astral territory of mind and imagination. First, monitor your breathing. Take regular breaths, not too deep or shallow, preferably in and out of the nostrils. Witches prefer the sacred number thirteen, so let's use that for counting. Visualize the oxygen entering your body as a soft white, blue, or other calming color of your choice. Begin counting your breaths in multiples of thirteen. With the inhalation, bring your attention to where the air meets your skin; let this be the first count. Immediately after counting thirteen inhalations, count the same number of exhalations, focusing on the point at which the breath leaves your body. Immediately after this, finish with another set of thirteen counts, this time not focusing on your physical body at all. Simply count and know that your regular breathing is supporting your being. After putting yourself in a heightened state of awareness, the core of the work begins.

4. **First person:** Before working on cultivating metta with anyone else, the healer must first work on him- or herself. Envision *yourself* sitting before you exactly as you are now. Your eyes are closed and your back is erect. See the clothes you're wearing now and try to form the clearest and most realistic image of yourself as you are in the present moment. If you have any "flaws," see them too—negate no part of yourself; you must see yourself exactly as you are. Let your mind construct the most realistic image of yourself. See yourself (both you and your envisioned self) surrounded in the light of metta, glowing and serene, illuminating the aura. Do not move on to the next step until this has occurred and you are content looking at yourself. If you are judging yourself, release those thoughts and allow them to move on. They only get in the way of feeling love. Once you are content, let your picture fade away and your mind slip back to blackness.

5. **Second person:** Next, envision someone *near and dear* to you sitting in front of you in meditation. This should be a person you already feel love for and whose presence you are comfortable in. See the person sitting just as you are sitting, practicing the same exercise. Envision him or her

surrounded in the same light as you surrounded yourself in moments before. The individual is at peace and you are at peace, aligned and balanced with the light of metta. Once you feel the same alignment come about this person, allow his or her image to also fade to black.

6. **Third person:** The next person you are to visualize should be a *neutral person:* someone who is real but whom you have never spoken to and have only seen in passing. It could be a clerk at a grocery store, or someone you've seen on campus, at the club, or downtown; it doesn't matter so long as the person is someone you know of but aren't acquainted with. Though you don't know the person, understand that he or she is a human with the same needs and desires as yourself—someone who deserves to be surrounded with the light of metta, regardless of his or her path. See the person as you did the others: meditating before you, surrounded in loving-kindness. Once you feel the individual's energy aligned with the peacefulness of the others, allow the image to once again fade away.

7. **Fourth person:** This will be the most difficult visualization of them all, but it will also be the most beneficial. The person to be visualized is someone you *have an aversion to.* This doesn't need to be someone you absolutely despise, but someone you are having problems with, at least at the moment. This could be a number of people: an old friend, a family member, or even someone you spoke to online. See the person sitting before you in meditation, knowing that he or she, too, exhibits human traits and is bound to physical form. Know that you have more commonalities than differences, at least in the sense of your both being human, and attempt to see the individual's "lighter side." Cast away negative thoughts you have for the person; let them be placed aside for the moment, unattached to any painful emotions. See the person surrounded in the light of metta, understanding that he or she needs this light as much as you do. Allow the individual to be surrounded in love, even if you feel he or she doesn't deserve it. This might take a bit longer to accomplish than with the others, but it's well worth the effort. Once content, allow the person's image to fade.

8. You should now visualize each person you reviewed in meditation. They should all be lined up and surrounded in the light of metta. See yourself sitting next to the person you love, next to the "neutral" person, next to the person you are having problems with. See the light glowing, surrounding all four individuals. Let each person's light permeate the other people. The same light emanates from each person and it now surrounds everyone as a single unit. All are surrounded with loving-kindness. All are connected and vibrate as one. Then let their images fade while you come back to center.

9. To complete the magick, see yourself (your physical self, not your visualized self) surrounded in Spirit's infinite light. See the light expanding from your own body to fill the whole of the room or area you're in. This may take a few seconds or minutes to accomplish. Next, see the light expanding into the rest of the premises, beyond you. See it expanding into the whole neighborhood, then into the community, the town, and the world. Perform this exercise as long as needed. Once you have visualized Gaia (the earth) surrounded in metta, let the light expand even further, through our solar system, permeating all planes and beyond to infinity. Obviously, we cannot actually perceive infinity in our human form, so simply project the energy and know that it is expanding evermore.

10. At this point, you're going to feel quite high. You will barely be connected to your body, having traversed the universe and all. Finally, slowly ground and center your energy. Bring yourself back from the stars to your geographical area, and finally back to your body. Take as much time as you need. Breathe deeply, letting air enter your lungs and rejuvenate your blood. Wiggle your fingers and toes, becoming aware of your physical self, and let your eyes slowly open. Odds are you'll have a nice grin on your face, knowing that you just lent a bit of enlightenment to yourself and everyone else.

IV
The Dark Arts

This chapter focuses on the magickal qualities of body art. Pagans and Goths share similarities of *creation*—Pagans manifest change through creative acts like magick and spiritual consultation, while Goths manifest change by creating art and bringing the internal outward. Dark Witches are artists, understanding the power of creation both magickally and physically.

Our image expresses how we feel. Other people's views of us are formed by their perception of our identity, much of which comes about due to the alternative clothing we wear. Obviously, Goths and other alternative people face persecution for just that reason.

On the other hand, we feel much more content and happy when we have the ability to artistically create ourselves based on our clothing, makeup, jewelry, and so on. The body truly is the temple; to decorate the temple is a sacred act. While the less informed would rather view our expressions as a rebellious way to shock the masses, others understand the spiritual necessity of art, be it in the form of body decoration or otherwise. Goddess knows we are *not* comfortable or happy wearing "ordinary" clothes, and feel a sort of torment if our stylistic expressions are repressed. Clothing and makeup accentuate not only our physical features but also our personalities. External alternative style allows us to break free of the ordinary and embrace the fullness of our spirits from the inside out.

After dressing for the day, it's a good idea to examine your appearance. Look at all the clothes you're wearing. Notice their patterns and stitching. Look at your jewelry and extra accessories, analyzing their symbolic meanings and inherent power. Look in the mirror at your makeup and set your intention for the day based on your external look. Let it empower you to carry you through the day (or night) with awareness, peace, and contentment. Know that *you* determine the magick you set forth throughout the day by what you wear.

Clothing

The clothing you wear determines your presentation, which in turn influences how others react to you and how you react to yourself. Though appearance is second in importance to music and philosophy, aesthetics in the form of physical presentation plays a large role in dark culture. Not only do we have an impact on the clothing we wear, but the clothing we wear has an impact on us. All parts of reality are made up of vibrational essence, which is the core of magick. Spirit is omnipresent, which most certainly doesn't exclude physical matter.

Also, the degree of art you decorate yourself with naturally may vary from day to day depending on current moods and pursuits. It's very important to choose clothing appropriate to the situation you are about to encounter and what will happen throughout the day. Gauge what you wear in accordance with forthcoming situations; you're bound to wear something different if you're hanging out with family instead of some alternative friends.

Clothing influences us whether we know it or not. As a prime example, some people have a tendency to slip into depression when wearing black, while others find it very healing and centering. Other accessories have a more noticeable effect on a greater number of people. For example, wearing sunglasses draws one's energy inside oneself, as the eyes (the windows of the soul) are not exposed to anyone else, even in the case of face-to-face interaction. Therefore, much less energy is exchanged with anyone who is interacted with. Similarly, wearing a hat tends to block energy flow in the uppermost crown chakra, keeping one's spirit more grounded in one's physical body. Wearing a spiked collar or bracelet induces some level of defensive (protective) behavior.

To continue these examples, the sunglasses don't have to just be worn, but can be worn with intent. Perhaps you are going through a healing process after a profound ritual and wish to lock energy inside of your body to better process the experience. Perhaps you've been overloaded with occult knowledge as of late and wish to stop discombobulating feelings by blocking the crown chakra for a period of time by wearing a hat. Perhaps the metal on the spiked collar or bracelet can be charged with the purpose of magickal protection if you fear that a negative situation might be encountered at some point in the day. You might also wear shiny clothing for protection and reflection, fishnet to keep energies secured to the body, or crushed velvet to evoke romantic vibes. If awareness is given to clothing and accessories and their direct psychospiritual effects, magick can be utilized to greater align with the energy of the décor. Anything can be enchanted with magickal energy. The possibilities are endless; you are the Witch, you are the magician, and you determine the magick.

To take these ideas a step further, into the realm of intent-based magick, something as simple as washing the laundry seems like an ordinary, mundane act, but, as with anything else, it can be transformed into a meaningful act of instant magick. As you toss your laundry into the washing machine (or the warm water, if washing by hand), see each piece of clothing as carrying a different ailment that you wish to remove from your life. Say something aloud or think to yourself, identifying the article of clothing as carrying your problem, to be cleansed by the element of Water. Even simply envisioning sadness or anger surrounding the clothes is sufficient. Communicate with the water, add a pinch of sea salt, and ask the undines to imbue the clothing with (insert your intention here).

Be sure to say a positive affirmation on the clothing after removing it from the washer or dryer to ensure that the negativity attached to the load initially is neutralized. Every time I fold a pair of socks, I visualize one sock as the yin current and the other as the yang. Folding them together creates unity and charges them with that energy. As I pull one down over the other, I think "protection" or "grounding" (the latter because you wear them on your feet) and make each a minor spell, trapping energy to be opened at a later day.

Luckily for us Goth types, we don't usually need to separate darks from lights and are afforded the luxury of doing a single load of wash! Dark colors help trap and secure energy, so it's convenient for us to perform instant magick of this type. Small magicks like this are part of the Witch's living path. When performing minor daily magicks, no circle need be cast and no gods need be invoked. Every bit of energy utilized throughout the day has an effect on forming reality. Even the smallest amount of intention helps create the future, each moment building on the next. Performing minor magicks helps us stay attuned to our spirituality, ever reminding us that the path is lived every day and isn't restricted to ritual alone. Our daily attire and the treatment of our clothing and adornments are two ways to energetically fuse magickal intention to the self.

Makeup

A Goth's motivation to wear makeup is quite different from the average person's. For Goths and other fashion-creative people, makeup is just as much a work of art as the clothing; the two go hand in hand. Instead of wearing makeup to fit in with the rest of society, many darksiders wear it for purposes of artistic creativity. Naturally, our makeup is often dark, thick, and symbolic instead of conformingly bland. If the face is the canvas, then the makeup is the paint. Because of our darker leanings, the makeup we choose directly reflects this.

The Books of Enoch are part of the Old Testament Pseudepigrapha, that is, ancient sacred Judaic texts that didn't "make the cut" during the formation of the Old Testament. The name Enoch, however, is referenced in Genesis. The Books of Enoch are apocalyptic in nature, but Enoch VIII does mention that *makeup changed the world!* I couldn't agree more. While Enoch may be referring to it in a negative way, I view the advent of makeup in a very positive light. The magickal use of makeup cannot be traced and is presumably primitive in nature. Ancient shamans and ritualists would paint their flesh with ash, blood, herbs, and plants to draw Spirit within, directly invoking specific energies. The presentation of the body would be out of the ordinary and would instantaneously attune the practitioner to divinity. To many cultures, painting the body declares the honor of tradition and spiritual communion.

Shamans of the Shipibo tribe of the upper Amazon decorate their faces with black and purple streaks, seeing the pattern as allowing them to astrally shapeshift into animal form and embark on intense visionary journeys. Ancient Egyptians would paint their faces prior to ritual or important events. It also allowed the pharaohs and those of high political standing to glamour their subjects with the appearance of agelessness.

These ceremonial and political uses eventually became fashionable for everyone in ancient Egypt.

Makeup-creative Witches carry on the spiritual practice of magickal makeup for Sabbatical and Esbatical rituals and other acts of meditation and magick. Applying artistic makeup brings a person out of the confines of everyday human existence. Applying makeup with magickal intention rekindles the ancient fire of its magickal use; just putting it on taps into ancient energy and reconnects the present to the past. Certainly, this form of artistic expression links the magick of the past to the magick of the present, allowing two moments in time to overlap.

So many people wear makeup these days for superficial reasons. Naturally, wearing makeup for reasons of social acceptance can serve to set the wearer apart from natural, spiritual rhythms and cycles. Applying makeup with artistic and magickal intention, on the other hand, can aid in aligning a person with specific spiritual vibrations.

Makeup transforms a person, accentuating features and creating new patterns, added on top of the already beautiful natural form. Makeup is art and is a spiritual declaration to the gods. Any wish can be manifested on the skin with makeup (or tattoo ink). In this sense, anything can be invoked into the practitioner, further allowing connection with forces of ultimate spiritual power. Additionally, makeup works on a subconscious level. The patterning and intention with which it's applied steadily influences the wearer throughout the day. Further, any onlookers who observe a person's makeup (or clothing, or any feature for that matter) develop an immediate and often subconscious perception of the wearer. This perception, which really is vibration and energy, bounces between the observer and the observed instantaneously, each person influencing the other in a split second's time.

You can draw on ancient worldwide spiritual practices by applying makeup before performing ritual. This makeup may be much thicker and more intense than everyday makeup. It can cover as much of the body as you deem appropriate, be it a pencil-thin line down the center of the face or a painting of the entire body. It should be even more representational than everyday makeup and should be totally guided by your intuition.

Ritual makeup will change for each ceremony performed. If you are doing a circle to align yourself with faerie energy, you may choose glitter and neon eyeshadow. If you are performing a ritual for balance, painting half of the face black and the other half white could be appropriate. To communicate with higher energies or strengthen psychic vision, a large lemniscate (infinity knot) can be drawn around the eyes with the loop's intersection resting at the bridge of the nose. To harness planetary energy, the symbol of the planet can be drawn on the brow. Virtually any intention can be solidified through the metaphysically conscious use of makeup.

Whether it's being used for ritual or for the daily grind, makeup can be enchanted with magickal purpose in mind. If you use a compact powder or a pressed foundation, draw magickal symbols in it with a pin. Concentrate on the energy you wish to imbue the makeup with while you draw, using symbols specific to the purpose. For a base or foundation that covers the face, the makeup should be imbued with any qualities you wish to carry with you throughout the day, such as protection and happiness. Enchant the makeup as you would any magickal tool. Form your own spell by creating an affirming chant and mini-ritual just for that purpose—and have fun doing it! Makeup doesn't necessarily need to be charged in a magickal circle, but it certainly can be. The amount of spellwork you do on the item depends on how much energy you would like for it to carry. By actively putting intention behind each and every *mundane* activity that we perform, we discipline ourselves to our intent to manifest our desires, not to mention the fact that turning the ordinary into the extraordinary keeps life interesting and magickal.

Makeup that is designed for specific parts of the face can be enchanted for purposes appropriate to the area to which it is applied. For example, if you have trouble communicating or forget to think before speaking, lipstick can be charged with the intention to aid in overcoming these struggles. Doing so can lend a hand in providing eloquence and clear speech. Eyeliner or eyeshadow can be charged with the purpose of sight, that is, seeing things clearly on a physical and psychic level. Doing so will allow the wearer to better notice people's subtle body movements and surrounding energy patterns, and perhaps better see the reality of a given situation. Even nail polish can be enchanted according to its specific color attribute in occultism; it is a great tool to invoke color essence for extended periods of time, especially considering that it doesn't wash off right away like other kinds of makeup.

A friend of mine, Kitty, takes advantage of the makeup application process by using it as a specific devotional practice. She is a magician who is devoted to her patron goddess Aphrodite. Aphrodite represents and embodies pure beauty in the Greek pantheon and is attributed with influencing emotional and physical love. For Kitty, each application of makeup is treated as a ritual activity paying homage to and aligning her energies with the patron goddess. In fact, she keeps her makeup and mirror on her Aphrodite shrine when not in use. This is an excellent way to align with the goddess on a constant basis throughout the day.

My Priestess, Estha McNevin, has similar views on the magickal and ritualistic properties of makeup and tends to pay strict attention to the actual patterns being created on the face. She will adorn her eyes and brows with detailed patterns and continue to create her elaborate eye makeup in a similar fashion in spirals, dots, and waves. In this process, which has come to be a daily devotional act to align with the Goddess, each swoosh of the lipstick or eye pencil represents spiritual alignment, each dot drawn represents a different point in magick, and each spiral traced represents a magickal current. Everything is imbued with intention, in the same manner that the ancients decorated their faces.

I fully believe that liquid eyeliner is a gift from the gods! It's incredibly versatile and can create virtually any design on the body. Like a miniature paintbrush with a foam or brush tip, it's one of the best tools for beautifying the eyes, lips, and other parts of the face. In addition to liquid eyeliner, one can use basic eyeliner, eyeshadow, lipstick, mascara, blush, glitter, foundation, and powder. The best makeup to use is something of good quality that flows well with the tone and features of your skin and facial structure. It's also best to search for makeup that is eco-friendly and is in no way tested on animals. Some major cosmetic companies that are cruelty-free are Clinique, Revlon, M•A•C, Avon, Chanel, Almay, Wet 'n' Wild, Burt's Bees, Jane, Jason Natural, Prestige, Bonne Bell, Estée Lauder, Manic Panic, Stargazer, Urban Decay, and GoodGoth.

The key to makeup art is to be creative. Do what feels right and makes you happy in your expression. Don't rush the process; allow your inner artist time to accentuate your form. Present your body as a spiritual creation to the world, decked out appropriately and magickally. Your body is your own to do with as you choose—fancify it and allow your inner self to manifest externally!

Makeup Styles

Babydoll

The best way to achieve the babydoll eye makeup look is to have the eyebrows shaved and then drawn on higher than normal. Eyeshadow, usually a vibrant or neon color, is then applied over the eyelids and worked up to the brows. This creates an intense, doll-like style, and is a great accompaniment to the babydoll style of clothing. The more exaggerated the makeup, the more intense the look. Drawing false eyelashes with liquid eyeliner is a great addition to this style. The babydoll makeup style is perfect to evoke childhood memories for the sake of healing or remembrance and to connect with the child side of the self that so many repress and forget.

Basic Smudge

The basic smudge is simple yet beautiful. Just apply eyeshadow of any color to the eyelids and beneath the eyes. The makeup can be smudged as high or low as desired and can also be created with a regular eyeliner pencil. The makeup can be smudged in any direction from the eyes. This style is often the base for additional designs. Adding extra designs is optional; it looks good with or without. The smudge can be slapped on quickly or styled with utmost precision. The eyeshadow can be all one color or a variety of them. Magickally, the basic smudge can represent absolutely anything you empower it to be. Just putting on a bit of plain dark makeup can be an act of dedication to the divine.

Blood

The blood-dripping effect can be created in numerous ways. I have found the best way is by using "dragon's blood" ink, which has a very realistic look about it. (Plus, a little goes a long way.) The only drawback is that it has the tendency to stain the skin for longer than expected. The second and perhaps most obvious method is to use fake Halloween blood. The shade and consistency of this stuff are pretty accurate, but its semitoxic qualities can be bothersome. Another option is to use red eyeliner. Unless it's liquid, I wouldn't recommend this method simply because it often tends to appear cheesy and unrealistic! Applying fake blood to the eyes can represent the death of cycles you wish to lay to rest. Each drop can represent the release of something in the past.

Butterfly

The butterfly eye makeup look is a rare one, but is very striking. This style of makeup can help the wearer tap into the realms of the fae. Butterflies (or "flutterbys") have long been associated with the faerie realm, and wearing makeup of this sort aids the individual in recognizing the astral realms. Butterfly makeup represents freedom and the flight of the soul. It can be worn to break free from bindings of the past. This look is especially worthwhile for chaos magicians; the "butterfly effect" is accepted as part of chaos theory, in which mathematician/meteorologist Edward Lorenz asked, "Does the flap of a butterfly's wings in Brazil set off a tornado in Texas?"

Cat's Eye

What better way to draw on the energy of our feline comrades than to decorate the eyes as such? The Egyptians knew a little something about the power of the feline and would decorate their eyes similarly to a cat's. In addition to invoking the energy of our ancients, the cat's eye is ideal to expand spiritual sight, working the energy from the eyes outward. The look is achieved best with liquid eyeliner, which lends to the smoothness of the effect. Extra eyeshadow can be added to intensify the look. Also, drawing short vertical lines from the inner points of the eyes downward can complete the cat's-eye style. If you have a feline spirit animal or wish to invite feline qualities into your person, this look is perfect.

Cat's Eye (extended)

A prominent variation of the cat's eye is something I call the extended cat's eye. It's similar in style to the regular cat's eye but the makeup is much thicker and more exaggerated. This theatrical makeup is the perfect addition to a dark-punk or deathrock getup because of its intense and stunning look. This style is achieved by using a combination of liquid or pencil eyeliner along with a significant amount of eyeshadow. Colors can vary, but the most common is black. Begin by covering the eyelids in eyeshadow and applying eyeliner beneath the eyes. Extend the makeup by drawing vertical points from the corners of the eyes, slightly descending on the nose. Finish by thickly brushing makeup in a swooping fashion from the outer corners of the eyes. Whether one swoop or more is created is up to the aesthetic tastes of each person. Magickally, this makeup style has properties similar to those of the cat's eye and is also ideal for enchanting in order to increase spiritual and psychic vision.

Dots

A number of dots can be drawn on the eyes or around the face to accentuate any amount of makeup already applied to the face. Sometimes a single dot is all you need to create a balanced look. Dots can be drawn in any pattern of your choice, in varying degrees of thickness. It's common among darksiders to draw a series of increasingly smaller-sized dots going down the forehead or descending from the eyes. Magickally, the application of each dot can be imbued with a wish, prayer, or spiritual purpose. Dots can be drawn on either lightly or as a thick pattern to create a tribal look. This tribal look is extremely beneficial in magick when aligning with primordial deities through shamanic ritual.

Droops

Droops are simply squiggly lines descending from the eyes. They can be drawn on with liquid or pencil eyeliner, or even smeared on with eyeshadow for a thicker appearance. Of course, I prefer to draw them with liquid eyeliner for a wispier effect. Droops look good accompanying some amount of eyeshadow on the lids, and can evoke feelings of sorrow because of the almost "crying" effect. For this reason, drawing droops from the eyes is ideal for releasing sadness or pain. If you're feeling more depressed than usual, drawing droops can be quite therapeutic. This is similar to the "blood" effect, but is considerably less visceral.

Eye-bar

Aside from the potential Geordi La Forge (*Star Trek*) side comments, the eye-bar (or "eye mask") is a unique and stunning look for darksiders. This makeup is drawn from one side of the face to the other as a horizontal bar, covering both eyes and the bridge of the nose. It's generally drawn between one and four inches thick. The eye-bar is best achieved with eyeshadow. The top of the bar is generally flat, while the bottom can fade off in lighter tones or be a sharp line. The sharp line at the top of the bar can be achieved by placing masking tape across the face (before applying any foundation, of course) and brushing the edge with eyeshadow. Additional colors look good blended into the bottom of the bar if the fading effect is used. I've also seen CyberGoths achieve this style with a series of vertical lines, creating a mysterious cyborg look! Magickally, this effect can be used to connect the energy of the two eyes, which, in turn, strengthens the astral third eye, leading to increased perception and psychic prowess.

Eye of Horus

The Eye of Horus is one of the most identifiable and spiritually profound symbols to emerge from ancient Egypt. It is, of course, associated with Horus, Egypt's falcon god. This style of makeup magickally draws upon the essence of ancient Egypt and is a perfect symbol to draw before performing Egyptian magick. The Eye of Horus is achieved by first outlining the edges of the eyes in black eyeliner and bringing the point to a "cat's eye" tip. From there, the lower curve and bar can be drawn, turning out best with liquid eyeliner or a fine-tipped pencil. Also, the eyebrows may be extended to match the line, and extra eyeshadow (usually grey or black) can be added to intensify the look. This style is the ideal design to connect with the Egyptian mysteries both inside and outside of ritual.

Eyelashes

False eyelashes can be drawn on the eyes alongside other designs to create an even more individualized look. False makeup lashes enhance the Babydoll makeup style quite nicely and create the effect of wide eyes. Any number of lines can be drawn in any length after mascara is allowed to dry. I find the look appealing with lines of various lengths drawn in a descending order from the outermost part of the eye inward. Exaggerated eyelash makeup also looks good with actual false eyelashes affixed. Similar to the "droops" style, false eyelashes can represent the banishment of unwanted energies and emotions. This is achieved by starting the eyeliner at the edge of the eye and bringing the line downward while focusing on magickal release.

Glitter

Though it is far more prevalent in the rave scene than in the Goth, glitter can create a fabulous look either by itself or in addition to other makeup. It can be applied thick or thin depending on preference. Glitter comes in every imaginable color and color combination—even black! Glitter can be applied beneath the eyes, around the temples, or on the eyelids themselves. The glitter can be shaped into a cat's eye or another form, or kept thin for a subtle sparkle. Glitter is associated with the faerie realm and is great to adorn the face with before engaging in magick associated with the fae, or to invite the wee folk to dance with you throughout the day, perhaps even giving you a glimpse of their subtle terrain. Glitter also can represent the starry sky, aiding the wearer in honing his or her connection to the cosmos, or a celestial deity like Nuit.

Siouxsie/Cleopatra

The style of makeup that has come to be known as the Cleopatra or Siouxsie has been looked upon favorably in the Goth scene since the '70s. Siouxsie Sioux was the singer of the legendary post-punk darkwave-Goth act Siouxsie and the Banshees, and is now the vocalist for The Creatures. Siouxsie has long been known for her influence on dark culture, not excluding her fantastic makeup abilities. Siouxsie's eye makeup is reminiscent of common portrayals of the last queen of ancient Egypt, Cleopatra. Spiritually, this makeup can be used to align with energies of ancient Egypt, imbuing a person with the ability to more comfortably commune with the old gods of the black land. The makeup can be achieved with a combination of heavy eyeliner and eyeshadow.

Spider Web

For a ghoulish look that invokes the energy of our spooky arachnid kin, the spider web is quite appropriate. It must be drawn with liquid eyeliner to get thin, wispy lines, and the spider at the end of one of the threads is entirely optional! The web takes practice and patience to get it just right. It can be as small or large as looks good on your face. Start at the corner of the eye, make a series of lines going outward, and connect them with half-circle loops to make the web. It may take a few tries to get this design just right. The spider web design also looks astounding when drawn above the eye, from the eyelid up to the eyebrow. Magickally, this may be drawn to capture certain energies and imbue them to your person, much like the material fishnet does. Just the same, it can be used to catch unwanted external energies, only to be washed off the face and banished down the drain at the end of the evening.

Spikes

Spikes can be drawn on the face to create an intense visual look. This eye makeup goes best with a spiked collar for similarity from the neck up. Spikes can be drawn with dark eyeshadow and look great brushed over with a lighter shade. They look great coming from the side of the face, forming false "sunken cheeks," or in the form of an extended widow's peak descending from the hairline. Holding a piece of paper to the face and applying makeup flush with the paper's edge is helpful in creating sharp, straight lines. The more detailed spikes may take some practice to get perfect. Spikes are aesthetically pleasing in symmetry; they can be drawn on either cheek and/or either eye for a balanced appearance. Spikes can be drawn to summon protective energies in an act of magick. Astral essence can be drawn into the spikes, certainly deterring harmful energies from your person.

Spirals

A variety of shapes like spirals and swirls can be drawn from the eyes to create a profoundly mystical effect. The best way to draw these on is with liquid eyeliner because of the detail required in their creation. Spirals can go in any direction from the eye. They can be big or small, overlapping or singular, many or few. The spiral represents all of life. It is one of the most sacred esoteric symbols, representing the cycles of life. All of reality works in spirals and cycles. To apply this sacred symbolism to the body is to attune to the dance of life. Want to manifest a good day when a bad one seems impending? Want to align to higher consciousness before ritual? Draw some spirals with the intention of riding the tides and dancing with the ebb and flow of existence.

Sunburst

The sunburst symbol is simple yet powerful. It can be drawn on with eyeliner alone or drawn atop underlying eyeshadow. As you apply it to your eyes, begin from the outermost point of the eye and draw a number of "rays" from the central point. Focus on the sun and the necessity of sunlight for sustaining life and existence. Yes, I know we're the more lunar type, but the sun deserves equal respect! The sunburst pattern can be drawn to attune with sacred solar energies, especially for fertility or sun-welcoming Sabbats. Upperworld solar gods include Pan, Helios, and Ra, to name a few. An individual deity can be aligned with, or the Great God in whole can be focused upon. Additionally, inner light can be drawn forth. Either way, the sunburst is an ideal pattern for the dark Witch to attune to for means of balance and strength.

Hair

It's entirely unavoidable: Goths love to alter, decorate, accentuate, and fancify their hair to no end. Hair is the most easily changeable piece of the body—what better way to express one's own changing emotional state of being than through a mutable physical medium? People of all persuasions tend to obsess about their hair. Alternative folk are just more frequent and radical in their style changes and choices, tending to alter their hair on a regular basis to fit their facial and bodily figures as well as their personal feelings and interests at a given point in time. We like to craft our hair crazily, like spiking it up, dyeing it various colors, and shaving it in odd places. Hair is a great way to outwardly express our feelings and can be easily utilized in magickal practice. Plus, a little change now and then always does a person good.

Throughout time, the head and feet have been considered sacred parts of the body. The head is the highest in elevation while the feet are the lowest, connecting that which is above with that which is below. Some ancient magicians are said to have kept their hair and beards long, seeing them as storehouses of the past and a direct linkage to personal energy patterns. Hair is located on the uppermost part of the human body, closest to the heavens. Hair also grows thickly above the genitals, our tools of procreation and sexual union. Hair contains our genetic structure. Each strand is like a time capsule in that it contains energies from the time it came into being from the follicle. Experience and emotions are energetically logged in the hair as it grows along with us.

A tonsure is a devotional act of shaving the head that is undergone to become a Priest or monastic in numerous spiritual cultures worldwide, including the system of Witchcraft I was initiated into. Each religion that makes use of the tonsure shaves a different portion of the head with the purpose of aligning the self both with spiritual forces and the community of practitioners (called the *sangha* in Buddhist traditions). It reinforces humility before the Great Ones and is aimed at dissolving ego. Some traditions stress leaving permanent tonsures, though others leave it only temporarily for acute purposes. The Samye Monastery was the first Tibetan Buddhist monastery to tonsure monks, having begun the system in the 800s. From there, numerous Buddhist orders adopted the system because of its effectiveness in securing initiatory adherence to a chosen way of life.

Some indigenous cultures alter their hair to mark a particular occurrence, like the death of a relative. To visually mark the grieving, members of some cultures (like some Chinese) will significantly cut their hair, while members of other Asian cultures (like some Indonesians) neglect their hair altogether for specific cultural reasons that have to do with the process of mourning. The ancient practice of altering the hair for spiritual reasons does not have to be reserved for indigenous cultures; we can certainly integrate their knowledgeable ways into our own magickal lives.

Hair has been used in magick since the get-go. The term "hair and nails" is popular in Craft when performing magick for oneself or another person. Both hair and fingernails contain DNA, the blueprint of one's genetic structure. What better way to tap into one's energy pattern? Magicians in antiquity called hair, nails, and other accessible body pieces to use in magick *ousia*. Ousia would be used to directly access a person's energy and manipulate it for magickal purposes.

Undoubtedly, magickal ethics must be employed when performing any working whatsoever. As Witches and magicians, we strive to create positive change and must be accurate in all we do, whether physically or energetically. Hair can be used in a number of ways; it may be burned for releasing, buried for earthwork such as grounding and centering, or boiled with herbs to attune a person's energy to properties of the plants. Pagan folklore says that burning someone else's hair draws that person to you. It is also said to curse the person whose hair is being burnt, though this works only if the intent is such. Combing the hair is said to bring storms if the weather is focused upon. Hair can be used effectively in magick when one reflects on the past. The fallen hair represents the release of elements of the past and is perfect for use in spellcraft.

When getting a haircut or trim, focus on releasing unwanted energies of the past. Each cut of the scissors represents the severance of an element of the past that is no longer needed for growth. Pieces of the hair then can be offered to the elements or left with trustworthy people to keep your energy disseminated and protected in many places. If the hair is long enough, it even can be donated to a nonprofit organization like Locks of Love, which provides prosthetic hairpieces for children afflicted by diseases that cause long-term hair loss. In this case, the hair should be smudged and cleared, which energetically prepares it for use by another person.

Our emotions are constantly and continually changing. A primary causal factor is the individual's surrounding stimuli and the mind's reaction to it. On a larger scale, human emotions change both monthly and yearly, in tune with the lunar and solar cycles. We may choose to alter our hair drastically or subtly in accordance with these tides. For example, during the tide of Samhain, we may choose to fashion our hair in a flowing, mournful fashion. Doing this may also be ideal to embrace dark moon energies that stress internalization. Hair may cover the eyes at this time to represent the internal energy of the season, when much of the world begins its slumber, awaiting springtime rebirth. This style is also good when feeling sadness, as it keeps your own energy inside you instead of projecting outward. Combing hair in front of the face, particularly over the eyes, can be representative of introspection. Doing so draws one's energy inward and keeps the aura close to the body. Since the face is the part of the body that receives the most stimuli, it acts as an emanating energy center. Placing hair in front of the face locks energy within, keeping it from going too far away from the body. For that reason, wearing this style too often can inhibit natural energies from flowing about the body and may drive a person to an excessively depressive state over time. Maybe emo kids have it right by covering one eye with hair—it definitely encourages internal versus external balance!

Hair can be styled in a number of ways to invoke magickal properties into the wearer. When styling your hair, put magickal intention into each brush stroke, each glob of gel, each formation of a spike, each snip, shave, and so on. Everything can carry your will. Create your own associations with different hairstyles!

I like to charge spikes with protection. They protrude from the head and, if charged properly, can "scare off" energetic intruders. Mohawks and deathhawks run down the center of the head and magickally can provide balance through alignment of both sides of the body. This metaphorically can align the polarity of yin and yang of the body's energy. Because the hair is raised or spiked, it also can represent connection to higher planes.

Knots and braids can be the focus of any spell. With each tying of the hair, chant a prayer, mantra, or affirmation to keep the energy sealed to your person. When you wish to release the energy, just untie the knot and send it on its way. For example, say someone is taking classes and needs extra luck on the next day's exam, feeling as though cramming just isn't enough. The hair could be knotted, braided, or woven in a magick circle the night before with the intention of remembering the studied information. During the exam, the hair would then casually be untied to release the pent-up energy, tapping into the intent of the previous night.

If you feel chaotic or low on energy, you can put some gel on your hands and wave it sporadically through your hair for a Robert Smith style. Or, perhaps the moon is full or a high sun holiday is being celebrated; spiked or colorful hair may be ideal to draw on the forces of the time. The possibilities are endless and are based entirely on your personal associations and the magick you give them.

Body Modification

Body modification easily can be considered a Pagan art form. Its roots are in tribalism and shamanic spirituality. Goths, punks, and others of alternative lifestyles are drawn to body alteration in order to separate the self from society. While this may not be the intended purpose for some, the subconscious mind understands body modification as a deliberate declaration to a powerful force. In this case, modification connects to others of similar minds. Astral threads connect all people across the globe whose bodies are modified, in a sort of primal bond, simply because they have undergone the act. If magick was intended and the modification was made into a ritual, then stronger interconnecting threads are in place. Everyone is interlinked on a metaphysical level, and the general consciousness of one person in a group affects the consciousness of other individuals in that system

Xavier and Angelus are always in the mood for some body mod!

and vice versa. I believe that engaging in body modification connects similarly minded people across the globe and is a reclaiming of latent individualistic tribal power.

While more and more mainstream Americans are saving their every dime and nickel for facelifts and liposuction, the alternatively inclined are saving up for tattoos and funky piercings. The difference between cosmetic and alternative body alteration is simple. Plastic surgery, fake tans, and the like are designed to make a person appear to have been born *naturally* "beautiful." Cosmetic surgery (aside from that done for medical purposes) actually disempowers a person by allowing others' opinions to determine the person's worth and view of personal beauty. Our type of body modification is different: it's not meant to look natural by any stretch of the imagination, but is a form of artistic creativity using the human body as the canvas. Many choose to alter their physical bodies for spiritual or emotional reasons. Alternative body modification is a creative individual expression, whether or not onlookers believe it to be freakish.

Altering the body with sacred intention is a declaration of spiritual devotion. It reflects a desire to rekindle connection to ancient energy and unify the self with the spiritual community in a world slipping so far away from naturalistic tendencies. To artistically alter the body is to bring out the spirit, and may subsequently force any observers to question their own identities.

Indigenous peoples across the globe have long practiced tribal body modification for reasons of beauty, initiation, dedication, declaration of status, and so on. In addition to the modifications described in the rest of this chapter (which are becoming more popular in Western society), the Mursi tribe of Ethiopia practices lip extension with plates. The Padaung peoples of Burma and Thailand practice visual neck extension with the stacking of brass ring coils that girls begin to wear at as early as five years of age.

Another Ethiopian group that performs tribal body modification is the Nuer tribe from Sudan. While in the past tribal members used less sanitary tools to perform the modifications, they now use razors and large safety pins. The pin is inserted into the epidermis and pulled out. When a small amount of skin is pulled out with the pin, it is sliced with the razor blade. This is performed in patterns all over the body, creating a beautiful stippling effect.

Westerners tend to enter a state of shock when observing these practices, but to the people of these cultures, such practices are absolutely accepted and part of ordinary life. It's no wonder that body modification is beginning to surface in the West, as this part of cultural identity has long been suppressed.

Though it's not commonplace to practice the aforementioned alterations in the West, quite a few other alternative means of body modification, such as the implantation of 3-D objects beneath the skin, are being practiced more frequently across the globe. Also, one of the most bizarre and unique forms of body modification is the forked tongue, which is the result of a tongue-splitting surgery. Also gaining in popularity is the surgical implantation of "horns" into the skull. These all require more advanced surgical procedures than do tats and piercings. Self-mutilation is not necessarily a negative thing, though it has a tendency to cross that borderline. When does altering the body become too much? The limits are different for everyone.

In addition to the types of body modification discussed on the next pages, the modern "Witch's cradle" also changes consciousness by altering sensory experience. Instead of subjecting the body to pain in order to induce an altered state, the practitioner is wrapped in a body suit, blindfolded, and suspended by a rope, free to move any way he or she chooses. The person is immobile inside the suit and unable to engage in any sensory experience but that of the mind. The Witch's cradle may have originated during the Witchcraze of the fifteenth to eighteenth centuries, in which Witch hunters would occasionally wrap the accused in a burlap sack, tie it, and toss it over a tree. The blind swinging would induce an altered state of consciousness, with the aim of gaining "confession" of Witchery. While this method was not exactly pleasant or positive, most likely it gave a handful of relatively modern practitioners the idea to attempt a similar practice for spiritual means, perhaps with the idea of releasing horrid connotations by giving them an actual spiritual meaning. This is one of the many forms of sensory deprivation, which can be very therapeutic and educational if done appropriately and carefully. This is the flip side of extreme pain induction, but the results differ very little. Feeling an extreme amount of sensory input and depriving the body of input altogether (likely causing emotional distress) are two means of achieving altered states of consciousness by removing the body from its ordinary sensory experience.

In the following sections, I will discuss the more common forms of visible body modification practiced in today's subcultural societies. These practices are telling of people's willingness to break free from social boundaries and let their creative spirit sidestep the norm by way of individualistic expression.

Piercing

We Goths love our metallic shinies! Piercings are beautiful, quick, and relatively painless. Well, maybe not painless—it depends on where you get "poked." The eyebrows are much less sensitive than the nipples.

Ancient Egyptians pierced themselves (and even the ears of their pet cats!), as have people of many other cultures throughout time. Piercings long have represented wealth, beauty, and rites of passage.

Modern jewelry pieces created specifically for body piercings are most commonly made of stainless steel, as it does not irritate the skin for most wearers.

The process of enchanting magickal body jewelry is identical to that of empowering pendants and other pieces of jewelry. However, you must be sure to sanitize and disinfect any piece after charging to ensure that no infections arise. If you already are pierced, then energy can be worked through the piercing without actually removing it from the body.

Some Pagans believe that piercings block the flow of vital bodily energy. I don't believe ancient shamans who practiced this felt the same way, just as many present-day

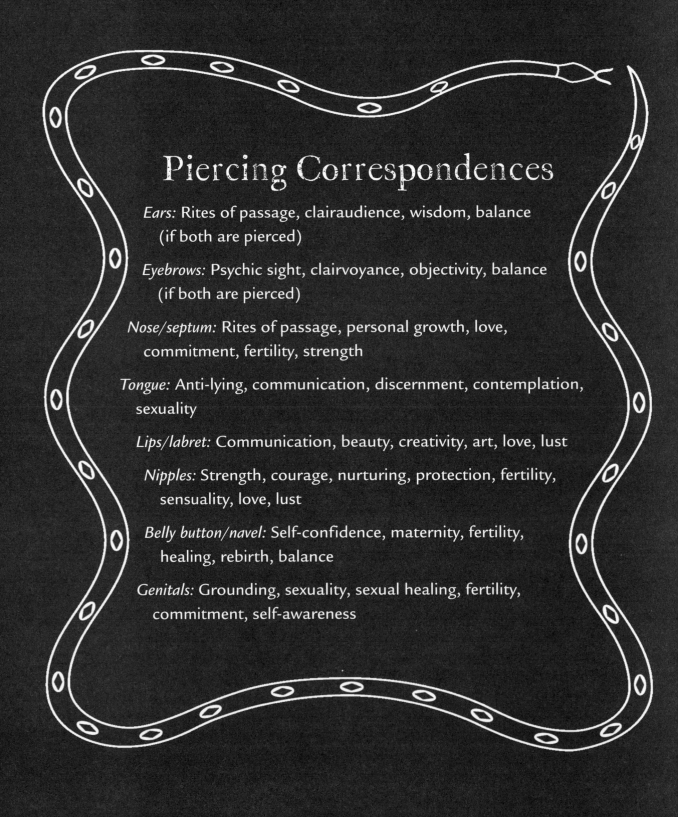

Piercing Correspondences

Ears: Rites of passage, clairaudience, wisdom, balance (if both are pierced)

Eyebrows: Psychic sight, clairvoyance, objectivity, balance (if both are pierced)

Nose/septum: Rites of passage, personal growth, love, commitment, fertility, strength

Tongue: Anti-lying, communication, discernment, contemplation, sexuality

Lips/labret: Communication, beauty, creativity, art, love, lust

Nipples: Strength, courage, nurturing, protection, fertility, sensuality, love, lust

Belly button/navel: Self-confidence, maternity, fertility, healing, rebirth, balance

Genitals: Grounding, sexuality, sexual healing, fertility, commitment, self-awareness

Pagans don't either. Pagans and spiritualists tend to be more aware of their own actions and the effects of their actions. While it may be easy for some to believe that body jewelry is trivial, Pagans have a way of imbuing each and every little thing with magickal intent. Body jewelry can be another tool in spellcraft if used with awareness and intent. I believe that piercings certainly can inhibit energetic flow in non-magickally minded people, because the currents are not directed with intent. Instead, lacking intent, the physical piercing itself—and not the meaning behind it—becomes the focus. Instead of magickally charging the modification as a sacred act, the art is left relatively meaningless, prohibiting full energy circulation.

While I realize that some people get their cheeks, neck, back, arms, and other areas pierced, some of the more common piercings today are listed on page 138, along with ideas of what they can represent, based on the area of the body, in terms of energetic correspondences and cultural associations.

As magickal folk, we must strive to get our piercings for both aesthetic *and* spiritual reasons. Figure out the meaning for your piercing before you enter the shop; may it be significant and powerful. As the needle enters your flesh, focus not on the pain but on your intent. Put yourself in a light trance. The rush of adrenaline will help project your intent directly into your body and weave into existence the essence of your miniature rite of passage.

Cutting

Several global tribes practice ritual cutting. Many people bear numerous slice-wound scars across their bodies in specific patterns. These markings show that the person sought help from a cultural shaman, tribal elder, or witch doctor who cut the person (with both participants in a state of trance) to release demons and disease through bleeding, or for purposes of undergoing a rite of passage.

Australian Aborigines have the longest-running unbroken culture in the world. Staying close to their ancient tradition, Aboriginal shamans undergo a cutting ceremony in which the tribal elder takes deep horizontal cuts across the chest. This signifies his advancement in the ways of understanding Dreamtime.

The pastoral African Nuer society has a ritual of life-changing body modification to mark the transition between boyhood and manhood for males of the society. Around the age of twelve to fifteen they undergo a ceremonial procedure in which an elder slices a series of deep horizontal gashes across the forehead of the young male experiencing the transition. These marks are called *gar*. These gashes create scars for life and symbolize one of the most significant times in a person's life. Ethnocentricity aside, these modifications are highly venerated among the Nuer as a dedication to their fellow tribespeople and the spirits of the land. Extreme body modification is viewed as a sacred act to the Nuer people and countless other tribal societies across the globe.

If a person of Western culture attempts cutting, he or she should do so with utmost care and precision, not for attention and certainly not for careless pain induction. Sadly, most Westerners who cut themselves do so out of depression rather than ritualism. They may carve slashes, words, symbols, or anything else into the surface of the skin for nonspiritual purposes, usually with the reason of directing internal pain to the physical body. People use razors, broken glass, knives, guitar strings, scissors, or nails. Some do it to gain attention from others by cutting in noticeable places. Those who hide their wounds well, on the other hand, are trying to get in touch with their body by inducing harm on themselves, testing their threshold of pain, trying even nonconsciously to understand the frailty of the physical form by undergoing a sensory—even dangerous—act of emotional release.

Taking time to carve and wound the skin moves energy from the mind to the physical body. Cutting on a regular basis out of depression is entirely different from practicing ceremonies involving blood magick, like shamanic rites of release and exorcism. Slicing the flesh in a state of sorrow is not glamorous and is *not* effective. I speak from personal experience and draw upon the experience of others who have also partaken. *Cutting yourself makes the pain temporarily physical*; it does not release the pain permanently. In fact, it adds to the pain, perpetuating it on numerous levels. We must discover the most appropriate ways to release what we feel, instead of causing more pain on another level.

If you are a "cutter," consider it an unconscious cry to reclaim your power through intensive magick, as well as a need to release built-up energy from your person. Carefully cutting yourself in moderation in ritual can be beneficial, if the energy is channeled properly, and is certainly the best environment in which to do so if you feel a pull toward letting a bit of blood. Cutting in a ritual setting with focused intention is much different from using a razor blade in the bathroom. For more information on the ritual use of blood, please see the "Blood Magick" section in the closing chapter of this book.

Scarification

Scarification long has been a part of tribal initiation. In addition to the stippling modification mentioned in this section's introduction, scarification is still practiced heavily in West Africa. Generally, the face is scarred with slash markings in particular places. Ash may be inserted into the open wound to darken the result. The scars represent the village, clan, and family a person is from, and are seen as a form of beauty. They also are recognized as a form of magick that changes the physical body to better access the spiritual, and can represent the completion of a rite of passage.

Scarification is common in tribes of people with dark skin tones, since tattoos don't show up as easily as markings left by broken skin. Tribal groups on the Middle Sepik River in Papua New Guinea incorporate into their mythology a view of the world as having been created from the mouth of a crocodile. To honor this myth, an initiation has been developed in which men and women of the tribe scar themselves with a series of short puncture wounds that, when healed, represent the scales of a crocodile. This connects them to the totem animal of the area, bearing deep mythological symbolism.

Forms of scarification have begun to surface in Europe, America, and other industrialized cultures. In modern scarification in the West, the top layer of the skin is carefully lifted from the epidermis, exposing a surface-deep open wound. The wound can be in any shape, even relatively detailed. The skin then heals over, causing a scar to form and securing the symbol as a different shade than the rest of the flesh. Scarification typically uses no ink or branding iron, though branding is another form of body modification making its way to the West.

Suspension

The art of suspension greatly draws upon native tribal practices. It is a form of *asceticism*, which implies extreme personal discipline, usually in the form of physical sacrifice, for the sake of spiritual devotion.

The annual Native American Sun Dance ceremony, practiced by many North American tribes, includes fasting, singing, ecstatic dancing, vows, and spiritual communion, lasting several days and nights. Many Native American cultures practiced ritual suspension as part of the Sun Dance until the Europeans outlawed their ceremonies. Now, some tribes are resurrecting these practices in their entirety to preserve their spiritual heritage.

In the Sun Dance's ritual suspension, tribesmen volunteer to be pierced in the back or breast area with talons, bones, sharpened wood, or skewers that are attached to a rope leading to a pole or tree. The practitioner dances and sings while suspended (or partially suspended, depending on the tribe). Energy is exchanged between the person suspended and the tree or pole, eliciting profound visionary experiences in the practitioner and drawing his spirit to the divine. Sacrificing personal comfort is seen as reciprocity with the earth for providing constant sustenance, honoring abundance of the past and ensuring that of the future. Tribes pay much homage and respect to anyone able to endure the sacrifice and come out with strength and power.

Many people all over the world are becoming drawn to neo-primitive practices that include the art of suspension. Wide and sterile stainless steel hooks are inserted into specific regions of the body, and the body is suspended above ground. Many hang from their upper back, which is the most common method. Some prefer hanging from the chest, which often is reported as the most difficult method, at times impairing the ability to breathe properly. Some practitioners hang full-body, with many hooks inserted down the front or back of the body from the chest to the legs. The skin supports the body weight, and the practitioner's consciousness is elevated beyond ordinary time and space. Underground clubs and venues exist all over the world where one can watch and take part in this extreme and controversial art form, which is absolutely legal and only practiced willingly.

As with the tribal practice, modern practitioners suspend themselves for spiritual reasons. Suspension provides a release of internal pain, lifting the suspender to a heightened state of consciousness transcending the physical body and the mortal pain attached to it. When the body goes into a state of shock, the mind goes elsewhere, serving as a vessel for higher spiritual vibrations to enter. The pain itself becomes lessened and even unnoticeable when the suspension is taking place. Much as when one is under the influence of transcendental meditation or mind-altering substances, the mind does not focus on the mundane aspects of life during suspension. Rather, the practice provides insight into the nature of reality, bringing visions and epiphanies to the person suspended.

Tattooing

The art of tattooing is ancient and can be traced back to prehistory. Visibly altering the body with dyes (vegetable and other types) was a worldwide spiritual practice at one time. Tattooing practices were seen in innumerable ancient cultures. Some of these include the Romans, Vikings, Incans, Mayans, Aztecs, Picts, Maoris, Polynesians, Native Americans, and other shamanic systems. Even the classical Greek philosophers (and magicians) Pythagoras and Galois were tattooed with sacred symbols. Drawings of many ancient Egyptian Priests and Priestesses show the rulers bearing tattoos.

In the Polynesian islands of Samoa, tattooing was the ultimate rite of passage for boys. Upon taking the sacred mark, a boy gained the right to speak in the presence of elders, get married, and do more than the most ordinary chores, which were reserved especially for the unmarked.

It seems the practice is reemerging at present as a worldwide phenomenon, symbolizing the resurfacing of ancient ways in the global community. With the rise of Christianity, tattooing and body modification of any sort were seen in a skewed, negative light, telling of barbarism and heresy. Most cultures currently don't view the tattoo as sinful or transgressive, but are accepting of it as a common expression that even may have spiritual connotations. Tattooing gives some people a link to their heritage and cultural roots. It can bring an ancient practice into modernity, reclaiming old ways that are suffering the threat of extinction.

For many cultures, bearing tattoos of deities, script, and symbolism is representative of everlasting devotion to a belief structure or set of ideas. Some cultures utilize tattoos as proof of initiation and social status and for rites of passage. Designs vary from culture to culture. Many adherents of Eastern spiritual paths get very detailed designs on their bodies that may cover a small or large portion of skin, often portraying a series of mythological events and rich tapestries of imagery significant to their culture.

Tattooing the skin permanently fuses the energy of the piece to the spirit. The body is the house of the soul, and sacred marks integrate the physical and the spiritual. This is why tattoos must be chosen carefully, not carelessly. Pagans and other spiritualists tend to mindfully choose which tattoos to affix to their bodies. It's essential that the design be symbolic and highly meaningful. Ink work can be a celebratory activity to mark important points in a person's life, like the finding of personal freedom, initiation, or spiritual realization.

The recipient of the art must carefully select the tattoo artist, as portions of the artist's energy pattern (both the person who is giving the tattoo and the person who drew it) become fused to the artwork placed under the skin. In most large urban areas, there exist professional spiritual tattooists who understand the ancient implications of permanently marking the body. If these people are not accessible, then a balanced and altruistic person at the local tat' shop can be great, so long as you have similar ideals and your energies don't clash.

The pain that accompanies the tattooing process isn't much of an issue in most areas of the body. The sensory experience can be utilized to enter into a trancelike state, as with any body modification, to attune to the purpose of the marking process. If approached with respect and awareness, tattooing can be one of the most beneficial and magickal rites of the modern Pagan.

V

Sex, Drugs, and Rock 'n' Roll

Social views on sex, drugs, and rock 'n' roll (or any impassioned music) have been skewed largely as a result of Christian doctrine. Many obsolete fear-based ideas still surround these topics, which at one time were viewed as sacred acts of divine communion.

Oh, to be young and surrounded with so many tempting sensory experiences! Engaging in socially taboo, risqué activities can be stimulating, fun, and sometimes dangerous. Extreme experiences have the ability to make us feel more alive and even more enlightened at times—a truth well understood by shamans and chaos magicians alike. Humans are given tools that aid in the progression of consciousness. This includes the three aforementioned taboos in the form of mind-altering flora from the earth, the human sexual system, and our unique ability to create music with the materials around us. Each is an experience of heightened perception and presents an opportunity to learn from the land, oneself, and one another when approached from a spiritual perspective.

Unfortunately, many of these tools have been either overused or overlooked, especially in these times. Intense experiences of reality can either lift us up or destroy us inside, but no matter what, doors of consciousness will open as a result.

In our youth, we don't know everything, no matter what we choose to believe. These experiences can be gratifying but not necessarily beneficial. When we are young, we are overwhelmed by the fact that truths into the nature of reality are constantly revealing themselves. We begin to see the greater picture of life a bit more clearly and, through involvement and experimentation, begin to determine our identities. Though we perceive life a bit more clearly, we still know only a piece of the puzzle at this time and mustn't fool ourselves into thinking otherwise. While extreme sensory experiences may be tempting and even rewarding at times, the line between *use* and *overuse* (or *abuse*) must always be kept in check.

To look at sensory experiences from an Eastern perspective, I turn to Tantra. Tantric practices have their origins in Hinduism. They focus on life's strongest experiences, like sex and death, as gateways to spiritual enlightenment. Tantra, which also has its own school of Buddhism, does not revolve around sex, as many Westerners believe. Practitioners make use of the body's energy in direct experiences, seeing them as vehicles of ascension. These processes are not enlightening in and of themselves, but open the self to the *possibility* of transcending mortal boundaries. Tantra strives to identify the self with divinity. Natural reality is seen as a complete emanation of divinity, and a Tantrika would certainly agree that sex, drugs, and rock 'n' roll are extensions of divine expression, which must be approached with respect and intelligence.

Gerald Gardner's original Book of Shadows includes information beyond ritual procedure. For example, it includes a list of "Eight Paths to Reach the Center" (see the sidebar on page 147), which is spiritual connection. These are referred to as the eight "Ways of Making Magick." This Book of Shadows recommends combining various points to reach the center, assuming that each activity will be practiced in the confines of a magickal space. In fact, it is mentioned that five additional things are necessary before using any of the Eight Paths, in order to practice the arts successfully. These are intention, preparation, invocation, consecration, and purification. Please reflect on the meanings of these points before reading on.

The information on page 147 can also be found in *A Witches' Bible: The Complete Witches' Handbook* by Janet and Stewart Farrar.

The Ways of Making Magick

from the Gardnerian Book of Shadows

1. Meditation or concentration.

2. Chants, spells, invocations. Invoking the Goddess, etc.

3. Projection of the astral body, or trance.

4. Incense, drugs, wine, etc. Any potion which aids to release the spirit.

5. Dancing.

6. Blood control. Use of the cords.

7. The scourge.

8. The Great Rite.

Number two on this list emphasizes chanting, while number five emphasizes dancing. Number four emphasizes drugs and similar substances as ways of "releasing the spirit," and number eight emphasizes a form of Pagan ritualistic sex. Gerald Gardner and his associates understood "sex, drugs, and rock 'n' roll" to be spiritual gateways—codes of ascension—and applied this knowledge to early Wiccan teachings.

Music of the Night

Goth music and style are becoming increasingly popular, growing in recognition every day. Even formerly "un-Goth" bands are embracing the style and portraying dark attributes without a firm foundation within the dark art movement. Experimentation is cool, but changing to a dark style because it seems like the neat thing to do at the moment dilutes the real significance of Goth, and the music begins to lose its touch. Nonetheless, this newfound persuasion often serves as a steppingstone into the realm of true dark music, culture, and expression.

Music (or "musick," as I sometimes spell it) is an expression from the soul. It is an exclamation of spirituality and connection to higher levels of awareness, to be shared with all who choose to listen. In this case, the lyrics and instrumentation do not necessarily have to refer *directly* to spiritual or philosophical ideas. As with any deeply personal art form, music is naturally written, composed, and performed from levels of heightened consciousness, bringing the internal outward through the medium of song. The result transports the listener to higher planes, swinging open the mind's doors of perception.

Everything that exists physically has its own energetic pattern. Everything vibrates at different frequencies, which is why herbs, stones, and metals are such great magickal tools. Everything has its own frequency that can be lent to any working. Just as physical objects have their own vibration, so do nonphysical things, including music. Music is restricted to the physical plane only by the instruments themselves. The patterned noise that comes about is naturally more astral in nature than other forms of art. For this reason, music serves as a profound spiritual medium and has been recognized as having these effects since the most ancient of times.

Music is one of the oldest forms of spiritual expression, used in literally all cultures throughout time. Early shamanic and tribal cultures used instruments such as drums, rattles, shakers, and gourds. The sounds and vibrations these instruments emitted were used for both celebratory and ceremonial means. Before humankind drew a solid line of division between the ordinary and the spiritual, all aspects of life were held sacred. Thus, celebrations and ceremonies took place for personal rites of passage (birth, coming of age, initiations, and death) as well as natural shifts (seasonal changes, phases of the moon, harvest, and fertility). Numerous cultures, especially in South and Southeast Asia, have elaborate musical ceremonies for invocation and spirit possession. Indigenous and native cultures around the globe use music for inducing trance states of consciousness. Certainly, Neopaganism strives to resurrect these practices and further attune the self to the cycles and patterns of life. All along the way, music has served as a central binding force between human and Spirit.

To tie in the magick of music with an ancient example, Pythagoras, an early Hermetic magician and mystical genius, is said to have studied in Egyptian magickal schools. He began an order based on the central teaching that mathematics is the science of reality. This fusion of mathematics and magickal practice is commonly referred to as *sacred geometry, arithmology,* or *mathemagicks.* Pythagoras's school was one of the first to use the pentagram, symbolizing personal connection to life's essence and the actuality of spiritual learning. According to these studies, all things in reality, including physical objects, thoughts, and ideas, are composed of vibrations. "All is number," and reality is seen as a series of geometric patterns funneling from a central source: Spirit. Part of being a Witch or occultist is to actively work on the development of spiritual sight—that which allows us to perceive energy patterns and synchronicities all around us. Pythagoras understood this truth and its connection to music. Not only is the whole of natural reality attuned to geometrical patterns, but music is divine patterning in and of itself. Pythagoras understood the intensely influential energy of music, recognizing its profound effects on the human mind. Pythagoras was one of the first ancient magicians to note in detail the spiritual properties of music.

Modern music draws on similar concepts, though usually in a much subtler manner. Singers and musicians generally focus their creative efforts on personally significant life changes, whether internal or external. Listeners may relate to the artists' creations and may be experiencing similar changes in their own lives. This empathic connection between the creator(s) and the listener(s) may very well help both parties experience and evolve with life changes, as with the ceremonies of our ancestors.

Goth music is characterized by its dark attributes. It reaches into the depths of the artist, the cobwebbed, hidden parts of the self, and pulls them to the forefront. In turn, the sound vibrations have this effect on the listener and present the opportunity to face one's deepest, most hidden thoughts and heal them with acceptance. This is not an easy process, but great healing potential lies in dark music.

An oldschool Goth friend of mine once told me that there are "three types of music: Goth music, non-Goth music, and music that Goths would enjoy but isn't necessarily Goth." I'd say this just about sums it up! Goth music in particular dares to stress and express emotionalism above all else. Since many artists do not fit neatly into the "Goth" category, the scene constantly witnesses multiple overlaps. Just go to a Goth club; one may hear London After Midnight or Specimen the same night as Tori Amos or Enigma! Of course there is nothing wrong with this, but much internal controversy arises within the scene as to what is and what is not "Goth." Personally, I feel part of the beauty of the scene is the indefinability and ambiguity of both the music and style, allowing leeway for interpretation and experimentation for all involved. So long as the expression stays true to the heart and soul, Goth has no need to worry about perversion or deterioration.

Nowadays, there are countless subgenres, sub-subgenres, and sub-sub-subgenres of both Goth and industrial music. To more easily define particular styles within dark music, genres have been created and built upon. These are briefly described in the sections that follow.

I use the elements Earth, Air, Fire, and Water to group Goth, industrial, and otherwise darkly music. Most artists include bits of all traditional elemental associations in their work, yet usually have one element or feeling presiding over the others. I have filed various musical styles and bands under certain elements for easy categorization, but their elemental associations do not by any means reflect the entirety of the music the band or artist creates. Because of the emotional nature of Goth music, nearly all of these artists are attuned to some extent to the element of Water.

Suggested Gothic Listening

Bauhaus. *Crackle.*

Christian Death. *Only Theatre of Pain.*

Cure, The. *Disintegration.*

Dead Can Dance. *Toward the Within.*

Depeche Mode. *Violator.*

Faith and the Muse. *Annwyn, Beneath the Waves.*

Fields of the Nephilim. *Revelations.*

Inkubus Sukkubus. *Vampyre Erotica.*

Joy Division. *Substance.*

London After Midnight. *Psychomagnet.*

Love and Rockets. *Sorted!*

Numan, Gary. *Exile.*

Sex Gang Children. *Medea.*

Siouxsie and the Banshees. *Juju.*

Sisters of Mercy, The. *A Slight Case of Overbombing.*

Sopor Aeternus and the Ensemble of Shadows.
   Dead Lovers' Sarabande, Face I and Face II.

Specimen. *Wet Warm Cling Film Red Velvet Crush.*

Switchblade Symphony. *Serpentine Gallery.*

Various Artists Compilation. *The Black Bible.*

———. *Goth: Music of the Shadows, v. 1.*

———. *Gothic Rock, v. 1–3.*

Earth

Bands and artists who helped spawn the movements we subscribe to could be categorized under the element of Earth, as they are the "roots" of the subculture. They are the fertile ground from which the dark musical evolution came about and continues to grow. They are the ones who sowed the seeds of alternative dark culture and should ever be minded as the forefathers of Goth! Bands that can be equated with the element Earth include those of the darker varieties within the post-punk movement, early deathrock and darkwave. Industrial bands and early electro-industrial fusion artists may also be considered "earthly" in their influence, and can encompass those belonging to the genres of early synthpop and EBM (electronic body music), the latter of which was created by the group Front 242.

Examples: Bauhaus, Sex Gang Children, Christian Death, The Cure, Alien Sex Fiend, Siouxsie and the Banshees, Psychic TV, 45 Grave, Kraftwerk, Einstürzende Neubauten, Tones On Tail, Specimen, Skinny Puppy, Nitzer Ebb, The Wake.

Pros: Grounding, satisfaction, dedication, recognition.

Cons: Über-seriousness, stagnation, isolation, ennui.

Air

In Witchcraft and Paganism, the element of Air represents intellectualism, creativity, and the workings of the mind. Music in the category of Air may include neoclassical and neo-Mediæval music that evokes feelings of our historical past with dark romantic imagery. Artists who utilize ambient experimental electronic soundscapes may also befit this elemental categorization, as could artists who tell stories through song. Some "visual kei" (Japanese visual/musical artists) bands that portray their artistic expression equally through both mesmerizing sounds and visuals also may fit well into this category, including those of the Japanese Goth, baroque, angura, and eroguro subcategories.

Examples: Rasputina, Qntal, Attrition, Malice Mizer, Dir en Grey, Voltaire, Delerium, Black Tape for a Blue Girl, The Mediæval Bæbes, Atrium Carceri, Audra, Coil, Jocelyn Montgomery, BlutEngel, The Crüxshadows, Lycia, The Tear Garden.

Pros: Intellectualism, study, thought, discretion, philosophy, creativity.

Cons: Ungroundedness, idealism, disconnection, arrogance, delusion.

Fire

The element of Fire represents passion, invigoration, motivation, and sexuality. Music that can be categorized here is progressive in nature, motivating the listener and pushing the mind to new limits. Genres that fall easily in this category include *modern* industrial, deathrock, dark-punk, EBM, futurepop, fetish, and powernoise. Artists who integrate elements of metal and hard rock are best aligned with this element. Also included in this category are bands that deal with apocalyptic and taboo-sexual themes.

Examples: Feindflug, URN, The Azoic, Hanzel und Gretyl, And One, Combichrist, Das Ich, Lords of Acid, Terrorfakt, KMFDM, Stromkern, Zombie Girl, Experiment Haywire, XPQ-21, Battery Cage, Pig, Neikka RPM, Angelspit.
Pros: Motivation, passion, love, lust, desire, excitement, drive.
Cons: Anger, rage, temperament, sexual indulgence, ostentatiousness.

Water

Genres that would best be considered part of the Water category include those of the darkwave, ethereal, and other categories. I almost willingly would classify all overtly Goth music into the element of Water because of its strong emphasis on the emotional realms, and indeed most bands that can be classified in more than one genre could be included under this element. However, Goth has many aspects that need to be considered and addressed when deciding to categorize music in this fashion. Though virtually *all* artists in dark culture tap this vein, there still remain those who emphasize emotion *above all else*. While all music touches the soul on different levels, artists who could belong to the Water category necessarily target the emotions, often causing listeners to reflect deeply on their lives, be it through tears, meditation, or contemplation. Water represents change, fluctuation, and movement, in addition to extreme emotionality, and music can be one of the most significant means of influencing spiritual progression through change. Many artists use the voice as an actual instrument (rather than simply singing), often allowing it to overtake the presence of additional instrumentation.

Examples: Sopor Aeternus and the Ensemble of Shadows, Diamanda Galás, Julee Cruise, Dead Can Dance, Gary Numan, Wolfsheim, The Smashing Pumpkins, Andalusia, Vas, Azam Ali, Monica Richards, Assemblage 23, Veduta.
Pros: Change, empathy, emotional support, openness.
Cons: Sadness, uncertainty, indecisiveness, melancholy.

Ritual Noise: Music in Magick

Whether or not to use music in ritual is entirely up to the practitioner. Some feel that playing music while in circle inhibits the flow of the energy being raised. In that case, the simplicity of silence is the grand conduit of spiritual energy. Silence is empty, allowing undivided concentration for the magician. Its essence is pure and uninfluenced, waiting to be formed by the caster.

Music can be used for raising or lowering energy. Certain types of music help the listener fall into ambience, while others wake up and invigorate the listener. Each has a different effect and easily can be applied to a ritualistic setting as an aid in creating a particular atmosphere conducive to energy working. Using prerecorded music in ritual is tricky. Most Witches who choose to do so ensure that the music-playing device and speakers are *outside* the boundaries of the circle, since the electrical energy of the player can mix with the energy raised in circle. The energy is naturally similar to the electrical currents the player emanates. What the practitioner is going for is an auditory influence, not a direct electrical link between machinery and magick. The music's influence should be through auditory means alone, as a guide for the workings at hand.

Some occultists prefer only natural on-the-spot music in ritual. That is, the musicians must be present, instead of using prerecorded sound. This is especially appropriate in celebratory rites like certain Sabbats. A bit of music may be played (or performed) at a point in a Sabbatical or Esbatical rite to strengthen the participants' focus. Most Witches I know like to end large rituals with a "circle song" or unifying chant, and may or may not use prerecorded music. Most Pagans prefer self-created on-the-spot music with the use of drums, rattles, flutes, bagpipes, and, of course, the voice.

If you choose to use prerecorded music in a ritual setting, I highly recommend listening to the whole song(s) before incorporating it into a rite. A lot of music is very dramatic and subject to totally change at any time mid-song; this especially holds true with the weird dark-artsy music that we listen to! Making a compilation tape or CD (or "black tape") for various moods is a great idea. You can make a mix in which the songs are attuned to the attributes of one element or a combination of the four. If you study the Qabalah, you can make a CD for each sephira on the Tree of Life. If you practice natural magick, perhaps a disk of elementally attuned tracks would be suitable. If you practice a particular ritual often (like one for protection or healing), you could make a disk that you feel embodies characteristics of the ceremony. A faerie mix would work wonders. For past-life regressions, a compilation of soothing classical symphonies may be appropriate. Dark ambient or serene New Age meditation music can add to astral projection ceremonies. There are a number of genres that aid in deep meditation. You could create a compilation to draw forth particular energies of the Otherworlds and astral planes. Take your pick and have a go!

If any song on the compilation you create is displeasing or off-putting in any way, remove it immediately! The energy must continue its flow without disturbance, and since the experience depends entirely on your perception of the audio (and thus influences the spiritual work), any hindrance can be detrimental. It's best to have it all carefully mapped out beforehand.

Most magicians prefer to work with music that does not contain vocals. The vocals add an entirely different feel to the ritual and generally are best avoided, especially because vocals are in place to evoke a particular type of mood, such as that which the artist was experimenting with at the time of writing the track. Just as much power, if not more, is conveyed through nonvocal song. Wordless music also leaves the energy less defined, leaving it more up to the magician's own interpretation. Some magicians prefer to work with music that does contain voice but no actual words. Chant music holds its own vibratory essence and easily brings the listener to a plane above ordinary consciousness. In chanting, the voice becomes an instrument not withheld by words; this is why it has long been such a powerful tool of the magickal arts. Latin and Greek Gregorian chant is one form of music that can add a mystical allure reminiscent of classical antiquity, and can positively influence metaphysical work.

The music played in ritual does not necessarily have to be at the forefront of the working. It can faintly influence the ceremony, serving only as background sound. In this case, calming music almost always is preferred—nothing too vigorous or upbeat. Good choices are minimal electronic, chill-out/lounge, classical, and meditative worldbeat. Pleasant music relaxes the magician, helping the person enter a trancelike state appropriate for working magick and honoring life.

Goth Crafting the Night

The night has long since fallen, and a glance out the window reveals the hazy stars. A waning Mother Moon makes a striking appearance in the speckled sky, entrancing your gaze. Not looking away, you take three deep inhalations, knowing the energy she gives is free for all who seek the ways of old. Her essence enters your lungs, your blood, your body, and your mind. Aura now illuminated, you know this will be a good night.

Having phoned a friend, your plans to meet at the club are solidified. Your closet is an ocean of blackness with spots of red, blue, green, and white. Many of your clothes are hand-sewn with some of the finest threads available on the market—well worth the money saved. An industrial-styled number strikes your fancy. It hasn't been worn for quite a few months, itching for another night on the town. You wear the same boots you've worn for a week—no worries, the footwear isn't nearly as important as the makeup.

Eye to eye with yourself in the mirror, you feel your face readying for detailed adornment. You are feeling especially shadowy this evening, selecting darker shades of blue eyeshadow. Charcoal eyeliner intensifies the look, framing your widening eyes. With liquid eyeliner, you draw swirls and spirals growing from the cornea, letting only intuition guide your brushstrokes. A dot on either side of the face provides symmetrical balance. With a small, clever smear down the side of the face, your makeup is gorgeous; it feels right and is complete.

The weather is nice, and your apparel portrays your personality. This is contentment. Right then, off we go; it's nearly eleven! As you reach the club, you see your friend pull up around back next to someone's nifty hearse. Perfect timing but not surprising; it seems as though everything works synchronistically. You meet up and walk in, presenting the bouncers with your ID and a few bills. The pulsing beat brings a slight smile to your face. Deep-toned vocals drown out some of the crowd's chattering. The bass permeates your being, vibrating the flesh.

Entering gracefully, a couple near the door looks your way, briefly admires your outfit, and resumes conversation. The bar is crowded, and the enormous cages on the walls of the dance floor are packed to capacity with dancers. More people have shown up this night than most. You've longed for a cocktail all week and order a double, figuring it'll hit the spot. To the right, the moving ceiling lights that are illuminating the dance floor flash above a pale young man in a skirt. You can tell he's had a long week by his blank stare and awkward energy pattern. He, like many of the attendees, has come this night seeking personal therapy by mingling with like-minded people. To the left, a violet-haired oldschool Goth is having a good laugh with her friends at the table. You've seen her before at the tattoo parlor but can't recall her name.

"Here ya go," the bartender says. "Have fun." After no more than two sips into the drink, a familiar beat sweeps the club. It's a track from a new album that hasn't left your CD player's rotation in about a month. As if by magick, you are drawn to the middle of the dance floor with a number of other nightkind, clad in black and lost in the music. Your eyes slowly close while your body becomes a piece of moving art. The rhythm takes your breath while the driving vocals nearly bring a tear to your eye. "Mmmmm," you think to yourself. "This is home."

La Danse de Mort

Goth, industrial, and darkwave clubs are some of the most unique and phenomenal gathering places in the world. Stepping into a darksider club is like setting foot in a distant astral terrain. There, individuals of all body types, ages, flesh tones, and stylistic tendencies embrace fashions of the past, present, and even future—not to mention the amazing array of makeup styles! The environment is truly like no other.

The club is a temple. It acts as a gathering ground for people who hold similar points of view and expressive interests. It's a magickal place, seeming like a world outside of the world, separated from the mundane monotony of everyday life. It's a place to meet new people who also love to share visions and experiences with others of similar persuasions.

The club plays a big part in networking individuals of similar philosophies and allows for extreme personal exploration. In the barriers of a dark club setting, the ordinary is left at the door as a paradigm of experience is entered anew. The club is a *healing* place, a place to discover yourself and others. Too many Goths put on the frowny face and look down on the experience altogether to prove something to themselves. It's okay and even healthy to be depressed at a Goth club, but it's even healthier to let the serenity of the night empower and heal you, filling you with uninhibited bliss.

In larger cities, many nightclubs offer Goth-friendly evenings. This provides an organized meeting ground for those in the culture, assuredly beating the stale environment of a twenty-four-hour diner. Some clubs choose to cater exclusively to the Goth-industrial crowd. Many others limit darksider themes to certain nights of the week. Most clubs are 18+ or 21+, but some cities have taken to hosting all-age Goth picnics, bowling nights, or movie nights so all can have something to do, even if it's not going out to dance!

Some Goth, industrial, and fetish clubs enforce a strict dress code, barring anyone who doesn't look out of the ordinary from entering. To an average person, this may seem pretentious and segregative, but if you think about it, if someone in tan khakis and a baseball cap entered the realm of a hundred dancing darklings, they'd stick out like a sore thumb! This instantly can bring down the vibe as a whole. A certain fantastical environment is sustained within club walls, which is why the experience is so mystical and magickal. When that mystique is shattered, the experience is altered. For a nondarksider who is going to a Goth club for curiosity's sake, I'd recommend just tossing on a black T-shirt and jeans before leaving the house, if for nothing else but to show your appreciation for the scene.

Goth clubs usually have DJs spinning who are educated in the movement's musical expressions. Some clubs simply play CDs from their collection, while others have in-house picks. Others use vinyl records to beat-match and rework the songs into a non-stop mix. A wide variety of dark and darkish music is played at the club, all of which evokes a variety of emotional reactions in clubgoers.

Depending on a city's demand, musicians and bands tend to frequent clubs and venues throughout the week. The artists may be well-known in the dark art community, in which case the ticket prices and audience attendance tend to be higher than average. In clubs that offer band space, local or independent artists usually play either to open for headliners or put on shows of their own.

The layout of each club varies in size and shape. Some offer two or more rooms or floors, each with a band or DJ playing a specified subgenre of dark music. This is appealing to a wider variety of people, as they can attend the club to listen to their favorite style of music while hearing and learning about additional styles at the same time. Any DJ can tell you that the club's music has a direct impact on the crowd. The musical energy projects to the minds of the attendees and determines their general mood, though this may happen on a more subtle or unconscious level. The aural work of art vibrates whatever intent it was created with, every song attuned to a particular energy pattern that weaves into the energy of the listener. This is why music is such an incredibly influential force!

It's especially humiliating and giddily fun when the DJ plays a cheesy and entirely *non*-Goth song at the end of his or her set, forcing the clubbers to leave with Gothic grins upon their white-powdered faces. It reassures that Goth isn't always perpetually dreary and that humor—especially the ability to laugh at oneself—is a necessity, even for those with the darkest of inclinations.

Veronika Sorrow, a recording artist, has been a nightclub owner in Los Angeles since 1994. Her club, Funeral, is L.A.'s only all-ages Goth venue. She has hosted a number of live performances and has watched the Goth culture evolve over time. When I asked about her club-owning experience and its spiritual implications, she explained to me that the club attendees' fashions, attitudes, and sense of belonging have fluctuated over time, evolving and devolving with trends and interests. She believes the Goth scene, at least in L.A., has come full circle and currently is in a progressive and unified state, noting the fact that teenagers are out on the dance floor feeling the same energy that the middle-aged dark elders are experiencing. This connection between the generations, founded in a deep kinship for music and community, is quite possibly the most spiritual aspect of the Goth scene as a whole. Music is one of the most important and unifying elements of Goth culture (music birthed the movement!), and the club scene is the ideal gathering ground to share the experience of auditory transcendence.

In addition to welcoming people of various ages, Goth clubs in particular have more leeway as to what is socially acceptable and what is not. If you want to do the "pull the taffy" dance all night, then do it. If you want to be a wallflower, people watching and chain smoking cloves for hours on end, go for it. Want to be the social butterfly sprinkling glitter on pouty people? More power to you! Just hang out and kick it with close friends? Hell yeah! If you are male and wish to dress up in a vinyl Catwoman suit with high heels and a whip, by all means have at it. Okay, so I've witnessed that last one…thought it was a bit odd but still exciting, ballsy, and respectable all at the same time. Just make sure that whatever experience you choose to embrace is done with self-awareness, enjoyment, and honesty.

No Goth club is the same, nor is it constantly utopian. When immersing oneself in a public setting, one must mind personal barriers and boundaries of both the self and others. If comfort and spiritual peace are not found in this setting, then it is best left behind. Creepy individuals with deep-seated psychological disorders are just as easily attracted to this unique type of setting as they are to Pagan gatherings or anything else out of the "ordinary." One must be very attentive to one's personal sphere of energy and other people's influence on it, even if everyone's drinking! Know your limits, and ensure that they are not manipulated or broken. Above all, you mustn't go to a club to just prove involvement in the scene; personal well-being takes precedence.

For small-town Goths, going to an alternative venue in a bigger city is rare and exceedingly breathtaking. While the experience may be a part of every weekend for urban clubbers, rural folks often are left dreaming of and anticipating another concert or club night. Furthermore, some Goths never experience the club aspect of the scene at all. Some have an aversion to large crowds or feel they've outgrown the club scene. For others, big city life is an entirely foreign experience, and the clubs that so many take for granted are left to the imagination. Along similar but reversed lines, those who live in a large city are often left daydreaming about what it's like to be surrounded by nature. Existing in a big city can prove to be beneficial in terms of community, but detrimental in the sense that everything has been seen; certain things begin to lose their meaning, like the diversity of people, ideas, and art. The big city can be cause for sadness, seeing that many things are losing their magick due to modern industrialization and capitalism. It's easy to feel all alone in a city crowded with bodies. For the Witch attracted to alt-culture, it's best to have a healthy balance of the natural world and the "concrete jungle," finding time to immerse oneself in the best of both.

Coming from a fairly small college town myself, I recommend to anyone seeking a fuller involvement in the scene that you check out a club or a Goth gathering. Do some research online, and talk to friends and acquaintances in other states. Track the touring status of your favorite bands and DJs. By any means possible, find a good club and experience the sacred energy. Do it for nobody's benefit but your own. It truly is a magickal experience that lives on in the heart of the dark Witch.

La Danse Macabre

On the dance floor, the ordinary planes are transcended through musical bliss, lifting the listener to states of heightened consciousness. Real, untainted magick lies on the dance floor.

While most people simply dance *to* music, Goths tend to *become one* with it. The act of dancing aligns you with the flow of the music. It is a process of synchronization of the self to the ebb and flow of the soundscape. The physical vehicle becomes a conduit for the energy of the music, further projecting its essence to the club and beyond.

The main difference between "Goth dancing" versus the vast majority of dancing in other subcultures is how the music is perceived and further directed, in how deeply the music is taken into the heart of the listener and how the listener chooses to conduct it. I cannot generalize this observation for all scenes, as there is still a wide variety of individualism in any given movement. Thus, an expression can be viewed many different ways. For example, many in the hip-hop scene do not see dancing as much more than booty-shaking mating calls and careless drunken behavior. For others who are more internally involved in that subculture, the music carries deep sociopolitical messages begging to be not just *listened to* but *heard* on many levels. Recognizing

Mr. Ibis and Dave at Club Ascension in Baltimore.

☥ *Sex, Drugs, and Rock 'n' Roll*

deeper messages embedded in the music of any subculture is a preservation of what music has always been: an expression of the higher self, the deeper self, the truer self. Tapping into the higher realms can be accomplished through embracing the musical expression present in all subcultures. Because so much Goth (and Goth-like) music is focused on emotional states of being, I believe it to be some of the most effective music for transcending the paradigms of ordinary consciousness.

Regardless of whether the music is created on the spot by musicians or prerecorded, dancing is a form of musical appreciation and an acknowledgment of others' successful creations as felt by the listener. The *real* dance is internal, in the mind, in the soul. Following this are the physical body movements that mirror the inner dance. Gothic dancing styles include twirls, swoops, swirls, bows, kicks, grasps, waves, and other dramatic moves. It really is quite a beautiful picture. Club dancing is not meant to be difficult or painstaking. It is not meant to be rigid or uniform. It is meant to be an uplifting, magickal act whereby the soul and the sound intertwine. The dance floor is a place of untouched freedom where the dancer is both allowed and encouraged to embark on his or her own type of neo-shamanic journey. The dance floor is sacred space. Followers of the Goth movement choose to pay strict attention to the music they listen to and the messages it gives.

As Pagans, we recognize the fact that everything we consume alters our consciousness on one level or another. Music must be recognized as a powerful and influential force worthy of respect and admiration. Dancing is but one way that music is given the acknowledgment it deserves. Dancing has been a part of Pagan practice since the beginning, harking back to native tribal dances and the pre-Christian European Maypole and fire dances. Some covens perform the deosil Dance of the Wheel around a bonfire to welcome back the light of the sun at the winter solstice. Numerous forms of traditional and modern dancing are included within general Pagan practices, especially at celebratory Sabbats. Modern Pagans also practice spiral dancing, wherein the practitioners weave in and out of a spiral pattern, kissing one another to seal the bond. From there, magick is projected and spirally woven into reality. Magick through dance is an intensely powerful way of connecting with divinity and aligning with the essence of what it means to be a Witch.

The practice of *ecstatic dance* has origins in shamanism. In it, the shaman or spiritualist enters a trance state when dancing, losing connection to the physical plane. In ecstatic dance, ordinary human sensations like pain aren't felt; the body and spirit are disconnected. Some ecstatic dancers draw a spirit animal into their own body, a process of astral shapeshifting and spirit assumption. Physically, they begin to take on the mannerisms of their spirit ally and enter its realm fully on the mental/spiritual plane. Their voice changes tone and style; their ordinary waking functions become transformed; the body becomes an untainted vessel for the spiritual. Similarly, many practitioners of tribal religions invoke ancestral spirits into their bodies while practicing ecstatic dance. The invoked spirits then give prophecy and insight to the observers and may answer questions, provide healing magick, or request offerings.

While ecstatic dancing may look a bit strange to strangers on the dance floor, elements of shamanic dancing can be incorporated into the dancing experience, either in the club, in your living room, in the wilderness, or before your altar. To be moved by music to this degree is to become one with it. So much club music, dark and otherwise, follows a musical pattern similar to that of ancient tribal-trance shamanic music, making an entrance into a mystical state of consciousness all the more accessible for the listener. To enter a state of ecstasy, the dancer must release absolutely all inhibitions and anxieties. Fearing criticism or judgment from onlookers in a club or ritual setting greatly inhibits the possibility of magickal alignment. If we can allow our energies to be untouched by negative energy from outsiders, we can gracefully enter a state of oneness with the music with little problem.

In the club, awareness must be given to both the physical plane (including everyone around you) and the spiritual plane. Though I wouldn't recommend full-on ecstatic dancing in the club—that is, releasing entirely from the physical body in dance—it's possible to enter this realm to a partial degree, the results of which are extremely spiritually rewarding. Wait for a song that really catches your attention and seems to resonate with your spirit. Move to a spot on the dance floor where, if your arms were to flail about, you wouldn't hit anyone else. Feel the beat of the song. Begin by moving a part of your body to the steady beat—your arms, legs, or upper body. Let a part of you align physically with the audio sensations. Perhaps industrial sounds lead you to dance in a sharp, mechanized manner, or ethereal music produces graceful, soft movements. Let the music speak to you, entering your mind and body. Once your body is moving steadily, take note of the other beats and noises layered around the main beat. Start moving another part of the body in alignment with this as well. This tends to come easier if you already are familiar with the song and its fluctuations in tempo. Close your eyes and let the music flood your body. At the same time, be aware that others may be looking at you. Don't give it too much thought, but beware that you are still functioning within the parameters of human society, albeit in an alternative setting. Magick and energy raising can be achieved on the dance floor in the guise of regular dancing; the two may be almost entirely indistinguishable, especially if one dances with these purposes in mind.

Let your awareness focus only on the music and your body's reaction to it. It helps to keep your eyes closed for as long as you can, glancing around only occasionally to center your body and not lose control. After a few times, you will begin to develop your own methodology for experiencing body-music oneness. You may end up experiencing visions or learning how to focus on conducting energy in everyday life. Let the experience take you where it will; let it be pure and magickal.

Magick can be cast on the dance floor. You needn't cast a circle or verbally call the elements (but you can summon them mentally!); the sacred space is there all around you. I remember weaving energy on the dance floor in a Denver club with a couple of fellow Witchy friends after a metaphysical convention. We would create energy balls, project them at one another, and transcend physical space by connecting eye to eye. It was one of the most amazing feelings I've ever experienced outside a cast circle, and I get the same ecstatic rush whenever people do this during my own live DJ sets. This, I feel, truly is utilizing the magick of music.

Energy can be pulled from above, below, and all around. As a Witch, you must be careful not to pull the energy from anyone else, but only from the earth, cosmos, and elements. Once connected to these forces, energy can be drawn into the body and projected as a wish, prayer, or spell. It can be projected at your friends, surrounding them in light. It can be refocused on any intention you choose. Perhaps the remnants of a spell are still upon your altar. Energy can be projected there to strengthen the spell. You can also visualize intention; for example, envision someone you know being healed of an ailment or finding the way out of a difficult predicament, and send a powerful boost of magick through yourself and in that direction. Pull energy from the source you deem most powerful and appropriate for the magick you're casting—perhaps from the moon, a body of water, or the core of the earth. I like to pull lunar energy through my body when dancing by visualizing the moon and quickly raising my arms upward and then downward. I focus the energy as it pulses through my physical body, entering from the sky and flowing into the ground below. I also like to invoke this same energy and then cast it out to the rest of the clubgoers to ensure blessings and a positive evening.

Unfortunately, there are those involved in the dark art and magickal subcultures who don't have your best interests at heart and must be guarded against. Some may slander you to their cohorts, while others may attempt to magickally manipulate you just because they can. This is silly, considering magick is resurfacing in order to change the world for the better and let people take control of their lives, not to hold back evolution, especially in movements such as ours. Nevertheless, there always will be the few people obsessed with power-tripping and selfish, pathetic, ego-based magick.

It's a good idea to build a sphere of protection before going to the club, or anywhere in public for that matter. For the particularly empathic or highly sensitive dark Witch, protection exercises may be performed before going out in order to build a wall of self-preservation, banishing harmful influences throughout the night. This will help ward off any potential attacks, should they occur. Odds are they won't, but it's good to secure energetic protection if for nothing else but psychological comfort!

Drugs

In our modern society, the issue of drug use is considered taboo, usually filled with stereotypical misconceptions. Many people avoid drugs altogether, even the most natural of substances. Still others misuse intoxicating substances, having only self-centered intent, ignoring any possible spiritual implications that a drug may have to offer. While these instances are extremes, they're very much a part of modern culture that is quite divorced from the original conceptions of mind-altering substances. For many ancients, the Middle Path was walked between these two extremes, emphasizing *use* instead of abuse, misuse, or overuse. This section will examine shamanic, ritualistic, and modern drug use and their significance to the magickal path and alternative lifestyle.

I must begin this section by saying that neither the publisher nor I nor anyone else associated with the research presented here is to be held responsible for what the reader does with this information. If what you do involves disobeying the legal system or causing harm to your body, it is your choice and is not advocated by this book. I believe that education about drugs is invaluable to spiritual people. Knowing about drugs and their effects is essential when walking a spiritual path. Whether legal or not, they are a part of every society, and their presence should be recognized so that wise and responsible choices can be made.

Physically, drugs affect the body by either mimicking a neurotransmitter, such as dopamine or serotonin, or by increasing the rate at which the neurotransmitter is released in the body. Some inhibit a neuron by blocking certain receptors in the brain, disallowing the regular flow of chemicals, in turn causing a high. In other words, drugs change chemical levels in the body, which in turn causes sensations of altered consciousness. Used in excess, drugs may cause permanent damage to the brain in addition to the area of consumption, such as the lungs or nasal cavities.

The earth has gifted us with tools to be utilized for very specific purposes. This view is accepted by most spiritualists, namely practitioners of earth-based spiritual paths like the indigenous/tribal traditions, Wiccans, and other Neopagans. Additionally, many followers of Eastern religions tend to accept naturally high-inducing substances as normative and not inherently polluting, unlike the general view of many Judeo-Christian monotheistic traditions. Though some of these spiritualists may advocate the intelligent use of natural drugs, chemical substances and designer drugs generally are looked down upon. When looking at shamanic and tribal traditions, spanning from times past to the present day, the influence of mind-altering substances mustn't be overlooked. Mind-altering plants are venerated because of the part they play in shaping native belief systems. Substance-induced visions are spiritual experiences, and because of their profound effects on the user, they are viewed as real and valid happenings, allowing the user to see alternate layers of reality that otherwise likely would remain hidden. These perceived levels are recognized and included in the cosmology of the particular indigenous belief system. It is for this reason that certain drugs are viewed as spiritual sacraments.

Shamanic Drug Use

Shamanic tribes have, since their beginnings, utilized hallucinogenic and mind-altering substances in ritual settings for esoteric purposes, including communing with the gods, taking astral journeys, deep healing, past-life vision, spellcrafting, prophetic divination, and learning secrets of existence too grand to put into words.

When tribal members would fall sick, shamans saw them as having lost a portion of their soul. Shamanic healers, past and present, work with patients to draw back their spirits from the Otherworld in the case of illness, in an act of spirit retrieval. Natural drugs are often used to assist in this process, opening the shaman's perceptive ability to see an illness, locate a spirit, gain visions, and execute healing processes.

Hallucinogens are classified as alkaloids, which are characterized by their bitter taste. This represents their toxic properties, which may be utilized as medicinal healers, or as poisons in overly large quantities. They have a molecular structure that includes two carbons and one nitrogen, and long have been used in methods of shamanic magick across the globe.

Ayahuasca is a Quechua Indian word that means "vine of the dead." This vine is used in Amazonian shamanic medicine to expand consciousness and increase spiritual connection through visionary experience. Ayahuasca refers to a combination of plants, not one singular compound. The plants are native to the Amazon River basin. Each mixture is unique to its maker, as each tribal shaman uses a different combination of plants for his medicine and uses a variable amount of each substance combined. The presence of two alkaloids seems to be common in all forms of shamanic ayahuasca. These are beta-carboline and tryptamine. Beta-carboline typically is extracted from the bark of the *Banisteriopsis caapi* vine, and tryptamine typically is extracted from the leaves of the *Psychotria viridis* bush, though different alkaloid plants with similar genetic structures also are used.

Ayahuasca rarely is administered by smoking, but rather is made into a drinkable brew or powdered into a snuff. When ingested by the Amazonian medicine healer, he begins to perceive the cause of the patient's illness. Once determined, the shaman proceeds with ritual cleansing and healing to target the root of the ailment that the ayahuasca mixture's vision presented to him. The shaman doesn't treat every person who comes to him for help, but of those he does, ayahuasca is administered only for specific cases, especially those rooted in psychological ailments. Most of these ailments are deemed a result of negative magick ("Witchery") or bad medicine. During the actual healing ceremony, the healer will "suck" the bad medicine from an area of the patient's body and blow the smoke of specific plants on the wounded area in a metaphysical process of purification. Ayahuasca enables intense visions in the practitioner, which is helpful to both the practitioner and the tribe.

The peyote cactus (*Lophophora williamsii*) long has been used by native cultures of the Americas. It grows no more than an inch above the ground (with much larger roots). The "buttons" contain mescaline, which acts as a strong hallucinogen. Peyote first was used by Mexican Indians, and the name is derived from the Aztec word *peyotl*. It was introduced to upper North American tribes around 1870, before Europeans came in contact with them. A number of Native tribes began to use peyote at this time, including the Comanche, Pawnee, Arapaho, and Kiowa Apache. Still, other tribes felt peyote was unnecessary in their practices, as with the Omaha, the Oklahoma Cheyenne, and the Menomini.

Peyote has a number of uses. Some peyotists (those who make use of peyote's medicine in accordance with tribal tradition) carry a button on them at all times as a magickal amulet against evil. Medicine healers administer the drug to patients and themselves to target and heal the cause of an illness or imbalance. It is particularly useful as a sedative and painkiller, and peyotists believe it is able to help heal any ailment. It can be administered by ingesting the buttons directly (dried or fresh) as a tea, powder, or poultice.

Some tribes partake in large peyote ceremonies in which all present are under the influence of the drug and gain visions as part of spiritual communion. If a peyotist does not gain a vision, he or she will experience telepathic connectedness with other participants or feel oneness with all things, transcendent of time and space. The peyotist does not focus on extraneous thoughts that arise, but instead remains focused on the meaningful messages being delivered by way of the substance. The intensity of the experience depends both on the amount taken and the tolerance of the user.

Peyotists say that there is no ending point in learning what the drug has to teach, because something new is learned every time. Because the effects vary for each person, there is no telling what experience the person will have. It must be assumed that the drug teaches each peyotist the lessons needed at the time. Because of its healing properties, a number of Native Americans feel strongly about preserving its use.

Members of the Native American Church of North America practice what they call the Peyote Way, incorporating it into many of their religious ceremonies. The church originally was established in 1918 as an organization to preserve the Peyote Way as a sacred and legal practice. There have been a number of laws passed in America in the last thirty years that limit the use of peyote. Laws against the use of peyote prevented people from employing the substance in their religious practices, which was devastating to the

Native American Church. Members felt as though they were facing further persecution against their natural ways. The legal system has created a roller coaster of ups and downs for peyotists, and the legality of the use of the cactus fluctuates with the passing of every new law. Currently, every state has a different law associated with the use of peyote by which native people are permitted exemption from some of the restrictions on the controlled substance.

Additionally, Native American spiritualists historically have smoked and chewed 100 percent natural, organic tobacco and maintained awareness of the herb and its effects on the user. In native traditions, high respect is given to tobacco's medicine, and its use quite often is moderated under special ritualistic circumstances. The Jívaro Indians of the Ecuadorian Amazon drink the juice of green tobacco leaves on a regular basis to maintain awareness of possible attacks from rival shamans. Tobacco has been used to maintain awareness in meditation and to induce ecstatic trance when smoked in large amounts.

There is little to no evidence that native elders had lung cancer or other diseases as a result of tobacco use; chemicals were not introduced as additives until the early twentieth century. Whether chemicals or prolonged addictions to the plant are the reason for disease, the plant is still a toxin. Tobacco contains poisonous alkaloids and is a member of the nightshade family, which is related to mandrake, belladonna, tomato, potato, and eggplant. It grows from two to nine feet high, with large, fleshy oval-shaped leaves, thick, moist stems, and funnel-shaped flowers. There are nine species of tobacco in North America. Wild tobacco (*Nicotiana rustica* or "Indian tobacco") is considered the most spiritually potent and is used specifically for ceremony, though all types are considered sacred. The herb opens doors to other realities, and the psychological results, including addiction, can be devastating if the user does not treat the herb with utmost respect.

The Mazatec Indians of southern Mexico make use of the psilocybin mushroom. Entire families will eat mushrooms together and gain experiences of connectedness and kinship. Mazatecs use mushrooms for specific reasons, like problem resolution, the curing of ailments, and vision quests. The use is most frequent among the tribe's shamans, who are respected as being attuned to both the healing energy of the mushroom and the journey to spiritual planes that it takes the user on. They make use of it only during the nighttime, citing that one can go mad if mushrooms are eaten in the light.

Because darkness represents the unknown, mysteries of life are more accessible to the user when under the influence at night. Personally speaking, I've had a few breathtaking visionary experiences observing the starry night sky (and faerie realms) with the help of psilocybin medicine.

The Mazatec creation myth speaks of mushrooms as having grown from where the blood of the Aztec god Quetzalcoatl spilled upon the earth, becoming the food of life and wisdom. Until recently, the Mazatec had no other form of medicine than the mushroom. They rarely are eaten by the tribe except in the case of illness, where the healing medicine is said to target any and every form of physical and psychological imbalance, which is similar to the view held by peyotists about their own sacred substance. Mazatec shamans use mushrooms to open themselves to see hidden layers of reality both in the macrocosm (the surrounding world itself) and the microcosm (the layers of the human body and mind).

Magick and Drug Use

Drug use has a long history in Witchcraft and magickal societies. The Witch's flying ointment is but one historical example of drug use for magickal means. The consensus among Pagans is that minimal drug use is acceptable if carried out in moderation and with necessary awareness. Most believe that drug use becomes problematic only if the line is crossed between use and abuse. Unfortunately, many users recklessly intoxicate themselves, unaware of the spiritual gifts a substance can provide if approached correctly. This is most apparent in bar scenes wherein people use alcohol for purely social reasons, often having a tendency to partake excessively. Deaths and injuries occur as a result of alcohol more than any other substance. However, controlled drugs generally are viewed as being much more dangerous. Much of this view is attributed to the government's portrayal of all illegal substances as being untouchable evils. Society, for the most part, believes this without question, strictly viewing all drugs and their users as worthless delinquents. This is not to say that drugs are not harmful, but to emphasize the fact that there are many types of drugs and varying degrees of effects—physical, mental, and spiritual.

Goddess knows Pagans love mead! Also called honey wine, mead is created through a process of fermenting honey, usually with the addition of herbs, to create a sweet alcoholic beverage. Many Witches use mead or another wine as part of "cakes and ale" in ritual, and those that have a family history of or predisposition to alcoholism prefer nonalcoholic mead, sparkling cider, or all-natural juices like pomegranate, apple, or berry. Traditionally, high rituals are ended with a feasting of cakes and an alcoholic beverage for the sake of grounding and communion. The cakes are charged as the flesh of the gods and the drink as the blood. Consuming the products represents the alignment of the self with the Mighty Ones.

Alcohol and other natural drugs do not exist just to "fuck you up." Everything is designed with a purpose, and each substance can serve as a conduit to channel spiritual energies and open gateways of perception in the user. Additionally, many natural drugs have physical and metaphysical healing properties, but many have toxic properties as well. This is one reason that utmost care must be employed when using natural drugs (as well as synthetic, of course) for spiritual or other purposes. If you have heard that the way to a profound spiritual experience is through drugs, I ask you to really give it some thought. If you have experienced drugs, then you have an idea as to what affects you in which way. If you have relatively no experience with drugs, then you have little idea of what doors substances can open in you personally. Perhaps a mindful high would be beneficial to you. At the same time, there are plenty of alternative ways of raising consciousness. Approach the idea of drug taking with caution and a good amount of research.

Drugs influence every single person differently. One person may try a substance once and immediately get hooked. Someone else may experiment with that same substance at various points in life and never get addicted. There is no way of telling how a drug will affect a particular person unless he or she experiments and comes to realize his or her own particular limits and boundaries. However, in all likelihood, it is better to avoid substances altogether if there is no spiritual or medical need to experience their effects.

Some people become dependent on a given substance because the euphoria induced by the drug acts as a substitute for spiritual experience. For many people, the effects of certain drugs mimic what would be a spiritual high. When a user feels his or her only outlet for expanding consciousness is through the substance, he or she will continue to use it to induce a similar effect. On a nonconscious level, the mind, body, and spirit are seeking freedom from the constraints of the everyday grind. This, for many people, is gained by way of use of a drug that seems to fill an unspeakable void. For the magickally inclined, ritual and ecstatic trance induce similar highs, but with a greater purpose. Those who become addicted to drugs, on some level, seek union with the divine but go about it improperly, knowing no other means of achieving bliss but through continual use. The thing is, once the substance has been experienced and spiritual doors have been opened, they never really fully close. This is also the case with numerous prescription drugs, especially mind-numbing antidepressants that almost always have permanent "zombifying" effects on the user. Doors of the mind are just waiting to be opened naturally, not necessarily through the use of more substances. Instead of recognizing this and going about proper ways to open these doors without drugs, people become dependent, unable to achieve the bliss of expanded consciousness without the substance.

Habits are difficult to break and must be caught early on before they consume the user. Some people get into hard drugs habitually for an extended period of time, finally discovering that sobriety—life itself—is the grandest high. This may sound like a cliché, but it is absolutely true. We mustn't constantly experience our lives in a diluted and ultimately false manner by way of drugs. I believe it to be extremely healthy to experiment with relatively harmless drugs as long as the user does not become attached to the feeling induced and is able to return to sobriety with no trouble whatsoever.

Most magicians claim that the best revelations come when sober, though they may use drugs sparingly as recreational or medicinal vehicles rather than strictly spiritual tools. Drug use should be entirely up to the magician him- or herself. Few magicians, especially Pagans, venture into the realm of synthetic drugs. Synthetic or designer drugs are chemically manufactured by human hands. Instead of retaining the pure essence of a natural plant, the substance becomes nearly completely divided from its original compounds. Witches recognize that each plant has its own spirit, its own vibration. Obviously, it is this connection to holistic qualities that explains why plants have been used in spellcrafting and potion making for so long.

Extended overuse of unnatural drugs creates a sort of astral "slime." This unhealthy sludge is difficult to shake and remains with the user on an astral level apparent during magickal work. Further, this energetic imbalance filters into other levels of the body, not excluding the physical. This can manifest as disorders, diseases, and neuroses.

Using drugs in a ritual setting is entirely different from using them at a party or semimundane social setting. The environment is completely different, and thus the drug's effects are variable. Some practitioners of magick use drugs exclusively in ritual settings. Many Witches I know smoke marijuana in circle and during meditation, using it ritualistically rather than just recreationally. Because of the minimal amount of negative effects and the profundity of positive effects *if used wisely*, marijuana is one of the most commonly used mind-altering substances in the world. Even the deities Bast (Egyptian) and Shiva (Hinduism) are directly associated with marijuana, and many traditional worshippers of these deities make marijuana offerings to them and smoke the herb as an act of divine communion. Indeed, smoking weed ritualistically with the intention of gaining insight into the nature of reality is on the complete opposite side of the spectrum from tokin' and playing video games.

Though I don't smoke much anymore, I recognize the role marijuana played in my spiritual development, as my first experiences of multidimensional awareness were induced simply by "smoking herb." I fully believe that marijuana medicine was the "push" I needed to really contemplate reality and our place in it. Though people open their spiritual senses through different means, the rewarding effects that the intelligent use of drugs can have on human consciousness cannot be ignored. I'm extremely grateful to have had spiritually expanding experiences with marijuana, magick mushrooms, *Salvia divinorum*, and the like, and in turn recommend to any spiritual seeker to consider natural drugs' properties as healing medicines before casting socially skewed judgment on certain substances. As amplifiers, drugs have the potential to be life-changing, either incredibly rewarding or incredibly destructive, depending on the user's approach.

Certain covens, training systems, and magickal orders strictly forbid the use of mind-altering substances altogether, both inside the magickal circle and out. Though most circles are not so severely straight-edged, the ones that are approach such a decision with the philosophy that mind-altering substances only work *against* the spiritual seeker.

Some groups forbid drug use only *within* the magickal circle. This is understandable, as one person's energy not only alters the entirety of the energy being raised and focused in the circle, but also may invite unwanted vibrations into the confines of sacred space. Depending on the drug used and its effects on the individual, doors of extreme perception may open. These doors can gracefully open or burst like a floodgate, again depending on how the drug affects the individual.

All participants in group circles must be completely honest about their current states of being with the other members involved. This includes being under the influence of a substance, even if the magickal procedure at hand is only celebratory in nature. Withholding information that may be significant to other members involved is just as good as lying. If a participant consciously neglects informing other members of his or her insobriety, that person is breaking one of the most important ethical principles of circle: Perfect Love and Perfect Trust. If everyone in the circle is tight-knit, a person's shifted energy should immediately be detectable. Either way, everyone involved should be aware of one another on multiple levels so as to know what sort of energy is being raised throughout. In some Sabbatical celebrations, particularly Beltane, the ritual ends in music, dance, and merrymaking. Liquor and other drugs definitely are not required to have a good time, but if one decides to partake, then utmost self-awareness must be exercised nonetheless.

Some groups of Witches and spiritualists gather to use certain drugs other than marijuana for specific spiritual purposes. Reasons include vision quests, astral voyages, energetic healing, and extreme divination, to name a few. In these circles, the drug use is entirely controlled and supervised. In the case of using something stronger than marijuana, a sober individual is usually present to "baby-sit" the users, monitoring the situation and helping anyone whose perceptions become overwhelmed. Precaution is always the best option to prevent the possibility of things getting out of control if a substance (especially a synthetic one like ecstasy or LSD) is being used in circle. Certainly, if a ceremony is centered on the use of a particular drug for spiritual purposes, then all participants must be aware of the other members' states of being, including their limits, before using and their states of being during the high.

No substance is inherently good or evil, beneficial or detrimental. In the end, the user is the determining factor. It is the user who chooses whether to partake of a substance or become enslaved by it habitually. It is the user who discerns between reality and ideology, and chooses whether to use a substance recreationally or spiritually.

Utilized cautiously and with total mindfulness, drugs have the capability of taking a person to uncharted planes of the mind and spirit. As a result of direct physical changes, one's perception of reality immediately alters as well. This alteration may be minimal or intense, depending on the substance and amount consumed. Just as positive drug experiences can be some of the most amazing, spiritually rewarding journeys imaginable, so can negative experiences be the most horrid and spiritually/mentally damaging. It is for this reason that if one decides to use drugs, the substances must be approached intelligently and respectfully.

If you are in a situation in which you feel using drugs would be a good thing, you *must* look at the situation from all angles to better gauge it. If any possibility is left unaddressed, it could become a factor contributing to a bad high. Negative triggers can be overlooked if the situation is not fully examined. Who will you be surrounded by in an altered state…are they people you entirely trust? What activities are planned for the day…could your high inhibit these things or make them better? What is the purpose of using the substance…is it for social acceptance, or as an escape from your worries, or is there spiritual reasoning behind it? How much will you use, and how will the substance affect you physically and mentally and thus spiritually?

What I'm saying is, be smart about what you do. Be cautious and aware of what you put into your body and how it affects the whole of your person. Every experience we have shapes us in some way—it may be grand or subtle, but either way, every experience we have shapes us holistically. When experience is amplified by a substance, it affects us to an even greater degree, and on the magickal path this is not something to be taken lightly.

Goth Culture and Drug Use

Drug addiction among members of the Goth scene is relatively infrequent, the most commonly used substances being caffeine, nicotine, and alcohol. One is likely to find quite a few straight-edged Goths, or those who choose to consume only legal drugs like the aforementioned, perhaps with a dash of cannabis (especially hash), opium, or magick mushrooms on the side. These substances definitely are not completely harmless but, if used in moderation, pose much less of a risk than "hard" substances do in the long run.

For most clubgoers, alcohol, if used moderately, provides "mental lubrication" and an opportunity to relax and unwind. Some people feel they need it to enjoy themselves more in public outings, as inhibitions are lessened and anxiety wanes.

Alcohol is used in moderation on many spiritual paths. It is not meant to be overindulged in, as is the norm in Western culture, which as a whole fails to see the spiritual benefits of alcohol, or any mind-altering substance for that matter. Like all drugs, alcohol affects every person differently. Some people can handle a bit of drinking, allowing it to affect them positively. For others, alcohol takes them to an internally dark place and propels them into a cycle of chaos, self-loathing, and negative projection.

Erasmus knows that absinthe makes the heart grow fonder.

Goths tend to gravitate toward absinthe, which was a popular drink in the nineteenth century. Its green color hints at its strong hallucinogenic effects, and it was used by poets and artists alike, including Poe, Baudelaire, Kafka, Rimbaud, Wilde, and van Gogh—all of whom are favored by many a Goth and dark artist alike! Absinthe is made from wormwood and a combination of other herbs, which are allowed to steep for a period of time in a strong alcohol, like vodka, or an ethanol (grain liquor), like Everclear. Jägermeister and Chartreuse also seem to be popular drinks in dark culture; their unique high-inducing effects and exotic nature definitely are most favored by the nightkind!

Hard drugs like cocaine, heroin, and varieties of methamphetamine definitely *do* work their way into Goth and Pagan culture from time to time, and when they do, it's usually a downward spiral for the user from there, unless the person's willpower is strong enough to pull him or her out without significant mental, physical, or psychological (and thus spiritual) damage. Hard-drug addictions have absolutely no place in the Craft; I also feel strongly that they have no place in the dark culture because of their devastating, not healing, effects. A fine line exists between use and abuse, and as spiritual aspirants, we not only have the opportunity but the *responsibility* to choose wisely…for the greater good.

The Temple of Love: Sexuality

Sex and sexuality have become hot issues in today's society. In ancient times, sex was viewed in quite a positive light. In ancient Asia, particularly India and China, sex was seen as an act of worship and a natural part of human existence to be used for both pleasurable and procreative reasons. With the rise of asceticism, both Christian and otherwise, personally sacrificial acts, including chastity, were becoming better known as a means of connecting with divinity. Because sex is pleasurable, the act itself became associated with distance from God, and a number of dogmatic restrictions came about as a result.

As old ideas died with time, the restrictive ties associated with sexuality and religion slowly were loosened. In the West, various Christian sects each had differing views on sexual practices; all were restrictive to some degree, but some were more liberal. Some believed sex was to be used for reproduction alone, holding on to the idea that pleasure equals sin. Others felt that homosexuality, masturbation, miscegenation, and premarital sex were sinful, but sex after marriage was appropriate to any degree. Gnostic Christianity, however, held the perception of the sexual union of the male and female energies as an act of spiritual connection bestowing God's blessings on both parties involved, instead of as a forced division between humanity and divinity.

Many people have sexual wounds rooted in the belief that anything sexual is inherently sinful, filthy, and wrong. For Pagans, this belief is anything but true. The more open we are to sexuality and its positive benefits, the more able we are to heal the wounds of shame and guilt accompanying the word sex. Given mutual consent, neither Pagans nor Goths are ashamed of sexuality, seeing it very much as an inherent spiritual gift.

One common misinterpretation about the Craft is that we partake in massive orgies and are sexually indiscriminate. This, of course, is not the case and most likely came about as a reaction to traditional skyclad (naked) rituals and fertility rites. Nudity has its place in Witchcraft, especially during solitary rituals, because of its association with being "naked before the gods," aligning the fullness of the uncovered self with spiritual forces. Witches also traditionally perform the Great Rite, a ritual procedure in which the male practitioner (or person honing male energy) draws the God into himself and the female practitioner (or person honing female energy) invokes the Goddess. While in a fully drawn circle, the two unite in sexual union, making love physically and, more importantly, astrally. This unifies the masculine and feminine currents, cultivating the energy of fertility, physically or mentally. Many Wiccan circles have now replaced the physical Great Rite with a symbolic representation, using a chalice to represent the womb of the Goddess and an athamé to represent the phallus of the God. As the athamé is lowered into the cup, the energy of divine union is secured. This is followed with sips from the chalice and various words of power. To Pagans, sex is seen as a metaphor of divine union and the connection between the heavens and the earth—that which makes up the Hermetic "as above, so below," and can be enacted actually or symbolically.

All animals, including humans, are attuned to the earth. As Pagans, we are aware of and utilize our natural abilities to influence its cycles just as it does to us. In premodern times, fertility rituals were enacted through sexual union to either help the crops flourish or produce magickally attuned children. These fertility rituals were performed in ancient times especially to encourage the growth of crops for the sake of survival. Sex magick would be performed in fields to add a boost to the current harvest. Upon climax, the energy would be sent outward to the land. It was assumed that the act of fertility between the couple would in turn influence agricultural fertility.

In this time of overpopulation and mass-scale farming, such rituals are not necessary in all parts of the globe. Instead, ritual sex is often used either to heal the land and the earth or as a means of encouraging "inner" fertility and personal growth. Still, many cultures live hand in hand with the land, not disconnected whatsoever, as their lives depend on the success of their farming. For these cultures, spirituality remains linked with precise land cycles, with religious ceremonies centered on external and internal fertility.

In her book *An ABC of Witchcraft Past & Present*, highly influential Witch Doreen Valiente explains that Witches do not believe in promiscuity any more than they believe in prudishness, explaining that both practices are extreme and are therefore unhealthy in the end. Pagans are extremely accepting of sexual diversity, but are careful and respectful of the self and others just the same.

In the Wiccan Charge of the Goddess, the Goddess is channeled and quoted as saying, "For behold: all acts of love and pleasure are my rituals." Sensuality and sexuality are gifts of Spirit and can be honored if approached with respect, awareness, and moderation. Sex magick should be performed between two consenting individuals of legal age. I strongly believe that *both* individuals making love should be aware if sexual magick is being performed—if one is uninformed while the other is manipulating the energy, it's not only invasive but irresponsible. If one party is uninformed of energy work, it may as well be considered magickal sexual abuse. Also, if a situation is encountered in which any of the members coerce or pressure another person into sexual interaction against his or her will, for "magickal" or other purposes, then the individuals at hand are *not* spiritually aligned and should be fully avoided.

A number of (but most certainly not all) Neopagans, Witches, and spiritualists have nonmonogamous or sexually pluralistic romantic relationships. Assuming that everyone involved is entirely honest, safe, and intelligent, this permits those involved in the "open relationship" to have more lovers than just one another. It's also interesting to note that the lovely Neopagan High Priestess Morning Glory Zell-Ravenheart, partner of the Wizard and author Oberon Zell-Ravenheart, coined the term *polyamory*. Now experiencing widespread usage, the word comes from the Greek *poly*, meaning "multiple," and *amory*, meaning "love." Whereas polygamy refers to a person having more than one spouse, polygyny refers to one man with multiple wives, and polyandry refers to one woman with multiple husbands, polyamory does away with all these, replacing the confusing marriage and gender implications with *love*. For more information on polyamory, I highly recommend Raven Kaldera's book *Pagan Polyamory: Becoming a Tribe of Hearts*. Kaldera himself is actually a female-to-male transsexual and is highly active in the transgendered and intersexed communities.

Both Western and Eastern mystical systems recognize the profound energy that is raised in sexual union and incorporate these realizations into their teachings. While Christianity views sex as sinful—somehow inherently tainted—magickal paths celebrate sexuality as a religious experience in and of itself. At the same time, sex is not taken for granted, overused, or taken advantage of.

Eastern metaphysical systems recognize the *kundalini*, which is Sanskrit for "coiled one." This is the vital *prana* (life force) latent at the bottom of the spine in the genital area (the base chakra). Metaphorically, two snakes are seen as resting here. When sexual energy is stimulated, the snakes rise and coil, entwining along the spine. Each snake represents a polarity, the yin and yang. When the snakes ascend, energy is projected upward through the chakras and to the cosmic dimensions. These associations can also be seen in the form of the caduceus wand that the Greek god Hermes (equated with Mercury and Thoth) is depicted as holding. The symbol of the snakes entwined around the pole, with the crown chakra bursting atop with wings, is still used as a modern medical symbol.

Sex magick is a very powerful force indeed. When two people come together in a physical bond, a certain essence is created due to the fusion of two energy patterns. This is also called the Twin Flame. The gender of the two individuals is insignificant, because both men and women have the ability to channel both the masculine and feminine aspects of divinity. Magicians from ancient times to the present have understood that the body is but a vessel for spiritual energies and, when used properly, is capable of channeling any frequency, be it high, low, good, evil, masculine, feminine…we are vehicles of Spirit.

When physical sensations increase during sex, spiritual gates open. During the time building up to climax, energy is woven between the two individuals and finally projected upward in a cone of power. Sexual energy originates in the base chakra, from which it ascends through the other chakras and out the top of the head. Where this energy is directed is entirely up to the couple.

Sexual energy can be focused anywhere, for any purpose. Elaborate rituals can be enacted to direct this energy, though most Witches prefer a more simple approach, unless they are in great need. The most commonly focused-upon items are sigils, which are crafted for purposes of specific intent. Extreme energy projection comes about when the couple gazes at the same image or envisions it in their minds in a process of creative visualization. The object is struck with a force of power coming about from the sexual union, or from the solo energy raised in masturbation. Energy is added to the object, and its intention is strengthened. Carefully chosen words of power also may be chanted rhythmically, aligning the caster or casters to the frequency of the spell.

Strangelove: BDSM

BDSM is an acronym for bondage, domination, sadism, and masochism, or bondage/discipline, submissive (slave)/master. Due to poor media portrayal, BDSM has become known to some as "Goth sex." In truth, the BDSM/kink lifestyle has proven to be appealing to people of all sorts of cultural and subcultural backgrounds. While it may have visual and sensual overlaps with Goth culture, the practice is its own unique entity. For many BDSMers, dark culture is part of their own path, though this doesn't hold true for all members of the scene. Many darksiders are attracted to the BDSM lifestyle because of its uniqueness and allowance for freedom of sexual exploration and expression. There exist bondage clubs and groups that share ideas and experiences through communion. Many Goth-industrial clubs also offer fetish nights so that those of similar interests can gather in a public outing. Some attendees publicly display their kink through their clothing, while others wear the gear for light experimentation or fashionable purposes alone. Most BDSM is practiced at home in the bedroom between two people. Complete honesty, mutual respect, safe sex, and contraception are absolutely essential with sexual experimentation.

To the onlooker, pain mixed with sex is a scary and forbidden thing. How could anyone get pleasure out of pain? At first, these practices seem to be inducing unnecessary harm in another person. However, each person's perception about the borderline between pain and pleasure is different. What is pleasurable for one person may be tormenting to another. BDSM is very much about free choice; each participant willingly chooses his or her own sensory experiences. All activity is entirely consensual. BDSM uses physical pain to heighten sexual or sensual experience. Some amount of pain be-

Pandora Naamah is drawn both to dark culture and the kink lifestyle.

comes interpreted by the brain as pleasure in a moment of sexual stimulation, as the threshold of pain is considerably decreased. Putting the perceived cruelty aside, BDSM also emphasizes compassion alongside pain, intermixing two extremities into a singular experience.

BDSM is certainly sexual, but is not limited to sexuality. The practice is rooted in sensuality and sensory experience over all else. One can be kinky without actually reaching orgasm, and one can reach orgasm without practicing BDSM. Because sensuality and sexuality often overlap and are intertwined to their own degrees, the two often coexist.

Some BDSM and fetishistic activities include whipping, spanking, biting, tying, hot candle wax, nipple clamps, shaving, rubber costumery, suction cupping, ball gagging, bloodletting, pinching, scratching, enemas, asphyxiation, titatsu massage, role-playing, sissification, electric play, fire play, needle play, and sensory deprivation. Not all BDSM-ers are attracted to these alternative practices, as many are fetish-specific. The word *fetish* originally referred to an object that had metaphysical, magickal powers, like a talisman or charm. The word has now taken on sexual connotations, referring to anything of a not-directly-sexual nature that induces arousal in a person. For example, someone may become fascinated with the act of shaving and integrate the shaving of bodily hair into his or her sexual practices. Fetishes are literally endless. At the same time, there is a borderline; if fetishes become a requirement for sexual gratification instead of an added pleasure, then the borderline has been crossed.

Though fetishism technically refers to the phenomenon in which a person is unable to fulfill sexual arousal without the incorporation of a specific item or situational element (like an inanimate object or focus on a particular body part), the term is better equated in modern times with an "erotic fascination" or "sexual accentuation." Most individuals drawn to fetishism and BDSM don't actually develop problematic, unhealthy psychological dependencies (called *paraphilias*), though some do. Oftentimes, simply identifying with other individuals having unique, non-vanilla sexual leanings is enough to curb a potential paraphilia and maintain healthy sexual experimentation. If you would like more information about BDSM and its connection to magickal spirituality, I highly recommend the books *Kink Magic: Sex Magic Beyond Vanilla* by Taylor

Ellwood and Lupa, and *Dark Moon Rising: Pagan BDSM and the Ordeal Path* by Raven Kaldera.

Gay, Lesbian, Bisexual, Transgender, and Intersex (GLBTI)

GLBTI is an acronym for gay, lesbian, bisexual, transgender, and intersex. People who identify themselves as such are prevalent in both the Goth and Pagan lifestyles. Many queers are attracted to Goth culture and Paganism because of the general acceptance in both communities. Please note that the word *queer* refers to a gay (including lesbian) or bisexual person and is in no way derogatory.

Neither Goth culture nor Neopaganism negatively judges other people spiritually based on their sexual orientation. To do so would undermine the definition of *alternative* in the first place. Because both cultures are so open, there is a crossover between the GLBTI community and the Goth and Pagan cultures. Many queers find themselves in harmony with the ideas presented in dark culture because of the emphasis on individuality and personal empowerment. Still, it can be a struggle for those drawn to *both* the Gothic lifestyle *and* gay social culture to find secure footing in both scenes simultaneously or feel as though they "fully belong" in either scene, as each expression is, at least stereotypically, distinctly different, and members tend to "stick to their own" more often than not.

In terms of Paganism, the Craft invites innermost healing directly into the lives of each practitioner—something invaluable to anyone who may have been disowned by family and rejected by friends, which are unfortunate side effects of coming out of the closet. There even exist a number of magickal groups reserved exclusively for practicing gay male Witches who are actively reclaiming their spiritual and sexual freedom and unique gifts. In Ohio, the annual Between the Worlds gathering is held for gay and bi Pagan men. There are also many Pagan groups and covens reserved exclusively for gay women. Pagans and Goths certainly have joined the rest of the world (two-thirds of cultures worldwide) in accepting same-sex love as a totally normal thing. In fact, a great number of cultures don't even *understand* the concept of "homosexuality" because they takes no issue with same-sex love, therefore not recognizing it as abnormal or distinctly classifiable. In India and other areas, people's first sexual experiences are, quite often, with a person of their own gender. In this case, it's seen as a natural part of growing up!

Gays, lesbians, bisexuals, transgendered, and intersexed people have been, throughout history, quite respected on the magickal path. They carry associations of both genders and thus are recognized as having the unique ability to channel the polarities of male and female, the powers of the God and Goddess. People of alternative sexual orientation once were seen as mystics, capable of harnessing immense strength and channeling Spirit directly. Because Spirit is androgynous, queers were aligned directly with the sacred source. Spirit is both masculine and feminine, but at the same time is neither. Deities are personifications of the Great All, and have been given appropriate character traits in each pantheon to encompass all aspects of reality, including homosexuality and the like. Numerous religions understand homosexuality and bisexuality as natural modes of being; even many Christians are accepting of same-gender attraction, seeing it not as something threatening or abnormal but as something natural, harmless, and based in love.

Homosexuality was commonplace in classical Mediterranean religion and culture. Many Greeks and Romans were openly bisexual or homosexual without any fear of a sexually judgmental society. In the case of battle, male-to-male love strengthened a bond of brotherhood among the men and was not viewed as anything more or less than just that. Many of the Græco-Roman gods had queer tendencies themselves, and homosexuality was readily accepted as natural and normal. With this bond, the men had stronger emotional ties and would strive to protect one another in wartime. Most of them would return to their wives and children if they made it through the battle. The emotions that bound them together as a community were different from the emotional ties with their lovers, so what is now seen as a homosexual bond was no more than an expression of masculine love and brotherhood. Græco-Romans in classical antiquity saw the ingestion of semen from one man to another as a noble "giving of power," and whether this was passed from one generation to the next or exchanged between peers, this notion of energetic exchange actually was seen as *reinforcing* the recipient's masculinity. The perception of sexual energetic exchange between two members of the same gender is not culturally restricted, and a great many other cultures practice just that today. Such cultural comparisons really make you wonder how Western culture has gotten so incredibly fearful, uptight, and sometimes unspeakably violent at the very thought of same-sex love.

The Roman emperor Hadrian was born in the year 76 CE. It is documented that he had a youthful male lover named Antinous, who later drowned for reasons unknown.

The two were (arguably) deified and praised as influential lovers and political leaders of the time. Their relationship is proof that homosexuality was indeed accepted in antiquity, even among royalty, before the rise of early Roman Christianity. There is also evidence of homosexuality being common in Celtic, Norse, and Egyptian cultures, to name a few.

The alternative sexual preferences of many figures in our past are often overlooked or negated altogether. A list of all the (known) historical gay or bisexual mystics, writers, composers, architects, designers, artists, actors, and so forth would be far too long for the pages of this book. Queers throughout the ages have been associated with creation and mysticism. Though the history books rarely teach homosexually positive messages, if you are of a nonstraight sexual inclination, know that you're not abnormal and not alone, and never really have been.

Gothic culture and Paganism are both bisexual in nature. That's not to say that every Goth or Pagan identifies with bisexuality (though many do), but both cultures are drawn to both masculine and feminine qualities, often choosing to see few lines of separation between the two. Many Goths are effeminate but identify as straight. Similarly, many appear to fit their gender roles "appropriately" but are gay or bi. Additionally, many Goths and spiritualists *refuse* to label themselves as straight, gay, or bisexual, seeing themselves as transcending social roles or titles of the sort. Some either have no interest in sex whatsoever (asexuality) or simply follow their heart wherever and to whomever it takes them, regardless of gender (pansexuality).

So many people try to fit their sexual orientation into a box in order to feel more secure. People afraid of being gay will act overtly and stereotypically heterosexual. People afraid of being at all straight will act overtly and stereotypically homosexual so as to negate the option of attraction between opposing genders and psychologically secure social identity. Neither extreme is healthy and is a type of overcompensation for insecurity. When one's sexual orientation overrides *all other* aspects of life through behavior, it's a sign that the person hasn't fully come to accept him- or herself. Acceptance is possible if the person is able to sever ties of expectations placed on him or her by society at an early age.

Drawing on the concept of overcompensation, a recent in-depth scientific study at the University of Georgia has proven something we've all heard. For this study, sixty-four men who identified as heterosexual were gathered for testing. Following a number of intricate survey questions, the men were classified into two camps: the homophobes, and those who were nonhomophobic. The men were not made aware of these categorical divisions when undergoing the experiment itself, which consisted of each person being isolated in a room with a chair and a television. The television would play heterosexual porn and gay male porn, each for a certain duration of time. A supersensory device wrapped around each man's penis would monitor the amount of blood flow (arousal) the penis received during each video. Lo and behold, the tests revealed that the men classified as nonhomophobic were hardly, if at all, stimulated by the gay sex scenes, whereas those classified as the homophobes scored significantly higher on the arousal scale during the gay scenes. This, among other physiological and psychological studies, reveals that those who are most intolerant of homosexual behavior tend to be repressing their own insecurities, and are overcompensating by portraying the culturally perceived antithesis of that which is feared in themselves.

One must identify with whichever orientation suits one best, even if that's none at all. Personally, I believe that everyone is bisexual to one degree or another, and that the issue is not about sex, but attraction. Many people get accustomed to being attracted to one gender over another and choose to identify with either heterosexuality or homosexuality alone. This forms a pattern of attraction and tends to bring about the idea of "fixed" sexual orientation. This works perfectly fine for most people, though recent studies in sexology have shattered the idea that sexual orientation is immutable. Though it commonly is believed that people are of one unchangeable orientation or another, sexual attraction actually changes frequently, to one degree or another. This may be significantly noticeable to some and hardly noticeable to others. Instead of there being a one-dimensional linear scale with heterosexuality on one end, bisexuality in the middle, and homosexuality on the opposite end, the newest and most appropriate scale used in the scientific study of sexual orientation shows a box divided into four sections including the aforementioned three, with the addition of asexuality. One's sexual orientation can be at any point of the spectrum and may change to a small or significant degree over time.

Do scientists know the reason for such diversity in sexual orientation? Nope. A number of ideas have been thrown around the scientific community, such as childhood upbringing, hormone levels, brain structure, birth order, puberty onset, and even the demonizing "homogene" theory. While these all have been considered and may interplay to some degree, the truth is that there are no black-and-white facts about the source of sexual orientation and that it remains true that "we are as we are and that's just the way it is." Over 300 species of animals, humans included, exhibit "homosexual" tendencies. It seems to me that sexual orientation is just about as biologically determined as a person's taste in music or ice cream. Do we really *need* a reason to explain sexual orientation, or is it something Western society eventually will be able to cope with? Homophobia wasn't popular until late antiquity and was largely a result of the misinterpretation of certain biblical passages. Can obsolete hatred be done away with as time goes on? I sure think so.

Queer-Friendly Gods and Goddesses

This is a list of gods, goddesses and other deities throughout many cultures who are associated with homosexuality and bisexuality; a number of them are transgendered, hermaphroditic, or androgynous in nature, or simply have been characterized as having properties that are both masculine and feminine. Many are associated with universal creation and fertility, both of which require the coming together of masculine and feminine energies. A few are queer-friendly but are not documented as having direct homosexual associations. Many thanks to my friend and fellow author Christopher Penczak, author of *Gay Witchcraft: Empowering the Tribe* among many other books, for assistance with this list!

Aztec: Tezcatlipoca, Tlazoteotl, Xochipilli, Xochiquetzal

Buddhist: Quan Yin/Avalokiteshvara

Celtic: Cernnunos/Herne, Gwydion, Macha

Egyptian: Horus, Isis, Osiris, Set, Thoth

European: Baphomet

Greek: Achilles, Apollo and Hyacinth, Eros, Ganymede, Hermaphrodite, Hymen, Hypnos

Greek/Cretan: Britomartis

Greek/Phrygian: Attis

Græco-Roman: Aphrodite/Venus, Artemis/Diana, Athena/Minerva, Hecate, Hermes/Mercury, Heracles, Pan/Faunus, Zeus/Jupiter

Græco-Roman/Thracian: Bacchus/Dionysus

Hawaiian: Kumukahi

Hindu: Agni, Bahuchara Mata, Ganesha, Indra, Ishvara, Kali-Ma, Shiva/Siva, Vishnu

Mayan: Chin

Native American/Inuit: Sedna

Norse: Freyr and Freyja, Loki, Odin/Woden

Phoenician/Canaanite: Astarte

Phoenician/Græco-Roman/Mesopotamian: Adonis/Tammuz

Roman/Italian: Bona Dea

Santerían: Yemaya

Sumerian: Asushunamir

Sumerian/Akkadian: Ereshkigal

Vodou: Baron Samedi, Damballah, Erzulie/Ezili, Ghede Nibo

Welsh: Bran

Transgender and Third Gender

A handful of Goths and Pagans are *transgendered*. This refers to any person who crosses the commonly defined lines of gender identification, including drag queens/kings and transvestites (who cross-dress as the opposite gender only on occasion), as well as those who are *transsexual*. People who are transsexual fully live their lives as members of the opposite gender from which they were born, completely identifying as such. Most transgendered people are born gay or bisexual in their biological gender, though a good number of transgendered and transsexual individuals are *hetero*sexual in their biological gender, thus becoming homosexual after their transition. Sexuality and gender are different issues entirely, and for a number of transgendered individuals, the two overlap little if any. Additionally, many transgendered individuals place little emphasis on the genitals beyond personal psychological comfort. Still, many go through expensive gender reassignment surgery, in addition to hormone therapy and various other cosmetic surgeries. By the same token, many decide against surgery, preferring hormone therapy alone or no treatments at all.

Many transgendered individuals believe their soul to be of the opposite gender in nature, and that they were supposed to have been born as a member of the opposite gender, thus choosing to embrace both the internal recognition and external expres-

Eden Wolf has a foot in either gender.

sion thereof. This belief is (arguably derogatorily) termed *gender dysphoria* in the West. It is possible that people with gender dysphoria carry over experiences from past lives into the present one and thus recognize themselves internally as the gender they lived in a previous life. Curiously, recent scientific studies of the post-mortem brains of transsexual individuals revealed that each person's physical brain structure and chemistry matched their "chosen" gender's brain association, whereas their biological gender expressed the opposite. As a result, the theory recently has been proposed in the scientific community that certain people's brains develop differently in the womb, directly contrasting the person's developing biological sex.

In several Native American tribes, like the Mojave in California, a ritual transformation was enacted when an individual chose to assume the role of the opposite gender. This rite of passage signified tribal acceptance of the person's new gender assumption. Numerous native tribes have held similar rites of passage for transgendered members. In fact, over 150 native tribes are documented as having recognized a third gender. In certain native tribes, transgendered persons were (and still are) called *two-spirits* or *berdaches*. The anthropological term berdache, however, is seen as derogatory by many tribes, who prefer to call GLBTI Native Americans two-spirits (a nonoffensive term originating in 1990). Because of the historical significance, I use the past tense here, though it should be noted that two-spirits are still recognized and often revered in current times.

More often than not, two-spirits were also gay or bisexual and chose to carry out specific social roles attributed to the gender of their choice. Two-spirits usually were born male, but this was not true in all cases. Some native cultures would permit them to marry a male or female, while at the same time, sex between two "one-spirit" people identifying as either male or female was a punishable offense. Some two-spirits held official roles like chief or shaman. They would perform rituals and carry out obligations exclusive to the two-spirits. They were revered and venerated as necessary keepers of spiritual roles and were believed to have been sent by the Great Spirit as people who understood both the masculine and feminine sides of human existence.

Once-male transgendered transvestites in India (predominantly North India) are called *hijras* and are devotees of Bahuchara Mata, the mother goddess of their community. Hijras are androgynous, presenting characteristics of both genders, and exhibit many similarities to the transsexual *katoeys* of Thailand (many of whose live performances are an enormous tourist attraction and Western curiosity!). Hijras live in various communal "houses," each of which is run by a guru. The guru provides newcomers (males who have decided to separate from society and embrace the lifestyle) with a name change and additional third-gender-specific roles. As a cultural rite of passage, hijras undergo a full or partial castration not only to declare their adaptation of the lifestyle, but also to set themselves apart from the majority of society and attain a very specific social role. Additionally, a large number of hijras are forced to either beg or embrace the role of a religious prostitute, which, needless to say, is a problematic part of the lifestyle and has presented their community with many additional tensions like sexual abuse and sexually transmitted diseases.

Though different from others, hijras hold significant respected religious importance; they even are positively mentioned in the Hindu epic *The Ramayana*. Groups of hijras preside over weddings in Indian society and are said to provide either extreme blessings or extreme curses to all involved, particularly the couple to be wed. Because they have forsaken their own fertility, hijras are viewed as having the power to either bless couples with fertility or curse them with infertility. Hijras also are said to have the same blessing/cursing power over male infants. Because of the recognition of their inherent magickal powers, they are both feared and held in high regard as a vital part of Indian society.

Despite frequent persecution, transgendered and biologically intersexed people are becoming more accepted in this day and age, as they were in tribal times. If one examines the current movement, a variety of self-identifying similarities are revealed between other cultural practices and those of the Western transgendered lifestyle. In regard to sexual preference, one cross-cultural similarity is the frequency of homosexuality in transgenderism. Certainly, most modern transgendered individuals are not typically recognized as spiritually significant members of society these days, nor do they usually participate in prostitutional practices or necessarily "taboo" behavior, aside from style of dress. I do believe that as the greater society begins to accept both T-girls and T-guys, a great amount of personal empowerment will flourish and the associated magickal abilities recognized in other cultures will become known once again.

To compare transgenderism with dark culture, some outsiders actually label the Gothic phenomenon as transgendered in nature. This sounds a bit too *Rocky Horror* for my tastes. The opinion likely is due to the predominantly "feminine" style of dress usually embraced by both females and males. Goth culture is culturally effeminate rather than transgendered, because most dark culturists identify as their biological gender regardless of their apparently feminized appearance. Just the same, visual and emotional expressions of gender (just like the *idea* of gender itself) are strictly *cultural* phenomena and vary across the globe. Luckily, transgendered individuals tend to be fully accepted by members of alternative scenes in the West far more often than not. At the same time, the majority of trannies I know, both male-to-female (MTF) and female-to-male (FTM), are virtually flawless, and it wasn't until some time later that I discovered their original biological gender. You never know who is who, or who "was" who. But does it really matter?

Intersex and Middlesex

The word *intersex*—which also is called *middlesex* and often is confused with *transgender*—refers to someone who is born as neither a biological male nor a biological female, which has to do with chromosomal development. Obviously, the person's sexual orientation depends upon "xem" (see page 195) as a person and in no way is determined by biological genetic makeup. Those born biologically intersexed always are either truly hermaphroditic (bearing ovaries, a vulva, a penis, and testes) or pseudohermaphroditic: "male" pseudohermaphrodites have testes and a vulva while "female" pseudohermaphrodites have ovaries and a penis. Pseudohermaphrodites exhibit a number of variations in genital size distribution (especially of the clitoris/penis glans), which is understandable because the female reproductive system is simply an "innie" of the male reproductive system and vice versa. Believe it or not, 1 percent of all births exhibit sexual ambiguity; that's one in every 100 people—an enormous number!

Westerners, unlike people of many other cultures worldwide, refuse to recognize a third gender (a cultural recognition) or a middlesex (a biological reality), identifying people as only "male" and "female." Because of this, most intersexed people undergo surgery and/or hormonal treatments to become members of one gender or another; many are not even *made aware* of childhood "gender correction" surgeries and treatments until much later in their lives. Similarly, most transgendered individuals choose to live exclusively as a male or female, rather than embracing a third-gender identity entirely. At the same time, many transgendered and intersexed individuals recognize themselves as being *both* male and female internally, rather than being solely a "male spirit" or "female spirit."

Gender-Neutral Pronouns

Many people have begun using gender-neutral pronouns in writing and speech. Replacing much of the sexually dualistic structure prevalent in modern English (not to mention the extreme sexual dualism present in other linguistic systems), gender-neutral pronouns simply do not indicate the gender of the person being referred to. It can refer to multiple people, as "he or she" would, or a singule person whose gender is unknown or who identifies as third-gendered or nongendered. Rather than getting into the politics of gender-neutral pronouns here and now, I'll present a list of two of the most commonly used pronoun replacements and leave the analysis up to the reader. Please note that the lists below refer to singular usage and include the pronunciations. For more information on gender-neutral pronouns, I suggest browsing the article of the same name on Wikipedia (a source quite frequently praised by scholars, believe it or not).

Common usage:	Replacement I:	Replacement II:
He/She (subject)	Xe ("Zee")	Sie ("Zee")
Him/Her (accusative)	Xem ("Zem")	Hir ("Heer")
His/Her (possessive adj.)	Xyr ("Zur")	Hir ("Heer")
His/Hers (possessive pron.)	Xyrs ("Zurs")	Hirs ("Heers")
Himself/Herself (reflexive)	Xemself ("Zemself")	Hirself ("Heerself")

Boys Don't Cry: Goth and Femininity

Emotionally sensitive individuals often are drawn to dark culture because the lifestyle actually *allows* people to feel the emotions they're feeling, not leveling any shame or guilt at them because of it. A number of Goth males have had the homosexual label pinned on them, whether they are actually gay or not, because of their own personal emotional awareness and outward displays of what many would consider femininity. Many males are drawn to the emotionally open ways of Goth culture and Paganism. They wish to break free of cultural boundaries forced on them from a young age. For so many individuals, direct involvement in alternative culture is a form of soul-level healing.

Males are taught from a young age to repress their emotions. There are "girl things" and there are "boy things," and one gender shouldn't embrace that which is assigned to the opposite for fear of homosexuality. Boys can't play with dolls or makeup; girls can't play football or be schoolyard bullies. Boys are taught that it is wrong to do anything not dubbed socially masculine and are trained to shut off their emotional centers. This training is passed down from generation to generation and the chain is rarely broken. This teaching ends up damaging the psyche and energy field, restricting actual development. It can make people bitter and judgmental with time, because genderizing actually represses individual freedom. While I realize these examples are generalizations, many parents raise their children as *gendered* beings rather than as *human* beings, which, if strictly enforced, is a social issue.

I recently had an interesting experience. I was shopping at a local grocery when a four-year-old girl and her mother walked past me. The girl turned around, stared at me for a moment, and said, "Mommy, is that a boy or a girl?" I was wearing a trench coat and heavy eyeliner at the time—not even a skirt or lipstick! Her mom said, "That's a boy, honey," and gave me an embarrassed smile. I smiled back but felt an immediate rush of sadness come over me. I felt self-conscious, nervous, and insecure. This feeling was then replaced with feelings of contentment and ease. "Maybe," I thought, "I should view this experience as complimentary, not degrading." The little girl asked her mother an honest question she had on her mind, not trying to insult me whatsoever. Perhaps she saw my style of dress and equated it with her learned idea of femininity. Perhaps, being a perceptive and untainted child, she saw a little beneath the surface and was able to recognize my energy pattern as having a more balanced amount of masculine and feminine energy than most. Whatever the case, I refused to feel guilty about the issue and saw it as a positive affirmation of my generally balanced state of being.

It's such a strange dichotomy: according to typical Western ideology, females in our culture are to be prim and proper, dolled up and extravagant, while males are to be stylistically careless and quite "ordinary." This ridiculous archetype is shattered with subcultural movements such as Goth, which do not seek segregation or separation between the sexes. Gender roles are not reversed in the culture, but are simply (and ideally) nonexistent.

If nature is observed, one will see that the *males* of the species are usually the most colorful of the sexes. Many male fish have much larger and more colorful fins, many male birds have larger and more colorful feathers, and so on. Perhaps some Native American elders have it right when they say, in terms of gender appearance and behavior, "Western man has it backwards."

Androgyny means either "exhibiting both masculine and feminine traits" or "indistinguishably masculine or feminine." Linguistically, *andro* reflects the masculine, while *gyny* reflects the feminine. This both-or-neither principle is reflected in the Pagan spiritual system. Androgyny is apparent in both Paganism and Goth culture. The God and Goddess are separate energies but are not apart from one another; they are one. They are genderized and yet have no gender. In Goth culture, a person can present masculine and feminine qualities simultaneously—in fashion, speech, art, and otherwise. Gender stereotyping is not very apparent in dark culture, and its members often refuse to draw lines of boundary between masculine and feminine.

The Gothic and Pagan lifestyles are very attuned to femininity. This, I believe, is because darkness is attuned to the lunar cycle—the cycle of the Goddess. In dark culture, boys can be seen in makeup, skirts, corsets, and fishnets. They also are far more willing than your average guy to cry in public and express their emotional state to others with no qualm. Emotional awareness and femininity have become closely linked because of the oppression of both over time. Again, this occurrence is *entirely* cultural and not inherently biological. In Paganism and Witchcraft, worship and homage paid to the Goddess directly link magickal people to their own feminine nature, inviting energies of both masculinity and femininity into the practitioner.

One interesting gender-bending practice seen throughout numerous cultures is called *couvade*. This refers to the practice of a man voluntarily taking on the characteristics of childbirth while his female partner is in labor. The man will go to a separate area and publicly "give birth." He will complain of pain and contractions, and scream and wail as if delivering a child. He deliberately will outscream the mother and will keep doing this until the baby is safely birthed. This mock-birth is actually an act of magick and is centered on a belief in malevolent spirits. Many cultures believe that certain spirits are jealous of human life and childbirth and will either steal the soul of the child or taint it with death and disease. The purpose of the couvade ritual is to attract the malevolent spirits to the male, drawing attention away from the female, lessening the risk of spirit affliction.

Cultures that practice couvade also have a keen recognition of how the mother's pregnancy influences not only her own mood and behavior but her husband's as well. There seems to be a curious connection between the emotions exhibited during the female's child-carrying and her mate's state of being. Both people's emotional states change, even if it's only slightly, during the female's childbearing. At this time, male partners in virtually all cultures have a shift in mood, even if the woman doesn't know she's pregnant at the time. The more eager the male is to become a father, the more synchronistic traits he will exhibit. His receptivity to this sort of change also depends on the compassion and awareness he gives to the situation. Changes of attitude in the male are shown to a lesser degree when the female partner is menstruating. These metaphysical ties hint that the line between femininity and masculinity may not actually be as well-defined as once thought.

VI
Magick

Magick is one of the most appealing and interesting aspects of Witchcraft. Some people find themselves researching the Craft solely because of its inclusion of magickal practice. Although many think otherwise, the actual practice of ritual magick is only a small part of Witchcraft as a whole. The Craft is, first and foremost, a spiritual system. Magick is certainly a very important aspect of Witchcraft and other forms of Paganism, but does not take precedence over spirituality. Rather, magick is *aligned* with spiritual principle, not a substitute for it. Understanding metaphysics and the general order of the universe are required for successful magickal practice.

The magick of the dark Witch draws upon nocturnal energies to weave intention into manifestation. The darkness is an extremely powerful force that can be utilized for all types of spiritual workings. The darkness is everybody's own experience—energies of the darkness are subjective in nature. When dark energy is drawn upon, the results can be miraculous, serene, and intense. Nearly anything can be accomplished so long as fear doesn't interfere. I encourage the reader to safely and knowledgeably experiment on your own. I offer this information on tools, protection methods, circle casting, and so forth as assistance in the magickal journey. At the same time, it's only brushing the surface of the magickal world.

Magick works. I don't intend to defend my belief in the validity of magick because I imagine that most of the readers have experience in the arts and are past the point of uncertainty in this field. If you are relatively inexperienced in magick and/or are uncertain about magick and its validity, I commend you. All too many people approach ideas and belief systems without questioning, researching, and experimenting. Blind faith is a downfall to any religion or way of life because all sound paths must be built on a foundation of experience. Otherwise, they're only daydreams.

Like most magickal practitioners, I find myself performing minor magicks every day. When running late to an appointment, I envision my path to be clear so that I may arrive in due time. If an ambulance passes nearby, I'm sure to project a good amount of healing light at the vehicle so that it may surround the person the paramedics are seeking to help. When washing dishes or taking out the trash (how mundane can you get?!), I make it a process of releasing old energy in order to embrace the new. Practical, minor instant-magicks can be performed at the drop of a hat. Projecting intention doesn't require forty crystals and a pound of charcoal incense. Every one of us is weaving magick *constantly* whether we know it or not! Every thought we have is an act of creation.

Spellcasting is one form of magick that is considered by Witches to be "amplified prayer." That's it. Though the formulas may be complex and the energy raised extreme, spellcraft is just like prayer work. Likewise, common prayers are spells themselves. The only difference is how much energy is put into each projection of energy. Spells generally contain more oomph than short prayers, but not in all cases.

When I was exploring Christianity in my early teenage years, a friend of mine at the time took me to a fundamentalist Evangelical church. After sitting through a series of seemingly endless and judgmental lectures, the youth pastor instructed everyone to take pieces of paper and write down the names of friends and family who needed the "guidance of the Lord" in their lives. Everyone did this but me (go figure!), and the pastor gathered the papers and put them in a shoebox. He instructed everyone to gather around the shoebox, hold their hands outstretched to it, and pray out loud simultaneously. I took note of how much energy was being projected into the box as a result of everyone's combined intent. They were, in fact, performing magick without even realizing it. This was an act of projecting energy to the people at hand, comparable to burning a written petition in a Pagan ritual. This, in addition to entering trancelike states, exorcising "demons," and speaking in tongues, confirmed for me that energy is energy and magick is magick, regardless of the religious skin it wears or the deity it serves.

Magickal Ethics

All religions have their own system of ethics. The word *ethics* is inherently subjective and a never-ending topic in philosophical discussion. What is ethical for one person or group of people may not be for another, and vice versa. Ethics is culturally relevant. Moral codes differ in every culture, society, and belief system. There is no universal code of right and wrong.

Magickal lifestyles rarely include a strict code of ethics and morality. In most forms of Witchcraft and occultism, accountability is placed directly on the backs of the practitioners themselves. This is an *enormous* weight of responsibility, but one that should never be forgotten as we go about our lives. The Pagan path is a very personal one especially in that each practitioner decides for him- or herself what is ethical and what is not. There are no commandments in the Craft. Ethical principles are not the same for every Pagan, but are personally determined instead. This is a lot of personal responsibility, which can be off-putting to those who feel more comfortable following another person's established code of ethics instead of their own. At the same time, some Witches feel more comfortable following guidelines like the Wiccan Rede or a similar moral code. Unlike most religions' moral codes, the Wiccan Rede is but a general guideline emphasizing "harm none," a profound yet simple code designed to influence the ways in which practitioners conduct their lives.

I believe that we inherently know the difference between right and wrong. Instead of expounding on this, I will say that each of us has absolute responsibility for our actions and reactions. If little mind is given to the way we conduct our lives, including how we treat other people, which industries we support, what food we eat, where we shop, which ideologies we proclaim, and how we conduct our magick, then we are not properly living the magickal/spiritual lifestyle. The cultivation of personal spiritual awareness necessarily includes personal ethics and conscious behavior. When the cycles we create are given sufficient attention, we become more self-aware and our lives are lived in greater metaphysical consciousness.

Dark Witches aren't afraid to use magick to curse if there is no other option. For a true Witch to perform a cursing, the situation must be extreme and there must be no other option. While many Witches and magickal practitioners are more comfortable sending healing light to any given situation, dark Witches understand that this isn't always the most beneficial plan of action. Witches do not find enjoyment in cursing other people; very, very few cases actually call for such magickal work. Sometimes a cursing can cause the greatest degree of positive change, though this isn't true for 99 percent of cases. While most people need only to see and embrace healing to enter its realm, for others it takes a universal bitch-slap to wake them up to that reality. For example, if a serial rapist were the target of magickal work, the last thing I'd want to do is send him love and light in hope that he would suddenly change his ways. Before that can rightfully occur, the perpetrator must be stopped in his tracks, even if it takes a "karma booster" to make that happen. Of course, this type of dark spellcraft must be well thought out before being executed. Magick is not nearly as effective (actually and karmically) without spiritual grounding and rational thought behind it. Casting unjustified spells only creates chaos upon chaos, which ultimately ends up being consuming, rendering the caster jaded and drained of power. Witchcraft is about flowing with nature, not going against it. Witches harness and help move the constant ebb and flow of the universe. At times this is healing and at times destroying; it simply depends on which is best for the greater balance.

I rarely perform cursing and have done so only a couple times in the past—both of which had positive outcomes after the magick was brought to fruition. If I ever need to perform a cursing or a crossing, I always add an element of light with the intention that "if cursing is not the best possible way to bring this person to a more enlightened state, may he (or she) come to that state with no ill effects." Both light and dark elements are required for successful magick, and the will of the universe mustn't be forgotten for the sake of one's personal agenda.

I maintain the belief that people studying spiritual philosophies and the magickal arts for purely harmful reasons (like cursing) end up ditching the material as fast as they picked it up, having grown tired of "inapplicable" ideas and failed attempts at selfish magick. Not to mention the fact that they never really "get it." If spiritual principles do not become interwoven into one's life, no satisfaction comes about beyond temporary egotism, and disinterest soon follows.

Once when I was just winding up a road trip to Portland, I came across a magick shop on the way out of town. I thought that spending my last few bucks on Craft goodies while helping out a local business would be a great way to end a fun week full of Goth clubs and cafés. I went into the shop, talked to the owner for a while, and found some neat Witchy items I hadn't seen anywhere else. Five minutes later, a very determined black-clad teenage girl stomped up the stairs and approached the owner very intently. "Lodestone?!" she demanded, obviously needing it for a spell of some kind, probably a love spell. The owner simply stared back at her, his eyes seeing through her façade. He reached under the counter and grabbed her stone, as requested. She took it from him silently, completed her purchase, and went on her way, black cloud and all. Her ego and delusion of power obviously had distracted her from the real point of Witchcraft as a spiritual path. I bit my tongue and decided not to tell her that, based on my observation, her spell would either be unsuccessful or go awry entirely because of her approach to the magickal arts.

This story demonstrates exactly what Witchcraft is not. I have no problem saying that this girl was not a Witch and that she, at least at the time, was far from actualizing spirituality as a living practice. This is not how Witchcraft is meant to be lived. If a person walks around scorning and disrespecting anyone he or she feels to be "lesser than thou," then no spiritual work is really accomplished. Rather, this behavior builds a cycle of self-righteousness, which ultimately is consuming in the end. At the same time, if a person embraces the magickal principles of the Craft and strives to live life in spiritual consciousness, then condescending behavior naturally is done away with.

Drawing on the above story, Qabalists would call delusions of grandeur the *Illusion of Tiphareth*. In Qabalistic terms, the sephira Tiphareth is a lower emanation of the highest sphere, Kether. Like a reflection of the sun on a lake, Tiphareth reminds the magician of his or her own potential to reach enlightenment. If this acknowledgment isn't heeded, the magician may mistake this emanation for actual enlightenment. Rather than seeing an affirmation of his or her gifts as a confirmation, the magician believes him- or herself to have metaphorically reached Kether, existing at the top of the metaphysical food chain. Behaviors accompanying the Illusion of Tiphareth are purely ego-based, pompous, and foolish. Must this display of delusion be perpetuated in the Craft?

Some people get attached to the idea of magick as a supernatural or special power, when it's really just as normal as eating and breathing. Magick is not a hidden world

Harmony summons the magick of the old gods.

you cross into after performing the right spells. It's very much integrated in one's everyday life. Everyone uses it regularly through thoughts and intentions whether they know it or not. Thought forms reality. Certainly, magickal paths, practices, and philosophies help us learn to *own* our inherent power and teach us how to utilize our natural gifts properly. Paths recognizing the reality of magick are designed to ground our powers and give us a greater awareness of our influence.

Will

In his book *Magick in Theory and Practice*, Aleister Crowley defines magick as "the Science and Art of causing Change to occur in conformity with Will." This may sound like a very simple and straightforward definition, which it is, but the magician must really dissect what these words mean in order to fully grasp the process. I have found Crowley's definition to be not too far off from many other occultists' personal view-

points, regardless of their level of respect for the guy. To analyze this statement, we must understand what Crowley meant by "Will." To draw a correlation with modern Witchcraft, the final stanza of the fifty-two lined Wiccan Rede is this:

> *Eight words the Wiccan Rede fulfill:*
> *An' it harm none, do what ye will.*

This is a modification of Crowley's spiritual principle "Do what thou Wilt shall be the whole of the Law." This is one of the primary phrases of Thelemic philosophy, which is said to have been delivered by spiritual means to Crowley and his wife while in Cairo, Egypt, on their honeymoon.

After his wife, Rose, began experiencing a number of instances in which she channeled arcane spiritual messages, Crowley administered a sequence of tests that showed Rose possessed information impossible to know without having done massive amounts of prior research, and apparently delivered to her from legitimate external sources. Crowley later identified these sources as the Secret Chiefs (Masters) of the Great White Brotherhood (Lodge), who are seen as ascended masters who uphold evolutionary consciousness on the earth plane.

The height of the Cairo working was Crowley's instruction to sit in a temple at noon for an hour on three successive days to receive a channeling from an external source. It was then that Crowley received a transmission that became known as *Liber AL vel Legis* (*Liber CCXX*): *The Book of the Law*. The book was later researched and declared genuine by a number of occultists. The being that delivered the information identified himself as Aiwass, who became recognized as Crowley's Holy Guardian Angel.

The cryptic Egypt-centered philosophies delivered in *The Book of the Law* became the primary teachings of the path of Thelema, the magick of which works to push the practitioner to individually find the way to connect with the higher, cosmic self, or God self, thus uncovering one's True Will (cosmic destiny) in order to achieve the Great Work: that which we are destined to achieve during our incarnation. Another message delivered through the channelings of Aiwass was, "Thou hast no right but to do thy Will," meaning that all things done in life in accordance with one's True Will are correct and spiritual, while anything done out of line and against one's Will is incorrect and thus sinful.

Like Crowley's channeled philosophies, the final line of the Wiccan Rede does not mean "go ahead and do whatever the hell you want." If we take the Thelemic definition of Will into account, we see that all acts of magick are part of our life's plan. It is reasonable to think that magickal practitioners help uphold the energies of the world in which we exist, because magick is our specialty, our destiny, our will. This includes taking full responsibility for any action we take. It does not mean pursuing all temptations and pleasures of the flesh, nor does it mean inviting ego or chaos above morality; at the same time, it doesn't mean disregarding them. It means *uncovering your destiny and following it accordingly through conscious thought.* One's destiny is one's life path—that which is *meant* to be accomplished. This includes both one's greater destiny or life's work, as well as every moment of being; that which constructs the bigger picture. Thelemic magicians call the accurate following of one's True Will the "Great Work."

Gerald Gardner and Aleister Crowley were in contact while developing their own magickal systems: Crowley, Thelemic magick, and Gardner, modern Wicca. They exchanged an unknown amount of material that helped one another form their magickal systems. They also interacted with other magicians and Witches of the time, who exchanged multiple ideas among themselves. We do know that Gardner was initiated into Crowley's OTO. While Gardner and Crowley's relationship remains more or less ambiguous to this day, it's speculated that the final lines of the Rede, which are seen in a similar form in Gardner's Old Laws (Gardner did not write the Rede we are now familiar with), are modifications based on Crowley's input. It even has been speculated that Crowley actually wrote most of Gardner's original Book of Shadows upon receiving payment to do so! Still others believe that Gardner modified Doreen Valiente's "The Witches' Creed" to form portions of his Old Laws, or that he created lines now integrated into the Rede as a combination of the Creed and the Thelemic Law. Other theorists who do believe Gardner had a strong influence on the creation of the Rede think that he simply borrowed lines from Crowley's material in the process of creating modern Wicca. For example, a couple of lines from Crowley's Gnostic Mass are used word for word in the invocation of Drawing Down the Moon, which is credited to Doreen Valiente, the first Priestess of Gardnerian Wicca.

In the Ostara 1975 issue of *Green Egg* magazine, Lady Gwen (Gwynne) Thompson published "The Rede of the Wiccæ" (which is the Wiccan Rede), attributing the material to her deceased paternal grandmother Adriana Porter, who was said to have gotten it from earlier sources. Is this the origin of the Rede, and if so, how did Ms. Porter compile her material? We do know that Lady Gwen's version was circulated among members of the New England Covens of Traditionalist Witches (NECTW). Regardless of the text's origins, which are as of now unknown, the idea of will in both systems remains very much aligned. They are very similar and carry the same message: do the life's work that you are meant to do.

Giving Thanks

Giving thanks to Spirit is one of the most beneficial and profound things that one can do. I've had a surprising number of people ask me lately, "How do you give thanks and show your appreciation in ritual?" The answer is actually quite simple: Do what you feel is right! Do what's appropriate for the situation, and honor the divine as you see fit, so long as it's in honesty and humility. If working with a particular deity, offerings should be left for the deity that previous cultures have deemed appropriate. For example, Hecate prefers apples, honey, and myrrh. I've found that Baphomet prefers eggs, tobacco, wine, and a few drops of the magician's own blood. Find out what offerings your patron deity or deities favor, and leave them outdoors or at the base of the god's effigy to take of the item's essence.

Many Witches leave offerings of blended herbs to the deities. Though not nearly as personalized, this is a great way to show thanks and ask for blessings. I like to carry a blend to the cemetery and offer it to restless spirits, power centers, and astral guardians of the land. In her book *The Circle Within: Creating a Wiccan Spiritual Tradition*, Dianne Sylvan suggests using cornmeal in addition to other herbs for a "general offering" blend. Some versatile additional herbs I've found include mugwort, yarrow, tobacco, mullein, and lavender. Such blends are also ideal for offerings in general magickal workings in which elementals are summoned but no actual deities are invoked. Offerings can be left after performing magick or simply to pay homage to the universe for providing you with abundance—it's never the wrong time to give thanks.

The most important part of giving thanks is the intention. As the offerings are made, contemplate the essence of the one to whom the offering is being given, and think about what this spirit or deity means to you personally. Allow the energy of actual gratitude to rise within you, letting it manifest before you in the form of a material offering. Your internal voice is heard; this is the essence of giving thanks and is a vital part of living the magickal life.

The Magickal Name

The secondary name, or pseudonym, separates the ordinary self from the extraordinary Self, and is used by many Goths and Pagans. Pseudonyms, monikers, or alternative names are not by any means required for Goths or Pagans, but the majority of us choose to use one to some degree. It's entirely up to the individual as to how often, and how much of, the name commonly is used. When someone chooses or is given an alternative name, that person decides how often, if at all, it is shared with others. Oftentimes for the dark Witch, one's Craft name is the same or similar to the name one chooses to use within the Goth scene.

Alternative names in dark culture usually are just called "Goth names" and directly reflect some aspect of the individual assuming the pseudonym. For Goths, I strongly advise against choosing a name like Azræl Abyss or Circe Nightshade! If you want to be taken seriously by Pagans and non-Pagans alike, I recommend your taking on a name that has a deep, personal meaning to you, one that really "vibes" with you, instead of a borderline comical-spooky name like Mistress Lilith Nocturnia-Dæmonica or Count NecroFetus-Lugosi the Third. The name should be meaningful to you, not simply designed to make an impression on other people! Now, this isn't to say your magickal name shouldn't sound dark and even glamorous, because, well, people like us have a natural tendency to be attracted to all things mysterious, spooky, and fabulous. Let your magickal name be individualistic and personally empowering, but not something with which to impress your friends.

In Witchcraft, the magickal name used publicly is called the *Craft name*. This name doesn't have to take the place of your birth name, but it can if you desire. It also doesn't need to be used publicly in all cases and situations; it can simply be reserved for other members of the Pagan community to use, particularly those with whom you practice your Craft from time to time (called the Outer Court).

The *Eke name*, on the other hand, refers to a name reserved for only your Inner Court, in other words, only people with whom you practice on a regular basis and whom you are very close to, such as the coven or a few tight-knit friends.

The *working name* is the magickal name that only you know. No one else, including those closest to you, knows your working name. It is the name known only by you and

Spirit. It is the name used in private, spoken aloud only when necessary, such as when performing a personal spell or a spiritually communicative act in a solitary circle.

It is a personal choice as to how often the magickal name is used. A Witch or magician may also have a personal sigil(s) used only in particular situations and aligned to his or her magickal name(s). Some people take on all three names: a Craft name, an Eke name, and a working name. For some people, the Eke and working names are longer versions of their Craft name. Others have different names altogether for all three, while some have no magickal name (yet) or take on only an Eke or working name. The usage is different for every Witch.

A number of dark Witches adopt an alternative "Goth name" based on their magickal name. My publicly used Craft name is Raven Digitalis, though I also have Eke and working names. I tend to go by either Raven or Colin (my English/birth name) to my acquaintances, the former of which is taken from my Craft name. While I realize that thousands of Goths and Pagans use the name Raven, I'm not about to change it for the sake of uniqueness because of its meaning to me as an attunement to my spirit animal guide. If your alternative or magickal name is quite common, consider changing it only if you feel that it's lacking in personal relevance. Otherwise, refer to yourself in whatever way feels right. The alternative name is yours to do with as you please, and intuition should be your foremost guide!

How does one choose a magickal name? Well, sometimes it's not always a conscious personal choice. There are numerous ways the name can come to you, the most common of which is meditation. In deep meditation, a number of signs, symbols, and messages may be delivered to the seeker. Sometimes, Spirit will convey to a person his or her name of power. This can be delivered directly, such as through a channeling, or discovered upon further research into the symbolism presented in meditation.

Other Witches discover their magickal names by realizing that certain words, names, or symbols eerily vibrate with them. Oftentimes, this is a nod from the universe saying that further exploration must be made. From there, the name is developed. The Craft name may be chosen based on numerological associations with your birth name or covenstead, or it can reference your spirit animal, power herb or tree, favorite season or color, a mythological name, a Latin word or phrase, and so on. The possibilities for the magickal name are endless.

It is good to note that the titles Lord and Lady (and High Priest and High Priestess) usually are restricted to the third degree in Craft traditions. Simply filling the role of a High Priest or High Priestess in one's own coven does not earn the title, nor do years of study alone. The process of working toward the Priesthood is generally formal and demanding, yet is different for every tradition. One should not crown oneself with a title that isn't applicable! Magickal names should be researched and made one's own through knowledge and soul-searching; exaggerated names of any sort have potential to degrade the sacredness of the magickal name.

Beware also when choosing (or being given) the name of a god or goddess. Many people take on names like Horus, Ishtar, Kali, Persephone, or Zeus without actually working with the deities or doing appropriate research. The Law of Reflection states that with repetitive use, a name becomes an astral link to an energy force, including a person. This is why invoking gods is so successful. Over time, astral substance has formed the deity as an embodiment of energies directly accessible through the use of a name; this is called an *egregore*. Every time someone calls you by a god name, it invokes a bit of that person's essence into your person. This could end up causing a serious imbalance over time. This is why magickal names, or at least portions of them, are kept secret or hidden by many, so as to preserve the higher self from receiving unwanted influence from outside forces. If your magickal name is aligned with your patron deity or one you often work with, it can actually be beneficial to take on a deity pseudonym, assuming the deity gives you permission and constant work is done!

I should mention that if a person's birth name (or the name being chosen for a child) is a god name, like Rhiannon or Diana, some serious investigation into the name's origin and its cultural associations in its magickal pantheon must be undertaken. Only then can an accurate division be made between the person's energy and the deity's.

Ritual

In the pentagram, the most widely used Witch's symbol, each physical element is represented, along with Spirit, resting atop the others as the uppermost point of the symbol. In one's daily life, every element is encountered and used. To magicians, this use goes beyond breathing air or drinking water; each element has an inherent essence that is available for utilization at any time. Simply tapping into an element connects its essence

Medicine Witch prepares an altar for weaving shadow magick.

to the practitioner. Contrary to what some may tell you, magick and elemental connection are *not* limited to ritualism alone. However, ritual has extreme significance in any spiritual path. This is one reason that Spirit is set aside as a unique element on the pentagram. Practitioners mustn't immerse themselves in the four elements alone, nor should they be consumed by philosophy or study without setting time aside to actively work with the energies. This is where ritualism comes into play as a necessary part of spiritual practice.

Ritual can be defined as a repetitive set of behaviors designed to communicate symbols to a society or group of people while, at the same time, inducing some sort of change. Ritual makes spiritual experience real, and is a constant in all cultures worldwide. It grounds ideas into action and allows one to become an actualized practitioner (as opposed to just a philosopher) of a spiritual path. Witches use ritual for a variety of reasons, including paying homage to spiritual forces, observing solar and lunar holidays, spellcasting, meditation, rites of passage, handfasting, and initiation.

In some public group rituals, too much emphasis is placed on the *structure* of the ritual rather than the *substance*. In my earlier Craft days, I witnessed many "empty words" being spoken in public circles and "empty gestures" simply undertaken for the sake of tradition. When no power is behind the words or actions, the ritual procedure remains ordinary instead of magickal. Plus, the lack of ambition turns away potential seekers! As a ritual practitioner, you must speak to and communicate with the directions, spirits, deities, and higher powers not as though they are unfathomable powers, which may or may not exist, but as if you were speaking directly to someone else—because you are!

Gardnerian Witchcraft rituals never were intended to be followed to the T. Traditional rituals provide a valuable outline for creating one's own rituals. Spontaneity is part of the fun of ritual! I agree with Richard Metzger, founder and publisher of the underground news source *Disinformation*, when he says that just because a ritual worked for someone else doesn't mean it's going to work the same way for you.

In actuality, preplanned circle procedures are only the framework of the ritual, not the most important aspect of it. Both solitary Witches and group practitioners must beware not to get caught up in the symbolic aspects of the ritual—the words spoken, the tools used, the incense burned, etc.—and instead focus more on the magick being raised and sent. For most Witches, there are no hard-and-fast, immutable rules; that's why Witchcraft is such a personal way of life.

Group Workings

Early on in my involvement in the magickal-spiritual community, I noticed a major problem in many public Craft circles: too much emphasis was placed on the framework of the ritual, rather than the actual point of it. There was an emphasis on what words needed to be said, which tools needed to be used, and so on. It's good (and necessary) to plan ahead and have a good idea of what is to be performed, who is to perform it, what traditional tools and ritualistic components will be used, and so on, but it mustn't stop there. The ritual, whether created by oneself or conducted by an outside source, should provide an outline of basic procedure. One should not feel as though this procedure is immutable or unalterable. Witchcraft allows freedom to incorporate our own methodologies! When entering circle, we must be willing to completely surrender to the energy at hand and make the experience our own—for ourselves, for the group, and for the community and the world. Participants should also know that unexpected inspiration may occur mid-circle, and they should be open to the possibility that elements may be added or changes may be made to the original outline if those who are hosting the circle deem it appropriate. When organizing group events, all things will come together exactly as they are supposed to be. Preparations for the ritual's goal, as well as ritual etiquette, must, of course, also be taken. Ideally, every single participant should be involved in the circle so that the experience isn't empty or unfulfilling. Group rituals are tough because of the number of attendees, though it should be kept in mind that it's off-putting for people to be involved in bland or impersonal circles because of the lasting impressions they make on participants' spiritual quests.

If you come across a spell and don't understand why it says you must use a certain ingredient, chant, or procedure, do some research before using it. If you don't know why you're using the ingredient or performing the action, then don't do it! It's not that "this ingredient mixed with this chant has this effect." It may, but that requires intention. The *ingredients* are not the power in and of themselves. Your intention fuels the power and awakens the magickal properties of the spell's contents, including ingredients and words of power.

Spells and rituals can be done for any purpose. You can use the framework of rituals others have had success with, or create new ones altogether. In the end, do what feels right. Follow your heart and seek to evolve yourself, your loved ones, and the global community through positive magickal action.

The Shadow Tools

Witches use a variety of tools (also sometimes called "weapons") in ritual. Each has esoteric significance and is utilized in magickal practice for various purposes. The tools I mention in this section are commonplace on the dark Witch's altar. Some of their meanings have been changed over time, though most of them frequently are used in magick by modern practitioners who understand the timeless significance behind them. Many are tools seen in literature on Witchcraft from the Middle Ages that had been used for many centuries prior.

The benefits of having an altar and tools are limitless. The altar is a place to come back to after the turmoil of the day and is always available as a place to ground and center personal energy. Magickal tools help conduct energy and center the mind. I have a separate room in the house set aside for ritual work. This temple room includes altars for each of the directions placed appropriately in the room with the proper working tools on them, and a fifth central altar serving as the representation of the fifth element, Spirit. Whether you have a temple space or altar, the area in which you perform your workings should be kept energetically and physically clean at all times, serving as sacred space in which the mind can be cleared. It's important that only a small amount of influence from outside sources be secured in your sacred space. If you live in a household that's *not* magickally accepting, then simply create a portable "shoebox" altar with minimal tools, like a rock for Earth, a feather for Air, a candle or lava rock for Fire, and a bit of spring water for Water, along with any items you deem personally spiritually significant. This mini porta-altar can emerge for Sabbats, Esbats, personal meditations, or spells.

If you are fairly new to the Craft and don't have an abundance of tools, be assured that you don't need to rush out and buy everything all at once. Trust your intuition; you may feel the need to own one particular tool before any others. The wand is the first tool a Witch usually receives or creates by hand. It is one of the "lighter" tools, whose energy is relatively harmless yet still powerful, depending on its characteristics and how it is utilized. The more complex tools come to the practitioner as studies progress. If someone hands down a tool to you, cleanse it and make it your own, incorporating it into your collection. I recommend getting one tool at a time so that you can spend a while getting to know each one, enchanting and physically altering it to fit you. A direct and personal connection to the item makes it sacred and magickal. Feel free to add written words of power, colors, stones, oils, wax, feathers, and the like to personalize the item. If you feel the calling, using a bit of blood to consecrate the tools is a great idea to bind them to your person, assuming they will be used by you and you alone. Each tool should be energetically charged and attuned to its individual purpose (the athamé for projecting energy, the cords for binding, and so on).

If you are lacking a certain tool you wish to possess but don't know where to start looking, send your intention out to the universe. Light a candle or a stick of incense, focus, and say, "I would like (name of tool) to enter my life, so that I may use it for the greater good. As I will, so mote it be." This will project your intention and draw the item to you in due time. Meanwhile, brainstorm and keep on the lookout for possible avenues to access the tool. The item may be found in a secondhand shop, online, at a retail store, in the woods, or passed down from someone else.

I must emphasize that *tools are not necessary to perform magick.* They are but items that hold specific meanings and may be used to conduct, focus, and strengthen the workings. They are wonderful components of and complements to magickal work. Nearly all Witches and magicians choose to have tools to assist in their spells and rituals, but the truth is that the only tool truly necessary is *you:* your intention, your dedication, and your spirit. All else is metaphor.

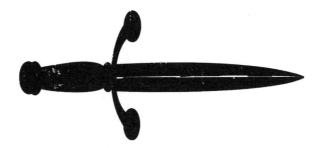

Athamé

The athamé, also called the blade or dagger, is one of the most important tools of the Witch. The athamé is a conduit of ethereal energy and is used to cast a magick circle prior to ritual and spellwork. The practitioner's energy is sent through the handle, and is both amplified through the blade and fine-tuned as the energy is condensed and exits the blade's pointed tip. The athamé is also used to create portals in the air, invoke the elements by tracing sacred symbols, and cut ethereal doorways in the magick circle. It also may be used to inscribe candles, or a separate tool may be used for physical cutting, such as a *bolline* to cut herbs or a *burin* to inscribe candles.

The athamé is used to conduct energy, but never to shed blood. Many athamés have dulled edges to avoid potential accidents. Some traditional forms of Witchcraft actually forbid blood from ever touching this tool and believe it to be tainted if this happens. Witches who work with blood magick use different, and ultimately safer, devices to break the skin. Additionally, the athamé traditionally is black-hilted, but the most important aspect of using the tool is its attunement to the practitioner. Use a dagger that feels right, fits well in the hand, and vibrates with you personally regardless of the handle's color or blade's length.

Broom

The broom, or besom, is one of the best-known Witchy tools. In old times, the broom actually was used as a masturbatory device by some female Pagans. In fact, some brooms have been found with a phallus carved at the end hidden in the straw. Not only did this relieve sexual tension (minus the splinters!), but it was also a sympathetic act of fertility. Because of the broom's long handle, it always has been associated with the penis, having implications as a tool of fertility for the land, the body, and the mind. Though much mythology surrounds the item's use in the Craft, its main modern associations are those of cleansing and protection.

The straw of the broom is used to sweep dust and unwanted/stagnant energy from a space. Many Witches "sweep the circle" initially before performing a magickal rite. Many Witches also keep brooms placed above or beside doorways to protect the household from potentially intruding forces. In the Pagan marriage ceremony known as the handfasting, the couple usually hops over a broomstick to sweep away negative ties of the past so they can embrace the newly created ties with one another.

Cauldron

One of the most maligned and misunderstood items over time, the cauldron has a long history in the Craft. The cauldron is simply an antiquated cooking vessel. As other methods of cooking gained popularity, the cauldron become exclusively associated with potion brewing, likely due to Early Modern pictorial depictions of demonic "Witches" using (then-common) cauldrons for black magick, as well as the portrayals of Witches in Shakespeare's *Macbeth*.

The cauldron unites the four elements: the herbs thrown in (Earth), the rising steam (Air), the fire used to heat the device (Fire), and the boiling liquid (Water). The cauldron also can contain kindled fire, flowers, herbs, or incense, and is not only restricted to hell-broth boilin' and bubblin'. Most people can't afford a gigantic traditional cast-iron cauldron, so they instead use a smaller device like a cooking pot or Dutch oven set aside specifically for spellcrafting and potion making.

The cauldron represents the womb of the Great Goddess. In Celtic mythology, Cerridwen's Cauldron of Knowledge (equated with the Holy Grail of immortality) was the metaphorical container in which the goddess mixed magickal potions of wisdom, transformation, and rebirth. Many Witches, and certainly Wiccans, adhere to a Celtic pantheon and carry over similar associations into their own practices. The cauldron traditionally is also three-legged, carrying associations with the Triple Goddess.

Cloak

When entering the magick circle, one transcends time and space to enter a world in which all acts are symbolic and all energy is consecrated. Ritual clothing greatly helps the practitioner enter this transcendental state. Clothing set aside exclusively for ritual use collects astral essence with each ritual and invokes higher energies into the practitioner every time it's worn. Plus, if the mind associates magick and mysticism with an article of clothing, just wearing the item brings the person to an altered state of consciousness almost instantaneously, much like applying certain designs of makeup prior to entering the circle.

Capes and hooded cloaks are ideal items of clothing for magick because of both their mystical appeal and their allowance of mobility, not to mention the fact that they can hide you outside in the dark if the need arises! Dark Witches prefer capes because of their aesthetic inclinations. Many like to sew magickal symbols into their capes to give them a more specific energy pattern. Capes and cloaks can be of any color; a magickal order or coven's own associations or a solitary practitioner's individual preferences often determine this.

Conical Hat

One of the most infamous features of the legendary Witch figure is the conical hat. The pointed hat actually used to be a fashion trend in the seventeenth century and eventually was associated with Witchcraft. Thereon, the cone-shaped "dunce hat" became associated with heresy and was equated to some degree with the horns of the devil (a visual desecration of the Pagans' horned god), likely because some conical hats had two cones emerging from the head instead of one.

The single-coned pointed hat represents the Witches' cone of power. The cone of power is the shape of the energy raised in a magick circle, spiraling from the ritual space upward. If one stands in the center of a magick circle and looks up, assuming that the boundaries of the circle are at least partially visible, a cone shape is formed from the practitioner's vantage point, projecting upward to the heavens.

The Wizard's hat is a variation of the conical hat and carries the same associations. Symbolically, the wearer is connected with the gods, the movement of the stars, and the celestial bodies. Pointed hats aren't just a modern phenomenon; statues and carvings from across the globe have been found that depict spiritual figures wearing pointed hats. In more modern terms, in addition to being sported by Witches, the pointed hat was depicted on a variety of gnomes and fairy tale princesses. Some people still wear Witches' and Wizards' hats (aside from on Halloween) at private Pagan festivals or for coven use, but usually steer clear of wearing them in open public circles where negative stereotypes could be held by outsiders. Nonetheless, the conical hat can serve as a wonderful energy-raising device if one can set aside the usual wicked Witch stereotypes!

Traditional Witches' cords (or *cingulams*) are nine feet in length and are usually white, red, or the primary elemental colors. They are used for a variety of procedures. The most common use of cords is binding, including binding abilities to oneself, binding energies to an item, or using a binding spell to keep a person from causing harm. Cords also can be used in knot spells to trap various time-space energies within each knot (usually to be untied at a later time), or tied a certain number of times as a focal item appropriate to a ritual's numerological associations. Cords also can be stretched between members of a circle to form what look like spokes of a wheel. The coven or group then circles deosil atop a cauldron, candle, or other projecting device in order to weave various energies into manifestation.

I have heard of Alexandrian traditionalists who practice the tying of cords on the body, especially the legs, to restrict blood flow. When restricting blood flow, the cords are tied tightly to bring altered sensations to areas of the body, thus projecting the practitioner into an altered state of awareness.

In old times, people's bodies were measured by cords. Traditional initiation ceremonies in Gardnerian Witchcraft include "taking the measures" of the initiate in addition to binding the initiate's hands and feet in a ceremonial rebirth. The cords are then given to the initiate to commemorate the rite of passage. Some coven leaders wear a cord around the waist for the purpose of securing magickal implements to their person or to untie the cord when needed in ritual. Cords are also gifted to a couple following a handfasting ceremony in which the couple's hands are bound together while words of power are recited to seal the declaration of partnership.

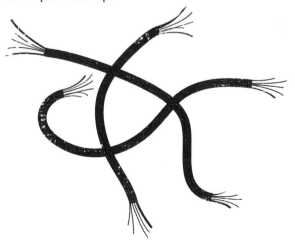

Garter

In many traditional forms of Witchcraft, the garter is used as a magickal item and as a badge of rank in a coven or training system. In some covens, only the High Priestess wears a garter, while the High Priest wears a belt or cord. In others, both the Priest and Priestess wear garters in ritual. Still others allow only the women of the circle the privilege because of their inherent connection to the Goddess. Traditionally, a coven's High Priestess is entitled to wear a garter with a single buckle when another coven breaks off from the original. With each subsequent coven hiving from those, the Priestess is entitled to bear another buckle. When she bears three, she is considered a Witch Queen. The term Witch Queen is almost obsolete in common modern Witchcraft because of its seemingly conceited overtones.

In the present day, the garter is associated with weddings. The bride's use of a garter may hark back to the Countess of Salisbury, who dropped her garter (part of everyday clothing) for Edward III to wear on his own leg. This very well may have had magickal significance or symbolism associated with Edward's protection of the Countess, not to mention his founding of a twenty-six-man order of knights soon thereafter (the number of a double coven: thirteen times two).

Grimoire

The grimoire is also called the Book of Shadows or the *Liber Umbarum* ("The Black Book"). Almost every Witch has a grimoire or something of the sort. It may be copied from a training system's book and/or compiled from personal study. The grimoire contains a wide array of magickal information, including Sabbats, astrological data, herbal correspondences, rituals, and spells. Many Witches have separate grimoires charting their own rituals and personal findings. Most practitioners go through a number of grimoires in their lives, often settling on a final book (or computerized "Disc of Shadows") including a vast amount of information learned through years of training and/or study.

Grimoires can be of any size or shape. I used to use a fancy journal, written exclusively in Old English, to document my Craft information. Later, a nineteenth-century wood-carved Bible came to me, the pages of which I replaced with blank parchment to make my own holy book. I also use a separate journal for channelings and another grimoire for information about my training system.

Pentacle

The altar pentacle is also called the *panticle paten* (or *peyton*). It is an altar plate that can be made of clay, wood, stone, or metal and is representative of the five elements of Witchcraft: Earth, Air, Fire, Water, and Spirit. The disc is inscribed with a pentagram (or hexagram, in some traditions) alongside other magickally attuned designs. Originally, it was developed by high magickal orders as a ritual tool and later was put into use in modern Wicca. The tool is used to invoke spiritual energies, presented in initiatory ceremonies, and also as a point of grounding.

Most Witches keep the pentacle in the northernmost part of the altar because of the tool's foremost associations with the element of Earth. Since the plate itself is composed of earth, both the pentacle plate and the symbol itself have gained associations with that particular element. Many practitioners also keep kosher salt or sea salt (a cleansing component in ritual magick) atop the pentacle to further attune the symbol to its element.

The practice of whipping, called flagellation, has a long history in religious practice, Pagan and otherwise. Self-flagellation is seen as a humbling act before the gods (or God, depending on the religion) to win their favor through an act of sacrifice. Some sects of extreme Christianity have been known to practice self-flagellation, even to this day. They see the pain induced as representative of the wounds the Christ endured and reenact bits of his torment on themselves to connect to the deity. In fact, members of one American sect practice annual self-crucifixion for the same purpose.

The scourge has other examples in history as well. On the Ashura holiday in the Islamic religion, Shi'ite Muslims mourn the death of their religious figure Husayn ibn Ali by ritualizing the pain felt at the time of his death. Painful and often bloody self-flagellation is practiced as a devotional act.

One noted group of fourteenth-century Christians, now commonly called "the flagellants," would go in processions from town to town whipping themselves heavily during the plague. They believed the Black Death epidemic was a sign of the apocalypse, and used self-flagellation as a final effort to ward off the disease…perhaps it worked.

The Witches' scourge is quite a bit milder than the early Christian versions and is quite "fluffy" compared to the ancient Roman scourge. Instead of being made of metal and knotted with hooks, rocks, and bones, it usually is now in the form of a relatively soft cat-of-nine-tails, and is *not* designed to tear flesh and punish heretics! The tails of a Witches' scourge can be made of leather, faux leather, or thick string. A number of knots can be tied in each string, each holding the energy of a different blessing the person being scourged should receive.

For modern Witches, scourging is also used as a tool to exorcise demons, diseases, and malignancies from someone, and a quick cleansing smack of the scourge is a requirement to enter the sacred circle for some Witches. While most Witches do not use the scourge in ritual to cause pain, some do. In traditional initiation rituals, the scourge is used to induce a small amount of sharp, momentary pain to remind the initiate of the vulnerability of the physical body and to increase blood flow to strengthen a trance. Being scourged also is believed to purify the soul. Many Witches choose not to use the scourge because of its common sadomasochistic associations—then again, most of us darksiders probably see no better reason than that *to* use it!

Scrying Mirror

The scrying mirror ("black mirror"), a close cousin to the crystal ball, is a tool favored by dark Witches and those who have natural divinatory abilities. The mirror can be purchased from an occult supplier or created by the magician him- or herself. The mirror is slightly reflective and black in color to act as a doorway or portal to the Otherworlds. Spirits can be contacted through this device, or issues of a person's past, present, or future can be focused on. Insight is gained through symbolism the diviner perceives on the mirror's surface. It's best to gaze at the mirror in a candlelit room with no images reflected on the surface.

Many practitioners keep the scrying mirror far and away from direct sunlight. This makes it completely attuned to nighttime energies and allows the item to be more connected with energies of a shadowed nature, aiding the process of divination. The mirror can be kept on the altar, either shrouded or visible, so divination can be performed during any nocturnal ritual. The black mirror and other similar divinatory devices most often are used in Esbats or during Sabbats attuned to scrying, like Samhain and the autumnal equinox.

Sword

The sword has magickal associations similar to the those of the athamé, but it is much larger in design. Thus it is used for harnessing greater amounts of energy and is the ultimate weapon of control within a magick circle. The sword can be seen as an amplified combination of the athamé and wand. Some Witches prefer to cast larger circles with the sword because of its length and visible durability. The sword often is used instead of the athamé for large magickal workings like global magick and weatherworking.

In some types of high magickal evocation, the weapon is used to banish and command spirits. Solomon and other classical magicians are said to have used swords in their magick for spiritual defense, assuming the item was imbued with just as much astral oomph as physical strength. Swords were made primarily of iron, a material that is believed to halt astral beings in their tracks and promote energetic nullification. In modern Wiccan terms, the item is used more for public theatrics and large-scale workings with specific alterations in mind.

Symbolism

The following symbols are some that I have noticed Goths prefer to wear as pendants and incorporate into their makeup application. All of these symbols have occult significance and can be used in magick and meditation.

Studying the symbolism of each item helps the practitioner tap into the energy that has been imbued in the shape over the course of time. Each symbol has its own astral essence that is accessible directly to anyone incorporating symbolism in magickal applications. Even the act of wearing a pendant, patch, or button in the shape of a sacred symbol imbues the wearer with its qualities. These qualities can be carried throughout the day by wearing the symbol or by using it for specific metaphysical purposes in ritual, with the symbol worn on the body or placed about the room as a point of focus.

Pendants bearing any of these symbols can be enchanted in accordance with both their symbolic attributes and the metals they are cast in. I will cover magickal associations with various metals in my second book, *Shadow Magick Compendium*.

Ankh

Egyptian deities often are depicted with ankhs in their hands. This symbol represents reincarnation and balance between the two polarities. The vertical handle is phallic, representing the masculine, while the ovular top piece is vaginal and represents the feminine. To practitioners of Egyptian magick, the vaginal portion is representative of Isis and the phallic portion is representative of her lover Osiris. Isis and Osiris are the mother and father gods of the Egyptian pantheon. The word *ankh* means "life," and the object serves as a talisman of protection and fertility. Early Coptic Christians used the *crux ansata*, which is akin to the ankh but usually is depicted as a bit wider and often shorter. Crux ansata basically translates to "cross with a handle," and symbolically it carries the same associations as the ankh.

Chaos Star

The chaos star represents chaos as a natural part of the workings of the world. The symbol is a variation of British author Michael Moorcock's "Banner of Chaos," popularized in his fantasy novels, and consists of two arrowed crosses placed atop one another, forming eight points emerging from a central intersection.

To the Greeks, Chronos was the god of time. It is believed that chaos sprang from Chronos at the dawn of creation.

Pan Gu, the creator god of Chinese mythology, is portrayed holding the "Cosmic Egg of Chaos," which actually is in the form of a yin-yang rather than a chaos star. My friend Eric, a Taoist chaos-punk of sorts, has a tattoo of the chaos star with a yin-yang on the intersection of the points. To him, this represents the balance of chaos and order in the natural world and is an affirmation that spiritual truth lies in paradox and divine dichotomy.

Cross

The symbol of the cross actually predates Christianity by many thousands of years. Variations of the traditional cross date back to prehistoric times, spanning numerous cultures around the world. Each culture ascribed its own meaning to the symbol, having associations particularly with balance, change, protection, luck, and wellness.

The traditional cross is commonly used in Christianity. In it, the vertical line is longer at the bottom than the horizontal line. Apart from representing crucifixion, it represents grounding and personal empowerment. The longest end can connect a wearer or user to the earth, and the other three ends connect to divinity as represented as maiden, mother, and crone or son, father, and sage.

Because of the cross's associations with the union of two polarities, variations of it long have been used as talismans of protection and balance. Each line represents an equal-opposite, the intersection being a balance of the two. Also, the four ends represent the four cardinal directions and four elements, both of which are recognized in the Craft.

The oldest and most earth-based cross is called the equal-armed cross, in which both the horizontal and vertical lines are equal in length. This is the most balanced of the crosses, representing metaphysical alignment and the balance of equal-opposite polarities. If drawn in a circle, the equal-armed cross becomes the astrological symbol of the planet earth. Thus, the symbol can be used for grounding and attunement to nature.

Though a few Goths like to wear inverted Christian crosses for their own reasons, Pagans generally don't wear the symbol upside down. To do so is seen as disrespectful to another group of people, just as someone wearing an inverted pentagram without understanding its meaning is seen as disrespectful to Pagans. The symbol most closely resembling the inverted cross commonly used in Paganism (heathenry, in particular) is Thor's Hammer, representing the power and strength of the Norse god.

Eye of the Dragon

The eye of the dragon represents, of course, draconic energy. Dragons represent power and protection, and this symbol can be drawn on an item, on the ground, or on doors or other pieces of property to imbue them with a boost of power and protection. Because of the eye associations, as well as the angular structure of the symbol itself, the eye of the dragon also can represent harsh and direct spiritual sight. With the point down, it's used to invoke energy; with the point up, it's used to send energy forth.

The symbol is Greek in origin. A variation of this symbol is the eye of fire, which is a diamond shape with slashes connecting the angles. Very little is known about this symbol except that the early Greeks used it for spiritual purposes. The eye of the dragon also is representative of the holy trinity—which is portrayed in innumerable forms across cultures—and can be applied to Pagan systems. Because the points are connected, the symbol represents the coming together of these three forces of reality.

Eye of Horus

The Eye of Horus invokes the mysteries of ancient Egypt. Traditionally, the Eye of Horus is the moon and is portrayed as the left eye. If shown as the right eye, it is the Eye of Ra, representing the sun. Both designs are ideal for Egyptian ritual magick and communion with the old ones of the black land. The painted form of the Eye of Horus is called the *wedjat*, representative of the falcon god's omniscience. Egyptians used the Eyes of Horus and Ra in the forms of paintings, carvings, and amulets.

At one time in Egyptian history, Horus and Ra were nearly identical deities, and their "all-seeing eyes" became associated with wisdom and spiritual clarity, much like the Buddhist Eyes of Truth. Both the Eye of Horus and the Eye of Ra stand as prominent symbols in the ancient Egyptian spiritual system.

Hexagram

The hexagram is truly the embodiment of the words "as above, so below," a variation of a philosophy in Hermeticism that later was adopted into Wicca in the mid-twentieth century. The hexagram also is akin to the Tibetan Buddhist *vajra* or *dorje*. This symbol represents supreme spiritual wisdom being balanced with mundane living, an integration of the highest and the lowest aspects of our own being.

In Judaism, the hexagram is called the Star of David, which often is misinterpreted as the pentagram and vice versa. The hexagram and pentagram do have similarities, but because of the hexagram's sixth point, a number of new associations are drawn. The traditional hexagram appears as the lying atop of two triangles, one upright and one inverted. When laid atop one another, lines appear across the empty triangles. The Hermetic alchemical symbols for the four elements traditionally are drawn in triangles. The Earth triangle is inverted with a horizontal line through it, the Air triangle is upright with a horizontal line through it, the Fire triangle is upright and empty, and the Water triangle is inverted and empty. When these symbols come together, the result is the hexagram, the embodiment of all elements put into a single symbolic form.

Additionally, each point of the hexagram represents a different planet utilized in ancient magickal systems: the Moon, Mercury, Venus, Mars, Jupiter, and Saturn. Finally, the sun rests in the center of the symbol. The hexagram often is drawn with the planetary symbols at each point.

Hexagram (Unicursal)

The unicursal hexagram is nearly the same as the traditional hexagram but differs because of a central point at which two lines intersect. This point represents the sun, and the other points represent the planets that rotate around this central point. This point represents not only the sun but also the magician him- or herself as the constructor of reality through magickal means.

I like to call the unicursal hexagram the *neo-hexagram*. It has a very modern, even electric, feel about it, and it can be drawn without removing the pen from the paper (or athamé from the air), unlike the traditional hexagram. This is where the word *unicursal* comes from: *uni* means "one," and *cursal* means "movement." The symbol was created by Aleister Crowley and is used most often by Thelemites today. A magician is able to draw the symbol in ritual with a wand, athamé, or fingers with a few quick, continual motions. Thus, it is especially useful when using invoking and banishing hexagrams during the quarter calls in ritual magick.

Lemniscate

One of the most powerful and best-known spiritual symbols of all time is the lemniscate. Also called the infinity knot, the symbol looks like the number 8 turned on its side. Like the circle, it represents the flow of all things—life, death, rebirth, and the fluctuation of reality including the tides of nature. It is drawn without pausing, just like the circle, but instead of having a circular shape, the figure is twisted into two ends, representing the polarity present in all things—yin and yang, if you will.

Like the yin-yang, the lemniscate represents the flowing nature of existence and is comparable to the Ouroboros, the image of the snake swallowing its own tail. Both hint at the fact that, regardless of what we may think, nothing ever dies or is born; all things in life simply *change*.

Moon

For Goths, the moon represents the beauty of night and serves as a reminder of the blessings the dark hours bestow upon us. Because we are connected innately to the nocturnal tide, the moon is the epicenter of our darker inclinations.

Since the earliest times, the moon symbolically has represented change. All aspects of change and transmutation have gained associations with this symbol because of its constantly shifting nature. This includes things like alterations in mood, death and rebirth, crop growth, seasonal shifts, and ocean tides. The moon also represents the mysteries of the blood through the menstrual cycle. Because women bleed alongside the moon's changes, the moon always has held associations with femininity and thus the Great Goddess. The triple moon represents the three phases of the Goddess in Witchcraft: the maiden (waxing), the mother (full), and the crone (waning). This probably is Greek in origin, having to do with the triplicate goddess Hecate. Numerous ancient cultures associated feminine deities with the moon, though some chose to ascribe male deities because of associations with hunting under the moon's light.

Pentagram and Pentacle

Wearing fancy pentagrams and pentacles is popular in both Goth and Pagan culture. Unfortunately, many people wear them for all the wrong reasons. Some people wear the five-pointed star to appear to be "spooky" or "evil," which is quite an insult to its original sacred symbolism. These people have bought into the idea that the circled star is a malicious or Satanic symbol and employ the image many uninformed Christians love to hate. In actuality, the pentagram has *never* been an evil symbol, as I'm sure nearly everyone reading this book already understands. In fact, early Christians used the symbol (likely adopted from Greek, Egyptian, or Græco-Egyptian sacred geometry) to represent both the five wounds of the Christ and the Star of Bethlehem. Yes, modern Satanists (who are different from "devil worshippers") use the inverted pentagram with Baphomet's head in the center. This was created by occultist Eliphas Lévi in his portrayal of the early European god Baphomet and had no Satanic associations (aside from the Church's) until modern times.

There is a long-standing debate regarding whether "pentagram" or "pentacle" is technically the correct term. Most Witches simply refer to their symbol as a *pentacle* only in order to avoid negative associations attached to the word *pentagram*, which some believe refers to a five-pointed star with a single point down. In actuality, the star itself is called the pentagram, while the circled star or altarpiece is called the pentacle. Additionally, the altar pentacle is called the *pantacle* in some high magickal traditions, signifying the element of Earth, and is used in Witchcraft with similar associations. The spelling depends on the translation and variation of the word.

A magickal practitioner is able to access higher states of consciousness and invoke divine guidance when using the symbol with the point upward. When the point is upward, it represents connection to the Upperworld, and when downward, a connection to the Underworld. In traditional Gardnerian Witchcraft, the inverted pentagram is used in second-degree initiation rites to symbolize the initiate's "going inward" and applying magickal wisdom to his or her life from then on.

No one can trace the definitive source of the symbol, but there are speculations that it originated in early Mesopotamia. In early Greece, the five-pointed star was called the *pentalpha*, referring to the five points that make up the symbol. Pythagoras used the symbol in his magickal order (c. 500 BCE) to symbolize purity and perfection. His initiates were said to wear a ring bearing the emblem to represent unity both among the members and with the universe itself. It also served as a mark of identification of the members. The Druids also used to wear pentagrams on their sandals; the Germans appropriately called this *Druttenfuss* (Druid's Foot), which eventually became translated as "Witch's Foot." In the seventeenth century, the Freemasons adopted the use of the symbol in their system to represent deity.

The pentagram represents all reality, interwoven and often bound with a circle. It is sometimes called the Star of Venus, as the planet Venus orbits the pattern of a pentagram in the night sky. The pentagram long has been used as a protective symbol, attracting positive energies and warding off demons, sorcery, and other maliciousness. In the story of Sir Gawain and the Green Knight, the main character's red shield is decorated with a golden pentagram for empowerment and protection in his endeavors. In this case, the points of the symbol stand for the five knightly virtues: friendship, generosity, courtesy, chastity, and piety.

And then, of course, the pentagram represents the five elements of Paganism, where traditionally the right-hand point represents Water, the bottom-right point Fire, the bottom-left point Earth, and the left-hand point Air. Finally, the uppermost point represents Spirit, ether, or God(dess). This "fifth element" binds the essence of the other four together, making the symbol complete and alive. The five points stand for the five physical senses, and the circle represents the sixth. The symbol stands for the human being: the bottom points correspond to the legs, the outer points the arms, and the top point the head. This can be seen in Leonardo da Vinci's *Vitruvian Man* painting. On a smaller scale, the pentagram represents the five fingers or five toes of the human being. These are some of the primary associations with the pentagram, but there exist additional correlations depending on the tradition or practitioner's personal point of view.

Skull and Bones

The skull and bones reminds us of the inevitability of death by representing change and our innermost self. In the human body, the bones correspond to the element of Earth; they are the core of our human experience. It's best to utilize this symbol with the focus of laying an aspect of the self to rest. I'd even go so far as to say it should be reserved *only* for the waning moon, Sabbats of the dying year, or performing magick of releasing (and thus death). Otherwise, it has the potential of attracting energies opposite to the vibrations being cultivated at the time.

The skull is a symbol of vitality because it's the most resistant part of the body to the process of decay. It also has been seen as the seat of intelligence, because the brain is held within. In Mediæval and Renaissance art, various saints and holy people were depicted as holding skulls, reminding the viewer of the vanity of the physical world, a *memento mori* reminding us that our time on earth is short and we mustn't be distracted by temporary pleasures of the flesh.

The symbol of the skull resting atop crossed thighbones was adopted by pirates and used on the Jolly Roger flag. It symbolized their strength and ruthlessness. The symbol also was adopted by Freemasons around the eighteenth century to represent the death of the ego in return for spiritual understanding and gain, and as such was used as a representative focal tool to strengthen the process of defeating the ego.

Tetragrammaton

A less common variation of the traditional pentagram is the Tetragrammaton, as laid out in this particular pattern. The word Tetragrammaton is Greek, meaning "word of four letters," and refers to the Judaic or Qabalistic "name of God." The four letters YHVH are placed in the symbol, usually in their original Hebrew script. This is pronounced "Yod-Heh-Vav-Heh," or Yahweh. Older traditions translate and pronounce the Hebrew word as Jehovah.

In older times, tradition held that if "YHVH" was written on an item, it was not to be destroyed or desecrated in any way. The letters themselves were said to imbue the object on which they were written with the essence of God, thus sanctifying the item as a holy piece. Many Jewish traditionalists, ancient and modern, do not pronounce the word whatsoever, so as to not desecrate the sacred name. The Torah, the Hebrew canonical text, consists of the first five scriptures of the Old Testament. In these writings, the name of God is substituted with Adonai, or Lord, which is read in place of the sacred name. To the Witch, any of the above names of God are aligned to what many earth-based magicians call Spirit: the essence of All That Is. Esoteric Qabalists

The Hebrew Name of God

and many Qabalah-influenced Witches additionally associate each letter with a different major manifestation of the Qabalistic levels of existence (Atziluth, Briah, Yetzirah, and Assiah), as well as with the four directions, the four elements, and the four suits of the Tarot.

The Tetragrammaton simply refers to the four Hebrew letters, and the symbol portrayed here is "that plus more," creating an enhanced representation of the energies portrayed in the letters. Planetary and other esoteric symbols are encompassed in this version of the Tetragrammaton, forming a profound and powerful representation of universal light. If drawn, worn, or used as an altarpiece in magick, it should have personal significance to the magician and should not be used lightly.

Triquetra

The triquetra, also called the *triquetrous*, means "three-cornered." It has been popularized in the last decade because of its Witchy use in the television show *Charmed*. The symbol is Celtic in origin but has gained associations with the Triple Goddess (maiden, mother, and crone) and Triple God (son, father, and sage). Numerous ancient traditions held associations with the trinity, all of which were religious, presenting three different sides of the divine. This was further divided into different, more humanistic associations like birth, age, and death; morning, midday, and night. Early Christianity took the symbol for its own use, ascribing the associations of the Father, Son, and Holy Ghost for means of conversion.

Some Witches of an Eastern esoteric persuasion even ascribe the Hindu trinity of Brahma, Vishnu, and Shiva to the symbol. The triquetra can be viewed additionally as a fertility symbol, with each corner representing a different portion of the mammalian reproductive system: the uterus and two ovaries as well as the penis and two testes.

The triquetra is a knotted form of the triangle and is often interwoven with a perfect circle in the middle. The representations are similar, yet have variations from culture to culture. Though the triquetra is Celtic in origin, it may simply have been a knotted variation of the Judaic/Hermetic triangle. It's also believed that it came about as a variation of the Celtic *triskele*, also used on armor by the Greeks. The triskele appears as three bent (running) legs coming together at one central axis. To the Celts and Greeks, this presumably referred to the physical prowess of the groups' warriors. This later morphed into the triskelion knot, which may have been the blueprint for the triquetra.

Building Protection

Dark Witches, and indeed Witches of all sorts, are sensitive creatures on many levels. We are aware of a multitude of energies all around us and tend to be more susceptible to their influences than the average person, simply because we know of their existence. Because Witches and magicians also practice magick, a great amount of energy is raised that has the possibility of attracting harmful forces. For these reasons, constant energetic protection is a *necessity* for any practitioner of the arts. This doesn't mean that we perpetually should be paranoid or expecting attack, but that we should have our shields intact "just in case." Goddess knows the cycles of life are trying; a little energetic protection doesn't hurt in the daily grind!

Through magick, we can construct energetic shields around ourselves to ward off both conscious and nonconscious energetic bombardments, be they psychological, emotional, or spiritual. Even the act of placing protection around the self has a nonconscious effect of steering the body clear of harm's way, possibly avoiding even physical attack. If the higher self is fully protected, it naturally will steer the lower selves, including the physical body, away from situations that would harmfully penetrate one's sphere.

The Circle

Some books on Witchcraft teach that a magick circle must be cast before attempting any form of magick or energy work, like meditation, visualization, or aura cleansing. I disagree. I find the circle to be extremely beneficial when working high or intense magickal procedures, but find it unnecessary—in the formal sense anyway—when performing spontaneous or minor work.

Hedge craft and folk magick differ from occultism in that they often are improvised, relying on intuition and the visible cycles of nature. Occultism and Hermetic mysticism tend to be based more on disciplined traditionalism and memorized ritual to manifest acute energies. Certainly, Wicca and other forms of Witchcraft now integrate elements of both methods (sometimes called "high" and "low" magick).

Some people are overly fearful of magickal attack and spend more time building the circle than performing the ritual. An exaggerated fear of attack can come from past experiences or assumptions about the danger of magick. It can be a good practice to fortify a space, but more often than not, the danger of actually performing a ritual is less than it's worked up to be. The amount of protection to be built depends on the ritual itself.

There is an infinite number of methods of casting a circle and creating a protective space. Play with different methods and see which works best for you; intuition is the best guide. Cast a circle when you deem it appropriate, whether it be for every working or only for Sabbats. It's common to use a variety of tools, chants, and words of power to help the process along. It's traditional to asperge the area with consecrated salt water, conduct energy with an athamé, and sometimes walk the boundary of the circle deosil with a representation of each element in hand. This helps consecrate the space and put the practitioner in a magickal state of mind. The space becomes a solid structure where esoteric activities are to be undertaken.

Circle casting may have its roots in ancient Assyrian magick; their baked clay tablets actually describe a procedure for securing a circular sacred space. They may have gotten this idea from the Egyptians, whom they conquered in 671 BCE. Circle casting is a common method of building a protective barrier—a rampart of protection—in both Witchcraft and other magickal paths, and it's difficult to determine its precise origin.

The circle is the most universal of all sacred symbols and has significance in numerous spiritual cultures. The circle represents the all—the continuous cycle of life, death, and rebirth—as well as smaller changes like waking and dreaming, eating and excreting, and inhaling and exhaling. It represents all of eternity and the whole of the universe. To early Greeks, the circle was the most perfect symbol, from which all things emanate. The planets themselves are circular in shape, as are many microscopic structures in the body. When this symbol is solidified around the body, energy inside is amplified and all thoughts, deeds, and actions held within become a sacred metaphor.

Widdershins: The Inner Sanctum

I find it appropriate to include a mention of widdershins in a book that examines the darker shades of Paganism. Widdershins refers to the casting of a magick circle of protection in a nontraditional way. Many Neopagans actually fear casting the circle widdershins (anticlockwise), because casting the circle deosil (clockwise) is traditional. Most Pagan books and teachers won't explain the ramifications of doing so. While casting deosil is the norm, and is extremely successful for solidifying an energetic barrier of protection, casting the circle widdershins also has its benefits.

Widdershins castings have their own appropriate time and place. Meditating on the subject, one can begin to understand the essence of widdershins. With a deosil-cast circle, the energy is spiraled upward, drawing on the energy of the Upperworld. For solar Sabbats and full moons, a deosil casting may be appropriate. Which direction the circle is cast depends on what types of magick or celebratory activities are to take place in the circle.

The ideal times to cast a circle widdershins are during the dark Sabbats, especially Samhain. Another good time is at the dark moon, when darkness is just waiting to be utilized and understood. Just beware—the gateways are very much open. Scrying and meditation are almost essential activities to perform in a widdershins circle. Because widdershins is the opposite of deosil, it represents reversal. Casting a circle widdershins is excellent for a banishing or releasing spell. If magick must ever be "undone" or a spell must be broken, this is the best type of circle to do so in. If a cursing or hexing must be performed, and let's hope that it doesn't, a widdershins circle is appropriate. Deep scrying also is especially powerful in a widdershins circle, as is any deep introspective personal work aimed at innermost transformation, that is, if the practitioner is willing to face his or her darkest side.

One can cast a widdershins circle before communicating with darker deities or before spells of banishment, like the dissolution of sadness. A widdershins casting allows the Witch to enter into the realm of shadows. The archetypal Dark Goddess and Dark God can be met in a widdershins-cast circle. Call them forth into the space to witness your rites of change, perhaps by using the Call to the Dark Mother and Call to the Dark Father at the beginning of this book. A coven or group of practitioners can even do a widdershins spiral dance at Samhain or the autumnal equinox, or at another time attuned to energetic release, to banish the unwanted to the ether.

In his brilliant book *Dark Moon Mysteries*, Timothy Roderick says that Witches dance the widdershins spiral at Samhain to honor a reversing cycle, moving spiritual energy out of physical form, thus aligning with the process of dying or releasing. He says that Neopagan spiritual systems celebrate the energy of death as a sacred transition, the energy of which is directly accessed in the widdershins spiral.

If one works with shadow magick, it is essential to experiment carefully with widdershins castings. They are the key to entering the Underworld and working with dark energies of any sort, whether internal or external. Working widdershins helps the dark Witch to more fully understand all aspects of the divine, both light and dark. Because of its Underworldly implications, a widdershins circle *must* be mapped out carefully; it has the potential of bringing the caster face to face with his or her own dark side. For some, this could be a nervous breakdown waiting to happen. For those who are ready, facing the shadow self can be a most beneficial healing experience.

Regardless of which direction a circle is cast, protection will be in place if enough intention is given to the process. Just be sure to say the usual words of power before, during, and after the casting process, and perform exercises that further secure the space as sacred. It's easy to feel that proper protection is not in place when working widdershins. If it is more comfortable to you, create a solid deosil circle before creating a smaller widdershins circle in the center of the traditional one. This provides balance, and can add an extra measure of security if done properly. In other words, don't negate the energy of the solid deosil circle by performing a widdershins casting; map the specific boundary line of the internal widdershins circle so its energy doesn't cross over into the deosil circle, thus possibly creating uncontrollable chaos.

I don't recommend that you experiment with a widdershins circle unless you are being trained to do so by someone with legitimate experience, or if you have been actively studying and practicing the magickal arts for at least five years and are both familiar and comfortable with the energetic makeup of a traditional circle.

A sweeping of the space should always precede casting the circle widdershins. To sweep a space before casting a circle is to remove stagnant energies and prepare the area for magick. The most common way to do so is with a besom (broom) charged for that purpose. Some Witches like to sprinkle black salt or black sand on the space so that it may be swept physically. The sand or salt absorbs further vibrations and is swept out of the space along with the stagnant energy.

I've found the widdershins circle to be most successful *within* a traditionally cast deosil circle. While the deosil circle serves as a rampart and solid sphere of protection, the inner widdershins circle simply takes the externally existing energy and spirals it in the opposite direction within. Instead of there being two solid ramparts, the inner circle builds on the outer. A traditional Witches' circle is nine feet in diameter; in this case, the widdershins circle should be built three feet in diameter at the center of the deosil circle.

Once the regular clockwise circle has been cast, the widdershins circle can be cast by raising and spiraling energy within, first inviting the Watchtowers as you normally would, just in the opposite order, standing at the edge of the internal circle being built. The elements now can be invited into the inner sanctum to lend their energies to this space within a space, and any deities being worked with can be called forth to mind the rite. You now can take your athamé or casting device, and spiral the inner circle counterclockwise, as the antithesis of the external rampart.

Once the widdershins circle has been built, say something like, "The inner sanctum is cast and serves as a spiral of protection in the names of the Dark God and Dark Goddess as I now weave this shadow magick." Follow with ritualistic activities appropriate to a widdershins circle, like banishing harmful emotions, etc., into a central source. If doing a releasing spell, it's best to keep in the center either a cauldron or a "banishing" effigy, into which unwanted energies can be directed. That way, the spiraling energy has an item to enter into. However, *do not stand in the center* of a widdershins circle. The widdershins circle follows the black hole principle: it sucks like a vacuum. You may end up inadvertently absorbing a variety of energetic vibrations, especially the stuff you aim to release! Be *very mindful* of the presence of the vacuous inner sanctum, and understand that it is a temporary second circle designed to banish, banish, banish.

When the circle is to be released, bring it down as you normally would, except walk *deosil* to ground it, releasing the elements in the opposite direction as invoked. I like to respectfully "push" the elements back from the widdershins circle, outside to the greater deosil circle or previously cleansed space. Say, "May the circle be open, never broken. So mote it be." Then close the external deosil circle as usual.

Protective Shields

Following is a list of a few of the more common energetic shields of protection, also called odic shields. Shields of protection can be constructed through visualization—

contemplate the variants of shields and carefully decide which is most beneficial for your own path. You also should determine how long you need the shield to last. More extreme shields, like the brick and iron walls, should be kept up only for as long as needed, perhaps only for the duration of a ritual. Keeping them up longer than necessary can cause serious disassociation between the magician and the outside world. Shields should be built between one and three feet outside the physical body, ensuring that the shield's energy will stay on the perimeters of the caster's own energy instead of fusing to it.

Brick Wall Shield: Used for introspection and serious protection. This is ideal for personal energy work, but beware that any energy released must have a way out.

Crystal Sphere Shield: Probably the best form of energetic protection for everyday life. This solidifies the magician in a crystal sphere, forcing harmful vibrations to be reflected and beneficial ones to enter. This should be maintained regularly.

Iron Wall Shield: Used only in cases of extreme psychic or energetic attack. This wall completely isolates the magician so no energy can penetrate or escape. This should not be maintained outside of a magick circle.

Light Shield: Used to keep the aura clean and project spiritual light to anyone. This method is relatively harmless. It can be used every day for spiritual alignment and is especially balancing for those who wear black clothes.

Mirror Shield: Used to reflect any possible attack, purposeful or not. It may be tailored to reflect only harmful vibrations and allow beneficial ones to enter. The biggest risks are reflecting necessary external energy and losing personal vital force as a result of energetic isolation.

Shroud of Invisibility: Used to render the magician invisible to other people or entities, especially within the magick circle. This is used by the Golden Dawn system of magick, and many Witches and magicians use temporary shrouds of invisibility in their daily lives. Longer-lasting shields such as these require intense energetic work to construct and maintain.

Tree Shield: Used to connect the magician to the power of the trees, whose roots are grounded deep beneath the earth and whose branches extend upward to the heavens. This can be considered Druidic or shamanic in nature and connects one's energy to the Upperworld (branches) and the Underworld (roots). It is best used in creative visualization practices within a magick circle; in other words, you'll want to keep rooted!

The Witch Bottle

The whole idea of a Witch bottle sounds vulgar to the average person. It's a pretty bizarre concoction, but it sure serves its purpose: *absolute protection*. Even in comparison to most Wiccan spells, this method seems strangely dark. The use of Witch bottles has been common practice through the ages. They have been found buried beneath doorsteps and near the hearths and fireplaces of old cottages, particularly in England. They date to the sixteenth and seventeenth centuries. This method of protection is just as powerful now as it was in old times. If you feel like someone or something is directing harm toward you, this bottle will be helpful in adding protection regardless of whether you recognize the source of the attack. It also is beneficial to create this bottle as a preparation for the possibility of future troubles or if you fear energetic invasion for any reason.

The spell is said to be broken only when the bottle breaks. Therefore, the maker must examine the bottle to be used, inside and out, to make sure there are no cracks in it and determine that the glass is thick enough to not break with heavy contents inside. The bottle itself can be as small as a baby food jar or as large as an economy-sized pickle jar, and the glass may be colored or clear. Do keep in mind that eventually it will be filled with urine and traditionally is buried or kept on a dark shelf. An oversized jar may be problematic if the bottle is designed only for you. If it's for a coven or household of Witches, a larger jar may be ideal. Again, check the bottle for cracks; if it breaks in the house, the results won't exactly be pretty or sweet to smell.

Align the bottle's energy to your own by adding ousia, like hair, blood, fingernail clippings, saliva, and sexual fluids. Your energy also becomes aligned to all the ingredients and will help you powerfully enchant the bottle. Because your essence is included in the bottle through your DNA, you must be certain to craft the spell with precision. What you ask for is what you get in terms of the bottle's usage. All of the ingredients are designed to catch harmful energies directed at your person and reflect them accordingly, either back to the sender or to the universe to etherealize the harm.

Suggestions for ingredients are listed at the end of this section. You also may add a small piece of paper rolled up with markings on it. Markings can include your written magickal name, your personal sigil, magickal symbols, or anything that represents your "being protected." It's good to draw personal sigils in the middle of an Ouroboros (the snake swallowing its own tail) to represent continuous protection through the cycles of life. It is preferable to add a boost of power by writing on a new sheet of parchment paper with "dragon's blood" ink, or any other natural ink if this is not available. Also, it's best that the bottle be created and enchanted within a traditional magick circle.

It's a good idea to include a couple of "light" ingredients in the spell to balance the energies so that the bottle isn't entirely dark. You can add an herb, a charm, a few drops of essential oil, or anything else that you feel is balancing. This will keep the bottle from being too weighted in dense vibrations. A good example of an herb to use is sage, which cleanses and neutralizes excessive energy. As with the darker components, state your intention when adding the ingredient(s) for balance, perhaps intending that the harm directed to you be surrounded with light and peace after being reflected and that it may have the opportunity to evolve in consciousness.

As a final ingredient, the maker's urine must be added. In the past, urine was used for a variety of purposes, including gaining control over an individual or situation, to shed negativity, to protect property, and to bind spells. Its addition to the Witch bottle draws on all of these associations. It is best to add morning urine to the jar, as the liquid would have sat in your body overnight, strongly collecting your essence. The bottle must be filled to the brim—depending on the size, this might take all day! To add even more power to this, you can drink before bedtime a specific, magickally charged tea whose ingredients are attuned to protection. The best protection teas are chamomile, mugwort, yarrow, peppermint, or a combination of these herbs. The tea's ingredients also should be charged according to your intention. After having been processed through your body, the urine will both carry the essence of the tea's magick and be attuned to the maker. Very powerful.

After charging the bottle in circle, the top should be sealed with black wax or electrical tape. The bottle should be either buried in the earth on your property or put somewhere out of sight like in the back of a closet. If you bury it, make sure the hole is fairly deep so natural soil corrosion and frost won't interrupt the spell. If kept in your house, it should be out of reach from children and animals and may be wrapped in black cloth to seal residual energy and increase the protection. This also will conceal the bottle should a curious visitor stop by and catch a glance of the kooky concoction.

Possible ingredients for a Witch bottle include "bat's blood" ink, black salt, black sand, shards of CDs or records, claws, eggshells, shards of glass or mirrors, graveyard dirt, nails, needles, pins, shards of porcelain, razors, sharp rocks, rust, safety pins, screws, and tacks. Herbs that might be used include belladonna, cat's claw, cloves, cumin, devil's shoestring, garlic, ginger, hawthorn, henbane, mandrake, mullein, nettle, nightshade, peppercorns, peppers, rosemary, Solomon's seal root, thorns, tobacco, twigs, and valerian.

The Lemon House Charm

Another protection spell high up there on the "spooky" list is the lemon house charm. This spell is notably appealing to the dark Witch because of its eerie look and magickal effectiveness. Also called the "pincushion lemon" or "industrial lemon," the spell is designed to draw harmful energies into the fruit through the use of pins as energetic conduits. It's fun to create a lemon house charm with your coven or another group of practitioners within a magick circle. The spell is simple and effective and is definitely visually appealing.

Pick or purchase a fresh lemon and a number of long pins; you should reserve about 200–300 pins per fruit. Enchant the pins with the purpose of conducting energy, and the lemon with the purpose of energetic absorption. A note on citruses: oranges represent the sun, while lemons represent the moon. For this reason, it's best to perform the lemon spell at night by candlelight, preferably during a full moon, so as to invite lunar energy into the working. Also, for added potency, use numerology to calculate the number of pins you plan on inserting.

Once inside a magick circle, begin the spell. Call the elements and deities as you normally would. Once under way, take a pin and say the words, "Negative energy to *here* instead of me." Every time you say the word *here*, push a pin into the lemon. Continue this for quite some time until the lemon is considerably full of pins. Once all the pins have been used, take black yarn or something similar and work it around the lemon, tying the yarn at both ends. Be sure to leave some amount of yarn at the top to allow it to hang from a nail somewhere in the house (like over the bed, doorway, or sink). Lemon house charms also make excellent Yuletide gifts, so if the spell is designed with another person in mind, replace the word *me* with the name of the person on whom you are focusing the protection when reciting the words of power. Be sure to keep the charm out of the reach of children and animals.

Over time, the lemon will harden and turn black. After about a year, the lemon will have absorbed all the energy it can take and must be discarded. When this time comes, remove the pins, wash them, and smudge them—they can be used in another spell once cleansed. Bury the lemon in the ground so the earth can take the icky energy far, far away. Then create another lemon house charm to carry you through the next year.

This spell is a variation of the Stregherian (Italian Witchcraft) tradition of gifting lemon charms as household blessings to ensure good fortune. The original version is explained in *Aradia, or the Gospel of the Witches* by Charles Godfrey Leland, which was written at the turn of the twentieth century. The text has become the cornerstone of Italian Witchcraft and is revered as a channeled document of Aradia, a supposed four-teenth-century woman later viewed as a demigoddess or female messiah who was sent to earth from higher planes to teach the arts of Witchery.

The first part of chapter 5 of the *Gospel* is called the "Conjuration of the Lemon and Pins," explaining that a lemon stuck with pins whose heads are of various colors always ensures good fortune for the person who is gifted with the charm. It says that if any of the pins has a black head, then happiness and prosperity will manifest, but with some amount of trouble. If you follow the traditional system, never buy black-headed pins when intending the charm as a gift. On the other hand, if you make a charm for your own home, perhaps you will choose black pins because the color is associated with protection. Personally, I have found multicolored pins to be perfect for gifting lemon charms and believe pins without colored heads (pure steel) to be perfect for personal charms. Experiment and see what works best for you…the results are übercool.

VII
The Death Current

Death is a fascinating topic. Both Pagan spirituality and dark culture touch death energy regularly to one degree or another. Earth-worshipping Witches and magicians honor the death of the season and the mirroring death of internal energies. When the season dies and when the moon wanes (thus the solar and lunar dying tides), personal energy one wishes to banish can be attached at will, aligning the psyche and the spirit to nature's death cycle.

Goths often are mistakenly accused of having an obsession with death. It's true that darksiders are more willing to contemplate the topic, reflecting on its reality and psychological implications, but it's rare that one becomes unhealthily infatuated with death. In a sense, many Goth types "dress as death" in a sort of corpselike or mournful fashion. On an energetic level, this subconsciously (or perhaps consciously, in the case of the magician) brushes death energy. Even natural occurrences like deep sorrow and reflection can pull a person into the abyss, touching the subtle planes beyond the immediate world.

Death energy is nothing to fear. Indeed, it is to be revered for its constant perplexity. This final chapter of *Goth Craft* will explore some topics undoubtedly of interest to practitioners of shadow magick. First, the topic of blood will be explored, followed by an obligatory entry on vampyrism, concluding with a study of the realms of death and the numinous practice of necromancy.

Blood Magick

Bloodwork is most certainly a part of shadow magick and dark Witchcraft, but is *not* something to be taken lightly or to be performed without caution and awareness.

Being introspective people, dark Witches are not averse to the prospect of shedding their own blood for serious ritual work that can produce actual change in one's own state of being. Although blood magick may freak out some magickal practitioners, dark Witches find it to be a natural, strong element of high-energy work. In fact, many dark Witches emphasize bloodletting as one of the most effective methods for working magick. This makes sense, because the blood contains DNA and is naturally linked to the magician on a multitude of levels.

Even so, many magicians and Witches are not interested in practicing blood magick. Some magicians use tears to amplify the intention of emotionally rooted magick. Others simply use saliva, hair, or nail clippings to provide an energetic link between the spell and themselves. But, I must say, blood is the most powerful ousia.

Blood holds ancient memory. In fact, it holds every memory of human existence within it. Drawing a bit of blood unlocks energetic keys buried within. Our current DNA is but a new combination of the same genetic structure of ancient humans. Because of this, energy lies dormant in the blood (possibly in the "dead cells"), waiting to be accessed. In fact, DNA-activated healing is gaining popularity because of its ability to expand consciousness and heal on multiple levels.

In the case of blood magick, it is simple to conclude that blood has the strongest direct link to a person. Blood is the ever-flowing substance encompassing the physical body as a whole, cycling and circulating again and again. It comes from the physical body and remains patterned to both one's physical body and the soul inhabiting it. Blood contains a person's ethereal essence through and through. Any magick performed on oneself or another person is naturally magnified with blood as a connecting substance.

DNA-linked magickal workings are part of what is called *contagious magick* in accordance with the Law of Contagion. That is, when an item contains a sample of one's genetic structure (including hair and nails), it has a direct link to the individual from whom it came. This theory may be extended to include the idea that any item a person touches or somehow is in contact with has a direct energetic link to the person as well. Even if the physical link is severed between a person and an object, an imprint still

Blood in Hinduism

It's good to know cultural comparisons when coming to your own conclusion about blood magick. The decision of whether to use one's own blood in magick is entirely up to the practitioner. In India and other Eastern countries, blood is seen as a foreign substance, something that doesn't usually surface or become visible. It is felt that blood is hidden beneath the surface for a reason and is therefore highly personal and a cultural taboo. When it does surface, it's seen as a polluting or impure element; something antispiritual and energetically toxic. Women's menstrual blood is also associated with extreme spiritual impurity, especially for many elite or conservative Hindus. This Eastern idea of blood as a taboo substance is apparent even in the birthing process due to the blood loss and afterbirth. Buddhism was borne of a Hindu society, and in the story of the Buddha (Siddhartha Gautama), his birth and many other factors of his life have become mythologized. The Sutta Pitaka, one-third of the Buddhist scripture contained in the Tipitaka, or Pali canon, contains the Buddha's birth mythology. In the mythos, Siddhartha was born clean, untainted by uterine water or blood. Afterward, he took seven steps to the north and declared this life to be his final incarnation. Other versions of this story speak of Siddhartha being born out of his mother's armpit. The armpits are similarly impure, but not to the extent that they bleed or emit fluid. These added mythological elements signify the purity of the Buddha as being born an enlightened soul whose influence was to be vast. In this tale, and many tales of war and bloodshed, it is apparent that blood is viewed negatively, as a toxin or pollutant.

remains. These ideas have been used in person-to-person magick since the dawn of time.

Not much blood needs to be shed. Because a single strand of DNA holds the entirety of our genetic makeup, one drop of blood is more than enough to add a boost of power and bind a working to the practitioner's energy pattern. According to some occultists, cutting yourself and extracting a small amount of blood is almost essential in any strong-willed releasing spell. It's a good idea to begin the ritual by saying, "May this cut (or prick) be the only pain experienced from this rite."

In magick, blood may be shed in moderation for deeply personal magick like encouraging an end to internal suffering. Blood provides an ethereal link to the magickal practitioner and sympathetic workings being performed. Many female Witches use menstrual blood in magick to symbolize divine femininity and connectedness to the lunar cycles.

Blood is one of the most powerful substances one can possibly use in magick. If a few drops of blood—menstrual or otherwise—are added to a personal spell bag, potion, or oil, or anointed on a burning candle, written glyph, or sigil, then the magick of the working immediately is amplified and bound to your person.

Adding a bit of blood to a scrying bowl is very effective for divination. When a drop of your own blood is added to a bowl of water used for scrying purposes, multiple doorways will open, and unseen issues of the soul will come into clarity if enough focus is directed. Diluted blood also may be applied to the edges of Tarot cards, runes, or other divinatory devices that are used *only* by the practitioner. I fancy a Book of Shadows recharge every year or so, in which I dilute a bit of my own blood with some ink and paint it on the outside edges of the grimoire.

Any bloodwork needs to be approached responsibly and with sterility. Cleanliness is a necessity, as any incision in the skin runs the risk of infection. As another forewarning, the precise place that bears the cut must be carefully mapped out to avoid hitting a vein or artery. This is very important when responsibly extracting blood for ritual use.

Because extracting blood requires cutting or pricking, there is a level of physical pain involved. When you break the flesh, it's a symbolic act. The pain felt at the initial incision triggers a reaction in the brain. The energy from this can be focused into the ritualistic procedure at hand, and the actual blood drawn can be its conduit.

Risks in Bloodwork

Bloodwork is extremely powerful. If a person can get past the socially accepted discomfort about bleeding, the practice can be utilized carefully to bring about extreme change. Emotions arise when the blood is shed. When the profound energy stored in the blood is accessed, it's like opening a floodgate. That's why a person must be *ready* to perform such work. This specific form of magick causes the hidden to become seen and the repressed to come to the surface. If practiced prematurely, the results could be overly intense and even developmentally detrimental!

Iron is present in blood, and this is something to take note of when working with blood in magick. Mars rules the metal iron and thus rules the blood. The properties of the planet Mars include motivation, strength, power, aggression, and even war (i.e., bloodshed). This is one reason why blood magick should be undertaken with much focus and care. If used improperly or out of anger, it could send the energies awry and into a state of discombobulated chaos. If used with focused intention and precision, it will add a multilayered boost to spellcrafting, providing an amplified and more personal experience of weaving magick and raising energy. In other words, plan any blood magick carefully and be seriously smart about it; an intelligent approach to potentially risky rituals is a key to mastering the arts.

Blood magick is very powerful but also can be dangerous. If someone approaches these practices with a high level of mental or emotional imbalance, the results can be devastating and unsafe, *especially* if the person is accustomed to cutting him- or herself due to depression. The energy of shedding blood in a borderline-suicidal state is completely different from the energy of shedding blood in a ritualistic setting. For those who don't approach these practices mindfully, the powerful energy released in cutting oneself has the potential to overtake the practitioner. This can lead to overuse and a lack of precaution when approaching this type of ritual.

Be very mindful of the amount of blood you use and how often you cut yourself in ritual. Analyze what purposes you have in mind when performing this intense form of shadow magick. Spells in which blood magick is used should not be frivolous, temporary, or superficial. Map out very carefully the area where you choose to cut yourself (*not* near a vein or artery), and decide if other people might possibly notice your cuts. I would not recommend that there be more than one healing cut present at any moment in time.

Please do not perform blood magick on a constant basis. The less frequently you shed blood in ritual, the more powerful the spell. This is due to the fact that a greater amount of personal energy gets built up in the body and energy field over time. If blood is shed more often than necessary, the practitioner undoubtedly will suffer a depletion of personal energy; not to mention that psychiatric help may be the next step if another person misunderstands the reason for the self-inflicted wounds. I highly recommend *no more than one cut every moon cycle.* Each cut or prick should be treated. Wash each gently and apply some antibacterial ointment to it, bandaging appropriately to avoid infection. Ensure that the blood that is shed stays in an area where others won't touch it unsuspectingly.

When I perform private handfasting ceremonies, the couple is to shed a few drops of blood into a glass of wine or pomegranate juice. I recall one handfasting ceremony in which, upon aligning the couple to certain Celtic deities, one of the now-partially-invoked participants cut a little too deep in the arm with a razor blade. Because of the razor's microscopic sharpness, added to the fact that he was partially out of body, we ended up having to exit the circle to make a quick trip to the emergency room for a few stitches. Luckily, the rite was carried on later that night with no problem—and plenty of blood was extracted to seal the bond. Lesson learned!

I recommend against using a razor or another ultrasharp tool when extracting your own blood. As in the previous example, if high energies are being raised, the practitioner may not have full conscious awareness of the physical plane, including the body. This can be very dangerous, even lethal. The safest tools to use for extracting blood are medical lancets, pieces of porcelain, or another earthen substance. The pieces should be used only once for sterility's sake, and may require a series of scratches on the skin to extract a little blood. This "scratching" allows the magician greater focus on the actual act of drawing the blood, and poses a much smaller risk of overcutting.

Recently, my circle started using medical lancets for the extraction of blood. Lancets are used by doctors for single-drop blood sampling and by diabetics for blood-sugar (glucose) level testing. One can purchase a lancing device along with a number of lancets, which are inserted into the device. Each lancet is disposed of after use, but the device can be reloaded. I prefer to use self-contained lancets, which are small plastic pieces containing a spring-loaded lancet. Like the lancets used with the lancing device, the needle is retracted immediately and only a single drop of blood is extracted. Both methods are virtually painless and sterile, and the pricks heal very quickly, leaving no wound. I think that lancets are the coolest thing ever for use in personal magick.

Empire of the Vampyre

It is only right for a section on vampyrism to be included in a book like this. I've heard the stereotype plenty of times that Goths have a perverse interest in vampyrism (or that all Goths *are* vampyres!). While obviously this is a broad generalization based on a handful of cases, the fact remains that, yes, many Goths are curious about vampyrism, or are involved in modern vamp culture. It has become alluring, romantic, and taboo in this day and age; its cryptic meaning beckons for research.

"Vampyre" is often spelled as such in dark culture to distinguish it from the fictional Hollywood "vampire." It's also seen as a more respectful spelling by some members of the vampyre community, as the more archaic spelling evokes Old English ideas of the very real—rather than idealized—image of the vampyre. Of course, this is not the case for all, and the spelling is considered unimportant by many members of the culture.

I will not discuss information about vampyrism that cannot be found on the Internet, at the library, or at a local bookstore, because I refuse to present any information that potentially could put certain individuals in harm's way. I will not discuss "deep-feeding" techniques, recite how to "become" a vampyre, or present speculation or idealization as fact. I do not seek to glorify, malign, or undermine vampyrism. The information presented here is from numerous public sources and offers only an overview of the general community. The true vampyric community is somewhat secretive for a variety of reasons, most of which are for the sake of self-preservation.

Much of the present interest in vampyrism, culture and mythos, is derived from the Victorian portrayal of the vampyre in Bram Stoker's *Dracula*, and its much later film counterpart starring Bela Lugosi. The vampyre long has represented the fear of both life and death, representing humanity's darker inclinations and embodying the trepidations of those in fear of losing their lives to the darkness.

Ever since the first tales surrounding creatures of the night arose, humankind has made them an archetype of evil and oddity. Vampyres are said to be repelled by

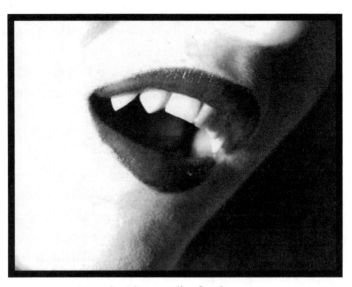

Vampire Kitten smiles for the camera.

garlic, crucifixes, and the ubiquitous wooden stake. Their powers are said to be super-human—they morph into bats at will and turn to dust if sunlight touches their frail skin. Obviously, these myths have just as much validity as Witches flying through the night, eating babies, and hexing everyone's cows.

Extreme romanticism has been attached to the image of the vampyre, and their portrayal as lonely, forlorn wanderers of the night just screams for sympathy and understanding. This is one reason people are attracted simultaneously to Goth culture and vampyrism; both represent elements of darkness and solitude. While true vampyres most certainly are misunderstood, they don't always seek social integration or human empathy. They have a strong sense of internal community and don't go around boasting about their lifestyle.

Elements of eroticism and seduction surround the modern romanticized ideal of the vampyre. The fanged biting has become a sort of sadomasochistic pleasure; intimacy is seen as the cure for their suffering. Sharing blood is seen as a bonding experience, linking the vital energy of two beings. Some vampyres do feed on sexual energy from the experience of orgasm, but most find this unethical if there is not mutual consent. In reality, vampyres are most certainly sexual creatures, but romance doesn't take precedence over other elements of life like survival, health, and well-being. Most vampyres regret their image having been dragged through the mud for aeons, yet understand it'll take lifetimes for their names to be washed clean.

Anthropologically speaking, numerous cultures attribute malicious spirits and their effects, like illness and sudden death, to the vampyre phenomenon. Similar characteristics are supposedly the results of Witchcraft, as well. Obviously, this is not the case from an occult perspective. The idea of vampyres and Witches as soul-sucking supernatural beings most likely has to do with mistranslations of words as well as cultural legends similar to vampyrism in the West.

It must be stressed that there are numerous types of vampyres. None of these types ascribe to the idea of vampyres as being lower-level astral demons, incubi, or succubi. These ideas are now, for the most part, obsolete. Though there exist plenty of astral nasties, demons, nonhumans, and the like, vampyres themselves simply are different entities entirely. They exist on the physical plane and function in this world. They are a lot like other people; the biggest difference is that they experience an energy deficiency that must be restored through energetic exchange. How this is achieved is different for each vampyre.

Vamp Lifestylers

There are some who are only interested in the vampyre lifestyle but are not actual vampyres. Such people, called "vamp lifestylers," engage in "vampyric" activities like drinking blood, getting custom-made fangs and contact lenses, sleeping in a coffin, and so forth, without actually being a member of the community. They are fans of horror movies, avoid the sun, wear only black, and have no problem talking to others about their fascination. If done out of sheer fun and honest interest, there isn't a problem. At the same time, a number of real vampyres who aren't too afraid to present themselves to others partake in the aforesaid activities. True vampyres have a problem only with those who claim to be what they're not, be it out of neurotic delusion or unrealistic cult behavior. Most of those who are all too eager to proclaim themselves vampyres (and try to convince others of it) are but vamp lifestylers.

Another group of people that get confused with real vampyres are role-players. These are folks interested in the *Vampire: the Masquerade*, *Vampire: the Requiem*, and other related White Wolf role-playing games (RPGs). These take the form of tabletop, computer, and live action role-playing (LARP) games, in which participants take on characteristics of the beings they've created and act under the guise of their creatures to give life to the story lines manifested. Few elements of these games are based on actual vampyrism and occultism, although portions of them are based loosely on occult practices like magickal prowess, types of beings, and mythos, which can be an exceedingly fun element when incorporated into a role-playing game. Role-players are not necessarily real vampyres and even fewer mistakenly *believe* they are. Unfortunately, some Pagans take portions of these games—such as certain beings, creatures, and abilities used in the games—as factual, making little distinction between reality and fiction, perpetuating ideas that they are one and the same. Honest vamp lifestylers are happy to embellish their love for all things vampyre, but are quick to make the distinction between fiction and reality.

Sanguinarians

Sanguinarians (or "sanguines") are blood-drinking vampyres. Instead of roaming the night in search of victims from which to feed, they usually satisfy their blood cravings by drinking animal blood (discarded from slaughterhouses), donated human blood, or even their own if the craving is strong enough. Harming people and animals for blood is simply unethical in every sense of the word, and most vampyres, like Witches, are not above personal ethics. Some psi-vamps (discussed next) satisfy their cravings by physically drinking blood if enough astral essence isn't readily available or if a positive bonding opportunity presents itself. At the same time, many sanguinarian vampyres satisfy their cravings by substituting physical blood with psychic/pranic energy.

For sanguinarians, blood is a craving but not a necessity. They can survive without it, though doing so can leave them weak and unfulfilled. The craving comes like any craving would for the ordinary human. The craving is not, however, for the blood itself. The craving is for the energy—the life force, chi, or prana—that the blood carries.

Some people mistake themselves for sanguinarians when they really have a blood fetish or psychological disorder like haematodipsia. These people aren't actually a part of the sanguinarian community but often get mistaken for such.

Psychic Vampyrism

Another vamp type is the psychic vampyre, or "psi-vamp." Often demonized, and also glamorized, psi-vamps have the natural ability to suck energy from people and places, taking it from other sources into their own energetic field. This can be quite dangerous for the giver of energy, especially if the giver is unaware of what's happening. If a psychic vampyre drains unwilling victims, the results can be devastating karmically. Additionally, an energetic bond is formed with each person energy is exchanged with or taken from.

Two specific types of psi-vamps exist. Some are born with the natural ability (perhaps carried over from a past life), but most develop the ability at some point in their lives. Most often, it is developed as a result of a traumatic experience. With this, a very negative, disturbing event will act as a catalyst for bringing about the desire to draw sustaining energy from external sources. Other individuals who develop the gift/curse of psychic vampyrism do so willingly through training, research, and experimentation.

Most modern psi-vamps have a code of ethics, taking energy only from willing donors or from the earth and cosmos, as Witches do. Others believe human energy is the only sufficient source and choose to work carefully with one or more partners who can safely and willingly provide energy on a regular basis. This, of course, takes a grounded understanding of the dynamics of energy exchange as well as emotional strength and mental stability. Ethical psi-vamps tend to believe that a person's energy is his or her own, and should not be drained from the person without direct permission.

Many do feel it permissible to perform "surface feedings," wherein the psi-vamp briefly takes a bit of raised energy from a large crowd in a process of quickly brushing the outer edges of the crowd's aura. If feeding from an individual person, the psi-vamp takes excess ambient energy from the aura's outermost layers. Surface feedings are quite different from "deep feedings" because unused energy is taken, rather than vital life force. Surface feedings are not invasive and don't deplete people's essential personal energy. Obviously, this shouldn't be performed at a Pagan celebration or something of the sort in which the energy being raised is directed at a specific source.

More and more people are becoming aware of the occurrence of psychic vampyrism. If you feel strangely and continually fatigued, saddened, or taken advantage of in the presence of one particular person, odds are that the person has the gift/curse of psychic vampyrism. Such people naturally gravitate toward those who can provide the largest amount of psychic drainage. On the other hand, the "victim" in this situation may be experiencing something completely different, ranging from delusions or paranoia to being afflicted by an astral larvæ or leech.

Many psi-vamps are aware of their ability, but an even greater number of these individuals are unaware of their unique gift/curse. Natural psi-vamps quite often are unaware of the extent of their abilities and may never uncover their true spiritual gifts in accordance with the ability. There actually exists a balance; they have just as great an ability to heal as they do to harm. Psi-vamps are catalysts of intense change and are most certainly natural energy workers. The positive psi-vamp uses his or her powers in a *projective* manner rather than an exclusively *absorptive* one. By projecting an energetic current of his or her choosing, the psi-vamp can influence people and situations at will.

To the readers interested in researching psychic vampyrism, I highly recommend the revolutionary *The Psychic Vampire Codex: A Manual of Magick and Energy Work* by Michelle Belanger as well as her outstanding anthology *Vampires in Their Own Words*. If you believe you have the gift/curse of psychic vampyrism, a huge amount of research and self-reflection must be done. Powers such as these are intense and must be honed properly to awaken their progressively transformational properties.

Dark Entries: Death Magick

Look deep enough in any cemetery at midnight and you're sure to see a Goth or two; just look for the candlelight! I believe it's safe to say that darksiders are more accepting of death as a natural phenomenon that's simply a part of living. I also believe it's safe to say that Pagans are aware of death's processes occurring constantly on various levels, including cellular, agricultural, and otherwise. Both Goths and Witches consider the reality of death as a beautiful and natural transition. While many believe that we glorify or are obsessed with death itself, this misconception comes from the fact that we choose not to fear death, but to embrace it as a sacred part of reality. We think about it more often and allow ourselves more time to contemplate its essence. When fires sweep the land, luscious greenery pops up from the destruction: an example of the death and rebirth process at its finest. Destruction spawns creation, and when life has run its course, it ceases to exist, and serves as a sacrifice for the (re)birth of others. The cycle continues and flows evermore.

By looking, appearing, and behaving differently, the dark Witch may remind others of their own mortality, that this life is temporary, and that there are great lessons to be learned by spending time on the earth plane. Goths subtly, and often unconsciously, remind others that life is but a temporary experience. By dressing "ghostly," a metaphysical link is forged between this experience and that of the Otherworld.

In modern Western culture, corpses are embalmed and preserved, poisoning Mother Earth, breaking her constant cycle. Mortuaries and funeral homes charge a family a high price to "properly" put their beloved to rest. Death is pushed aside, away from the eyes of the masses. It is crammed away in nursing homes, generally apart from the rest of society. People are no longer exposed to the reality of this transition and therefore pay it little mind. Aging goes unacknowledged and death itself is denied. As perhaps one consequence, violence in turn is glorified on television—the revolting all-American pastime. Death is portrayed as romantic and the concept both idealized and de-emotionalized.

In actuality, another individual's death is a very difficult process. Losing someone you love can be nearly impossible to come to grips with, as we often project so many of our own emotions onto other people. A part of ourselves dies along with a loved one's passing, and simply being unable to answer the questions *Why?* and *What's next?* is often reason enough to be tormented for many years.

In the ancient world, death constantly was given attention, and the dead were honored accordingly, in the belief that the dead still had strong sway over the living. Cemeteries were called necropolises, or "cities of the dead." They were sacred lands where the restless dead would wander and that the Great Ones oversaw. It's curious to note that even atheists still carry the tradition of bringing offerings of flowers to their deceased loved ones. This shows not only that death expands ordinary thought by pulling on emotional strings, but that longtime spiritual practices have inherent validity, even in the most unreligious of folks.

Death is considered to be the greatest of all mysteries and is, according to Oscar Wilde, second only to the mystery of love. What happens after we die? Is there a soul, and does it live on when the physical body ceases? Because natural science studies only the concrete, it would have us believe that once the physical body ends, there is no more experience to be had. This linear view of life is actually relatively new in the minds of humans.

While we are still incarnated on the earth plane, the afterlife can only be left to speculation. At the same time, though rare, some people do have vivid memories of the transition between life and death, which tends to either come from intuitive knowledge or from personal near-death experiences. A countless number of individuals who endure near-death experiences, which include physical death and revival, report various occurrences. These include astral projection, a "reviewing" of the present life, and "the light at the end of the tunnel," among other experiences. While these may be hints as to what's next, there's no saying what is to come. Even experienced necromancers often have trouble getting clear responses from the spirits they communicate with, especially because the spirits communicate "on the level" of the necromancer (and are thus bound by human perception).

It would be silly to think that death is the end... to think that once the physical vessel ceases to function, consciousness also dies. This is the easiest and simplest conclusion to come to about death: there is no continuance; consciousness comes to a complete stop. However, if we look at the process of nature and the cosmos, we see that everything works in a cyclical nature—nothing is linear; nothing ever really ceases to be. Greenery grows from the land; it dies in autumn and is reborn in spring. Our cells are constantly dying and regenerating; life is beginning again. There are no voids in reality; everything has its own essence. Though a very Taoist notion, balance is always the central point and is what all of reality comes back to. If something like human consciousness departs the earth, a corresponding energy must fill the void. This is regeneration. This is not to say that our souls remain attached to our human desires and preferences; these are mundane aspects of life and the soul continues as an energetic pattern disassociated from present experience. It often is theorized that the soul, when reincarnated, exhibits similar patterns of behavior as in previous lifetimes and is born into a number of similar life circumstances.

After death, I would imagine that we transcend the normal parameters of human experience and ascend to a connection with oneness—the whole of the universe. Time and space then are nonexistent. We become only energy, waiting to be recycled into the system. Energy may be astrally sorted onto various planes, and the human ego shed. If this were to happen, the "self" that was once known would be left behind. Our lower mental selves, or personal identities, are determined by our energetic pattern when we incarnate in human form. From there, the energy—which really is just a fractal manifestation of the infinite in the form of a person—follows its vibratory pattern by forming opinions and discovering interests aligned with the pattern of the spirit.

Through the whole of our lives, we develop an identity and personality, and that is what I believe is shed at death. If death is not accepted and the human "ego" experience is held on to, then the person becomes an earthbound disincarnate or ghost. Otherwise, what can be called the True Self is realigned with oneness and returns to the vastness of infinity before once again being sorted through reincarnation. But then again, we have no way of truly knowing what happens when life ends, and these are only my personal speculations.

A strong spiritual message accompanies the raw reality of death. Impermanence and change are directly experienced. Nothing is forever. We can only assume that all things happen for a reason. Death is the opposite of birth and is just as beautiful a change.

The Requiem

Burial rites have been performed since the times of the Neanderthal (130,000 to 30,000 years ago) and are, of course, practiced currently with much elaboration and care. These rites vary in every culture. Many indigenous and traditional cultures use drumming to attune to the energy of the departed soul and send it on its way. In drumming, life is celebrated and transition is recognized. The sound of the drum is attuned to the element of Earth (into which the body decomposes), and its rhythm can bring the listener to an altered state of consciousness. Naturally, drumming is thought to echo into the Otherworld, being heard on many planes simultaneously. In death ceremonies, the hollow resonance symbolizes the finality of death, and the beating of the drum is aligned to the beating of the heart and the rhythm of life. Drumming also serves to push the spirit of the departed from its liminal habitat (earthbound disincarnate) into the world of the dead.

The South American Amazonian Yanomamö is one of the few tribal cultures whose ancient ways have been preserved almost entirely. Surprisingly, it is virtually the only tribe that does *not* use drumming in its ceremonies. Instead, tribe members rely almost entirely on dance and chanting as ritualistic instrumentation. The Yanomamö also practice endocannibalism. When a member of the tribe dies, the body is decorated and then burned with all of the deceased's belongings. The next year, the remaining bones from the cremation are finely ground and stirred into a porridge or juice that the entire community consumes. This keeps the energy of the person circulating in the tribe while his or her spirit is released to the Otherworld. No sign of the deceased's body or physical existence remains, cutting the ties between physicality and ascension.

The Berawan tribe in Borneo creates rhythm and percussion during its loud, elaborate funeral ceremonies using instruments like gongs, xylophones, rattles, and sticks in addition to constant drumming. Participants dance and chant; the whole ordeal can be heard for miles in the forest. Noisy ceremonies such as this are not exclusive to death, but take place during any rite of passage, such as birth, tribal initiation, and fertility festivals similar to Pagan Sabbats. For the Berawan (and other tribal cultures), grieving is expressed very little in funerary rites. Rather, tribe members come to terms with death through celebration and ritualism and accept it as a cultural and spiritual reality.

Some members of the Dayak peoples of Borneo neglect to cut or style their hair or care for their body after a loved one dies. They will neglect bodily care altogether: no bathing, washing, changing clothes, or anything else. Harvard anthropology professor Peter Metcalf noted in his ethnographic fieldwork that this practice is in place so the deceased's loved ones can resemble the corpse. Because the deceased can no longer care for his or her body, the family members imitate it. They believe this will prevent the corpse from becoming jealous of the living and deter the deceased from taking the living to the grave alongside him or her, as it would appear to the spirit that his or her loved ones are also deceased. The family also leaves offerings of food, drink, cigarettes, and materials to bountifully send the corpse into the afterlife and persuade the deceased to overlook the living and not take them along to the gates of death.

Many cultures use the color black in their death rites. Black symbolizes the mystery of life, the darkness of the earth, and the loss of consciousness—the entrance into the Otherworld. Other cultures use white in their ceremonies to signify the paleness of the skin and whiteness of the bones associated with the physical body's decay.

In addition to black and white, red is the third most common color used in death rites. Red symbolizes blood and the connection between the self and the earth. Red also may be associated with death in that sunsets often cast various shades of red upon the sky; Græco-Romans even believed that departed souls leave the earth when the sun "dies" every day. Red is the color of menstruation, a monthly "death cycle" for women, and represents the fullness of the blood mysteries of the Goddess.

The Wiccan passage-into-death ritual is called Crossing the Bridge. The soul of a person is seen as crossing a bridge from the physical plane to the afterlife. The Legend of the Descent of the Goddess often is read at this time as well; some even reenact this Pagan tale as a theatrical play to better show the cycle of death as a revered process.

When a Pagan is in his or her last stages of life, the person's spiritual family gathers around him or her to perform various rites in order to guide the dying person into the afterlife and come to a place of acceptance themselves. Pagan death rites are performed both as a person is dying and at the burial service or wake in commemoration. Pagans have no strict code of conduct for performing death rituals and will tailor the ceremonies to the dying person's tradition and personal beliefs.

Often, a Priest or Priestess is invited to oversee and help conduct the rites of passage. Instead of performing rites that comfort only the living, participants' personal discomforts are set aside as much as possible so that *the dying* individual can be focused on during his or her transition. The Priest, Priestess, or overseer might read passages from a variety of books, including the Tibetan Book of the Dead, the Egyptian Book of the Dead, or Starhawk's *The Pagan Book of Living and Dying*, to name a few. The family may play instruments, chant, perform ritual, and meditate with the dying person to make the last days pleasant, and then peacefully usher the passing soul into the great beyond.

The Afterworlds

All religions have their own views on what happens to the soul upon death. Every tradition throughout history has its own afterlife theories and mythos. Recently, I heard of a theory that the soul, upon leaving the physical body, must travel to the Pleiadian star system and interact with the extraterrestrial Pleiadian race. When the physical body dies, time and space are transcended and traveling between galaxies and dimensions becomes normal and natural. Included in this theory is the belief that humans are "star seeds," which came from the Pleiades. Because the Pleiades are believed to be our creator gods, our spirit must interact with them, coming back to the source before journeying onward in the cycle. It is believed that these beings seeded us on the earth alongside a number of creatures, both plant and animal, from various dimensional star systems to create an amalgamated ecosystem of many beings. It may seem far-fetched, but seriously, who knows?

An afterlife abode mentioned in Pagan circles is the Underworld. The Underworld is the realm of chthonic deities recognized in ancient Mediterranean religions as the place to which souls voyaged after leaving the body. In classical times, it was called the dark earth, or the land of darkness beneath the rest of the world.

In Græco-Roman mythology, the Underworld serves as the place souls enter upon physical death and is recognized as a liminal territory where the soul exists before being appropriately sorted. This often is called Hades, which is also the name of the Underworld's ruler god. Hades, the god, is Persephone's consort, as well as the brother of Zeus and Poseidon.

One of the Underworld's many realms, which is comparable to the biblical Heaven, is the paradise Elysium, also called the Elysian Fields or the Isles of the Blest. Another is the punishing Hell-like realm of Tartarus, and a third is a Middleworld of sorts called the Fields of Asphodel, in which the spirits live as shades in an "in-between" state, having been neither villainous nor virtuous in their human lives.

Græco-Roman mythology includes detailed descriptions of the layers and levels of the Underworld, the sorting process of the soul, and the role the gods play in life after death. In that sense, it's similar to the Norse or Ásatrú view of souls moving through the various worlds of Yggdrasil upon death.

The ancient Egyptians' version of the Underworld was known as the Duat (or Tuat). This is seen as a world consisting of various planes, including Amenti, where the soul would be questioned upon death before either entering the Hall of the Gods (a heavenly realm) or being eaten and permanently destroyed by the crocodile god Ammut. The outcome for souls was seen as being dependent on their approach to life and living, things they had and had not done when incarnated, as well as their reverence for the Great Ones.

The ancient symbol for the Duat was a five-pointed sunburst shape within a circle, very similar to the Hermetic/Pagan pentagram. Egyptian pharaohs and other members of royalty would prepare their whole lives for this judgment and secure themselves a good afterlife. The recognition and mythologization of death was prominent in Egypt. Life and death were seen as equally important states.

Ancient Hittites recognized primordial deities as dwelling in the Underworld alongside spirits of the dead. The Semitic Akkadians called them by the name Anunnaki, who some current esoteric researchers theorize to be a race of alien beings incorporated into classical mythology, possibly actually belonging to the "twelfth planet" (called Nibiru, Wormwood, or Planet X), which is not scientifically recognized as part of our solar system at present. The Hittites had a unique method of communicating with Underworldly spirits and deities. They would dig a deep pit in the earth that was used to leave offerings to the deities and spirits below. They would stand in the pit and perform communicatory exercises, necromantic and otherwise, believing that contact was made much more easily when being physically closer to "their terrain," beneath the earth's surface level. Pits were used as gateways for the spirits to move from the earth plane to the Underworld, and from the Underworld back to earth. This type of chthonic magick was commonplace in the society. People would summon Underworldly deities not only for oracular work but also to present them with offerings and convince them to help purify living quarters and bestow blessings.

Tibetan Buddhists prepare at length for the time of their death, feeling that "in order to know how to live well, one must know how to die well." They, and many other traditional Buddhists, believe that the soul experiences a series of afterlife *bardos*, or transitional states. It is even believed that humans exist in one of these temporary stages, called the "bardo of existence."

Tibetan Buddhists believe that there is a post-death bardo period lasting forty-nine days in which the soul of the deceased faces various choices and challenges. At the point of death, the soul astrally projects from the physical body, viewing his or her own body and surrounding friends and relatives performing ritual around the newly dead. When a person is dying, he or she is believed to be extraordinarily sensitive to sound and energy. Because of this, prayers, mantras, and recitations from the Tibetan Book of the Dead are of utmost importance for the dying person's well-being in the afterlife.

After entering a state of pure mind and emotion, the soul of the dead enters a bardo, wherein he or she is faced with two lights. One light is extremely bright, nearly blinding. Most spirits are said to be very frightened by this light, though the tradition states that it is the light of pure Buddhahood—absolute enlightenment—and is ruled by Lord Vairochana, the ethereal Buddha of Wisdom. Because this blinding light frightens most souls, they choose to take refuge in a smaller, dimmer light off to the side. That light represents rebirth and reentrance into the cycle of Samsara (suffering). The concept of these two lights most likely is taken from the Hindu belief of the light of the sun and moon appearing at the time of death. If a person is drawn to the sun, he or she is said to enter heavenly realms, not returning for a future incarnation. If a person takes the path of the moon, he or she enters the cycle of earthly rebirth. Both Buddhism and Hinduism believe that one also encounters a number of peaceful and wrathful deities upon death, which may very well be manifestations of pleasures and fears of the conscious mind. Both traditions also believe that when a person is reborn, he or she is incarnated as a particular being in a particular set of circumstances based on his or her precise energy pattern, having come from lessons learned and deeds accomplished in the previous lifetime. Death is seen entirely as a transition, just another stage rather than an ending.

Wiccans and Celtic Pagans refer to the upper afterlife plane as the Summerland. This is opposite the Shadowland, and both planes coexist on the astral plane. The Summerland, called the Land of Eternal Summer, is associated with the Celtic (Welsh) view of Arran, the uppermost level of the afterlife world of Annwfn (Annwyn). The mythology surrounding Annwfn comes from the Welsh poem "Preiddeu Annwfn," and, because so much information was lost with the coming of Christianity, often is equated with the general consensus of the Celtic afterworld belief system.

Arran, the Summerland, is a heavenly realm of pure joy and oneness, the energy of which is pleasant and serene. The season is always summer and fun is always to be had. It often is associated with Avalon, the "Isle of Apples," and is linked to the legend of King Arthur.

The Celtic Middleworld, seen in a bit more optimistic light than the Græco-Roman version, is Cær Feddwid. This is seen as the "kingdom of intoxication," where wine flows and enchanting music eternally plays. Also present is an elixir of life that the inhabitants drink to sustain existence in this realm.

The third and darkest layer of Annwfn is Cær Wydyr, the desolate, gloom-ridden Underworld of Celtic mythology. This realm also can be called the Shadowland. All souls here are lost, wallowing in ignorance, emptiness, and loneliness.

Wicca, which greatly draws on Celtic mythologies, naturally recognizes the Summerland. Pagans of other cultural leanings may not identify the afterlife experience as the Summerland or Shadowland. Instead, they would base their ideas on their own individual belief systems. Not all Witches and Pagans agree on what happens to the soul when one dies. All simply understand that the soul lives on, existing in the Otherworld for a period of time, usually prior to reincarnation.

The aforementioned belief systems are just a few examples of the numerous conceptions of the afterlife from various cultural perspectives. Virtually every cultural mythos includes a version of an Upperworld, an Underworld, and sometimes a Middleworld. More than likely, the multicultural beliefs in these Upper- and Underworlds are rooted in shamanic practice, wherein the layers of the astral plane were known and perceived. It's surprising how much mythology overlaps among cultures throughout time, and how similarly the afterlife experience is viewed worldwide.

"Gateway" by OakRaven Photography. Model: Shelby.

Memento Mori: Necromancy

Because of the intrigue surrounding the reality of death, people study and philosophize about it in order to come to terms not only with the passing of loved ones but also the reality of their own impending death. Throughout time, people have sought to communicate with ancestral spirits for specific reasons. Communication with those who once were physically incarnated can be called *necromancy*.

Necromancy is not common practice in Wicca nor in most forms of modern Witchcraft. It takes training, dedication, and caution to accurately hone this ability. Some experienced Witches incorporate necromantic practices into their magick, but most have no need or desire to do so, unless it's for rituals on or around Halloween or upon the immediate passing of a loved one

Necro-, or *neku-*, simply means "the dead," referring to a person or persons. It comes from the word *nekros*, meaning "corpse." The suffix *-mancy* comes from the Greek word *manteia*, meaning "to prophesy." The term thus refers to a divinatory art form.

The word *goetia* originally was synonymous with necromancy but over time came to refer to the art of summoning dæmons (the sorcerers were called *goētes*). Grimoires of the magick of King Solomon are extant, including *The Goetia: The Lesser Key of Solomon*, which is concerned with communion with otherworldly dæmonic entities rather than the spirits of once-living humans. This is not actually necromantic work, but a form of interplanetary evocation. It is important to distinguish between necromantic magick and other forms of spirit communication. In modern times, the word necromancy is used loosely to refer to any magickal working in which the magician somehow makes use of the souls of deceased human beings or interacts *directly* with the energy of death itself. This general term is recognized even among some modern scholars on the topic, despite its linguistic roots emphasizing divination in particular. Modern practitioners tend to deem intentional communication with the dead to be necromancy, including communication with ghosts and the act of mediumship.

Ancient Necromancy

In classical times, the philosopher quite often was also a magician. The Greek philosopher Pythagoras taught, among many other things, that dying people had a better ability to easily communicate with the dead than did young or middle-aged people, as their souls were departing from their bodies at the last stages of life. Pythagoras claimed to have received prophecies from the dead, particularly in his old age. He would drink water from an underground well (attuned as a physical doorway to the Underworld) to communicate with chthonic spirits and gain prophecy. One of the prophecies he received was the fall of Athens. Pythagoras's main goal in necromancy seems to have been simply that of prophecy, with no ulterior motives. His intentions were not self-serving nor mundane, but held importance to himself and the greater community. His perceived encounters presumably served as the bases for some of the philosopher's teachings in his magickal order. Græco-Roman society is the most appropriate culture to look at when studying ancient necromancy, considering the number of mentions of the art in literary texts throughout time.

Mentions of necromancy began to appear in Mesopotamian texts around 900 BCE and extend to the transition into Coptic Christianity. Many of these mentions have to do with the dead appearing to a person in dream. There is no evidence of necromantic practice in Egypt, Anatolia, Levant, and other East Mediterranean cultures until the time of the reign of the Assyrian king Esarhaddon (c. 600 BCE). Because Mediterranean cultures showed evidence of necromancy at a later time than did the Mesopotamian cultures, it is theorized that they borrowed the idea and practice from the Mesopotamians. This most likely was due to King Esarhaddon's expansion of the Assyrian empire, reaching and thus influencing areas like Egypt. Evidence for necromantic rituals in Greece also shows up at this time, suggesting that they also may have borrowed the practice from early Mesopotamian cultures.

The Greek Magical Papyri, which date between approximately the first and fourth centuries CE, include a number of necromantic spells that certainly were practiced by magicians in antiquity. Spells such as these likely were traded, bought, and sold by magick-practicing aristocratic men, taking into account that they were virtually the only people educated in reading and writing; most of the peasants remained illiterate.

PGM (*Papyri Græcæ Magicæ*) IV 2140–44 is probably the best example of an "executable" ancient necromantic spell. It is called "Pitys the Thessalian's spell for questioning corpses," and describes a method of communicating with the dead, which is to write "AZĒL BALEMACHŌ" on a flax leaf. The ink is to be made of red ochre, burnt myrrh, juice of fresh wormwood, evergreen, and flax. The magician is then to put the completed flax leaf in the mouth of the corpse to induce oracular communication with the departed spirit. It is a very short spell, compared to most of the rest of the PGM material, and its simplicity is profound considering the goal. It doesn't describe what the magician can do after summoning the spirit, but says only *how* the magician can get the spirit in his or her presence. The discovery of possible reasons behind this must be left up to cultural analysis. The ingredients and procedures for this ancient Greek spell aren't nearly as arcane and even humorous as many of the other translated PGM workings, which rarely are practiced by modern Græco-Roman reconstructionists. Curiously, most modern Witches put little if any stock in these ancient spells and many consider them magickally obsolete. If nothing else, they are at least fascinating historical writings!

In literature, necromancy more often than not has been portrayed in a slanderous light. It's usually equated with Witchery, and it's the Witchy women in classical literature who raise the dead and work spells with people's dead body parts. For example, in second-century CE Roman author Lucian's sixth book of the *Pharsalia*, we encounter the Witch Erictho, living in Thessaly. After the battle of Pharsalus, she is portrayed scavenging the cremation grounds, gathering bones, ashes, and body parts of the newly dead, and she even kills someone herself to obtain the materials. She is an old and vile-looking stereotypical hag and in the story reanimates the corpse of a soldier by performing a spell so that he may foretell to her client the outcome of the battle. The soldier's ghost first appears next to his corpse and refuses to fulfill the spell until Erictho threatens the spirit, causing it finally to reenter the body to answer her questions.

Homer's *Odyssey*, a mythological heroic tale that came into written form around 700–650 BCE, is the earliest detailed mention of classical necromancy. Because of its inclusion in a fictional piece, it's only right to assume that necromancy was practiced, or at least considered, at the time.

In Book XII, Odysseus had just begun his journey to the house of Hades. The demi-goddess Circe had just instructed him to voyage there to consult the shade (ghost) of Tiresias, a Theban prophet. Upon reaching the Underworld, Odysseus first encountered the spirits of his newly deceased friend as well of as his mother, whom he mournfully was shocked to encounter in the realm of the dead. After Odysseus gave offerings to Tiresias, the spirit revealed to him a prophecy about returning home to Ithaca, mentioning the trials and tribulations he would have to endure to preserve his own life and eventually reach home.

In this case, the motivation behind necromantic ritualism is self-motivated but doesn't support destruction of anyone else for the sake of self-gain. It's surprising and reassuring that in this case necromancy is not portrayed as a malicious endeavor, though it is still dark and controversial. The *Odyssey* also crowns Circe as the first Witch in literature to incorporate necromantic practice into her "bag of tricks."

One of the most commonly known (and arguably only historical) documentations of divinatory necromancy is in the Bible. Samuel was written in the Greek archaic period, specifically the eighth–seventh centuries BCE, and was set in approximately 1050 BCE. The passage is in Samuel 1:28 and talks about Saul and his encounter with the Witch of Endor. Samuel was dead, his body burned and spirit released. The passage mentions that Saul had banished all the mediums and spiritualists from the land but still wished to find a medium who had the power to summon his acquaintance back from the dead.

His attendants told him of a Witch in Endor to whom he could inquire. Saul disguised himself and sought out the Witch. Upon summoning Samuel from the dead, Saul bowed before him, asking for advice as to why the Lord God no longer answered to him. Samuel, clearly upset by the disturbance, explained that Saul had not obeyed the Lord and now was being punished through God's silent treatment. He also predicted the future, including the fall of Israel to the Philistines, as well as the death of Saul and his sons.

Additional classical literature showing now-ridiculous depictions of the "evil nature of women" reveals to us the social context of the time. Depictions similar to that of the *Pharsalia*'s Witch (aforementioned) are seen in the writings of Theocratus (the Witch Samytha), Horace (the Witch Canidia), and Apuleius (the hags in *Metamorphoses: The Golden Ass*). Are these, in addition to portrayals by the Church, the source of the stereotypical view of the Witch we have now? It certainly is feasible. At that time, women (even the goddesses) generally were seen as men's property and were inherently tainted and thus more likely to fall into a cycle of malicious behavior like Witchery and self-motivated necromancy. It's also worth considering that men of the time had an insatiable desire to be fulfilled by a woman through marriage and childbirth for the sake of companionship and procreation, as well as acceptance by the community. I believe that one reason literary depictions of feminine necromancy are portrayed in such a negative light is that men of the time wanted their desire of women to seem miniscule or nonexistent, so as to not show signs of "weakness" or dependency. In reality, there probably were more male practitioners of necromancy than females.

Necromancy is a relatively obscure topic when studying the classical world. It is rarely mentioned in anything but fictional stories, and the accuracy of the information in those tales cannot gauge the actual practices of the art in that time. However, the information suggests that, yes, necromancy was incorporated into ritual and practiced alongside other forms of magick. Because of the limited documentation, assumptions founded in comparative research tend to be the most accurate assessments of the place of the practice in Græco-Roman society. Ancient necromantic practices mentioned are both similar and dissimilar to modern practices of the art.

Modern Necromancy

Modern necromancers seek contact with and understanding of death energy. A lesser form of necromancy is practiced on the holiday Samhain, when the Witch communicates with his or her ancestral spirits and leaves libations and offerings for their departed souls. Commemorative altars and shrines are constructed with the loved ones in mind, and offerings are left to satisfy their spirits. This sometimes includes one-on-one communication with the soul of the departed individual, and is still considered a lesser form of necromantic communion.

Some Witches, as well as a number of other magickal practitioners, engage in necromancy much more regularly. Modern necromancers don't limit themselves to divination from departed spirits. To do so would be self-serving and disrespectful to the energy of death. Instead, they will practice anything from transcendental meditation on death to releasing earthbound spirits (those trapped on the earth plane, often called ghosts). Modern necromancers work with death energy in its many forms, including the personification of Death himself.

Death energy traditionally is personified as an archangel named Azræl, who, according to Hebrew/Islamic mythology, is both the psychopomp and the record keeper of life and death. With the birth of every human being, he writes the name in his giant grimoire; when a person dies, he erases the name. He is said to have 4,000 wings and as many eyes as there are people on earth. When a person dies, an eye blinks. As with all deities, Azræl's form has been mythologized and personified, and is highly symbolic. If worked with ritualistically, his form most likely will appear differently to everyone, based on personal interpretation of the energy of death. Many see him simply as a grim reaper figure, which is a modern form commonly associated with death of any kind. The grim reaper itself is said to have its origins in sixteenth-century France, when an artist depicted what he felt was the personification of death.

Azræl's name means "he who helps God" in Hebrew. In the scripture, Azræl was said to have brought God (YHVH) a handful of dirt to help create Adam when the other angels refused to, heeding earth's warning against it. Some theorists believe that the name Azræl comes from a person named Azra, who was devoted to spreading the divine lessons of God following the Babylonian Exile. Additionally, the Angel of Death is given alternative names in different scriptural cultures, each of which gives its own, often similar attributions to his essence.

Regardless of origin, the energy of death has been personified through Azræl's name throughout time. When necromancers work with Azræl, they work with society's anthropomorphous image of death to uncover the truth of the dying process. A certain vibrational force has been attributed to the energy of death, and even if a practitioner doesn't believe verbatim in Azræl's original mythology, the energy still is accessible through Azræl's name because of social associations that have built up significant amounts of energy around the being. Because death so often is socially feared, many necromancers have found that Azræl's image has become tainted and his spirit saddened. Necromancers seek to remedy this as much as is in their power to do so, paying homage to the beauty and necessity of the death cycle. For people like us who have an inherent admiration for the dark and mysterious, working positively with the Angel of Death may prove a bit easier than it would for most.

In what is called *high necromancy*, the practitioner performs a communicative ritual in the presence of a corpse. The corpse serves as a conduit for death energy. The physical body is a shell for the soul, and when the soul has been removed from its frame, death energy lingers about it until the body is fully decomposed (or cremated) and has returned to the earth. When a person or animal dies, the energy of death is immediately present, permeating the body and the room in which the person or animal passed. Communicating with the Angel of Death is, however, highly effective in this case. This is why high necromancers prefer to work directly in the presence of death energy.

Performing ritual with a corpse isn't exactly easy or desirable—even for a Goth! Please don't rush out and try it. A graveyard, crypt, catacomb, or mausoleum is an ideal place to feel death energy, even if full contact isn't made directly in the presence of an "empty shell." A rule of high necromancy is to not cause harm to another being, especially for the purposes of magick. This includes *no* human or animal sacrifices. Something as absurd and cruel as performing ritual homicide not only induces cycles of horrible karma but also renders the death energy impure. It is also a horrible insult to Azræl, who would have taken the soul in due time. Murder has *no* place in the magickal arts, even necromancy, and it would be foolish to think it does.

If someone performs high necromancy in the presence of a body, the person or animal worked with must be given absolute respect in the process, and it's ideal if the person or animal died from natural causes (having naturally endured the process of dying). It takes a very particular type of person to perform this type of magick. The rituals are *very* intense and exacting, and pose the possibility of either lifting someone to extreme (and *not* always pleasant) states of consciousness *or* damaging the person's soul if performed improperly or in the wrong state of mind. Because of the risks associated with high necromancy, I won't include any rituals dealing with that form of magick in these pages. However, I have included a meditation on the Angel of Death. This is a necromantic rite that poses little risk to the practitioner, yet is quite effective in that it is a face-to-face experience with death energy as performed in the confines of a sacred space.

Another misunderstood element of necromancy, in addition to murder and violence, is *necrophilia*, which is defined as an erotic attraction to corpses, usually including sexual intimacy with a dead body (in modern terms). To necromancers, this is considered a defilement of the beauty of death energy and is an act of extreme disrespect to the Angel of Death. High necromancers don't seek sexual gratification from empty shells. When a person passes from his or her body, the energy lingers until all of the tissue is completely decomposed. Even then, traces of a person's energy are stored in bones and don't ever actually leave. To perform sexual acts with a corpse is not only disrespectful to the soul of the person who once lived in the body, but is also, well, pretty high on the scale of "what the fuck."

For those who wish to further research the implications of modern necromancy, I can't recommend highly enough the poetic and Gothic work of writer Leilah Wendell.

Encountering the Angel of Death (Meditation)

Most of humankind fears death, and this makes Azræl's energy dense and mournful. Azræl has not always appeared this way, harking back to a time when death ultimately was accepted and embraced, not pushed aside or romanticized. Death energy is the energy of transition and is the rawness of the loss of life. Death energy is the liminal stage between this incarnation and the next, and is something to be respected and worked with carefully.

The following meditation is aimed at making contact with Azræl. For some people, this can provide comfort and acceptance of the reality of death, particularly if someone you know is dying or recently has passed. This ritual is actually a form of minor necromancy and is a great introduction to the essence of the necromantic arts. Written out, it seems brief. Performed, and with enough time left between each step, it can last for much longer, even for many hours. Everyone's experience will be different. This is simply an outline for sparking temporary contact with the personification of death. Read through the ritual first and see if it's right for you. If now is not the time, save it for later down the road. If it *is* the time, approach it with caution and honest soul-searching. Your intuition will tell you if you're ready.

This meditation should not be performed carelessly or nonchalantly. It should be performed in Perfect Love and Perfect Trust; if there is great fear in your heart, then it will fail. This is not something to do at a slumber party, nor is it a way to make you a more powerful Witch. If performed properly, it will make you more aware, accepting, and reverent of death—and thus knowledgeable of life. It should be performed only if you are seriously contemplating the mysteries of the afterlife. This working should be well thought out, planned, and finally embarked on, keeping in mind that the time eventually will come when the Angel of Death will take your hand once again.

During the working, it is preferable to burn jasmine incense, which is said to be appeasing to Azræl. It is ideal to light a black candle or be surrounded by a number of them. You also should secure a nice piece of dark-violet amethyst to cup in your hands during the meditation. You can hold melenite, apache tear, dark tiger's-eye, jet, or a combination of any of these, in addition to the amethyst. It also is beneficial to use an elestial stone (also called a "record keeper"), which is any stone with a number of terminations or jagged points along one side. If using an elestial stone, smoky quartz is a great option, as very few stones are capable of forming this design.

It's a good idea to surround yourself with sprinklings of graveyard dirt ("graveyard dust"). Simply go to a cemetery and gather a handful of dirt from any part of the land. Be certain not to accidentally desecrate any area; even a few pinches will do. Be respectful when gathering the dirt. Tell the spirits that you wish them no disrespect, and that you are gathering the dirt to honor and connect with the energy of the Great Beyond. It's a good idea to leave a small offering as well, like an apple, tobacco, cornmeal, or any flower. This will appease the spirits and inform them of your intentions.

If a cemetery is not accessible to you for one reason or another, then graveyard dirt may be substituted by a combination of as few or as many of these herbs as you'd like: mullein, valerian, patchouli, sage, and nightshade. Grind these into a fine powder and sprinkle them around your ritual space before performing the rite. This will aid in communication with Azræl by securing the space with the subtle vibration of death.

If you use nightshade, be very careful when handling it, and pick it up afterward so no one will come in contact with it later.

The best time to gather or create the dirt is at midnight on a new moon. If going to the cemetery, beware of traveling spirits. They come out in hordes when the veil is thin on the new (dark) moon and may not always have your best interests in mind, especially if they feel threatened. Midnight on the new moon is the ideal time to perform this meditation. There are three nights of the new moon. It would be a good idea to either gather the dirt during one month's new moon, allow it to charge on your altar for a moon cycle, and perform the meditation the following month, or to gather the dirt the night before the "official" new moon, while still in the dark moon tide, and perform the meditation the following evening. I recommend the former, as the wait between moon cycles is a good time to reflect on the goals of the meditation and further research the energy of death.

It also would be beneficial to use animal teeth or bones, or even pieces of fossil, by keeping them with you during the ritual. Death energy is still imprinted on the bones and is thus accessible in ritual. If you have a long bone to use, it may be consecrated as a wand and used in the same manner as when casting the circle. Just *don't* make it your magick wand for every ritual; its energy is quite specific. You also can use a small branch of an evergreen yew tree for the same purpose. This (preferably) should be freshly cut; it must be cut only with the tree's permission, with thanks given to the tree's spirit or dryad. All parts of the yew tree are quite poisonous, so be careful if you choose to use this.

As with all meditations, this may be prerecorded, memorized, or read softly in monotone by an accompanying friend. A strong circle should be cast beforehand, including calls to the Watchtowers and a strongly enforced rampart of protection. Do not make an internal widdershins circle, as discussed in the previous chapter. Though this meditation is not designed to put you at risk, a practitioner is more susceptible to unknown energies when working with this type of magick. Also, it's ideal to wear all black and powder your face a pale white, applying some eyeshadow around your eyes and slightly on your lips. Doing so will help invite Azræl's presence and bring to mind the necessity of death as a sacred aspect of life. "Dressing like the dead" shouldn't pose too much of a difficulty for most readers.

1. After constructing the sacred circle, begin by situating yourself in a comfortable meditative position before your altar or in an outdoor sacred space. You must face the west. The west is the direction where the sun descends behind the horizon and is thus the direction associated with death.

2. Take slow, deep breaths to calm and balance your energy, in turn lowering your vibrations. Meanwhile, clear your mind of any unnecessary thoughts. Your only thought should be that you, as a spiritual being, wish to make contact with the essence of death itself. Gradually make your breathing slower, longer, and deeper. Stop breathing for a moment at the peak of each inhale and exhale. This will change your normal breathing pattern, further aligning you to the sensation of departing the body. Feel free to vocalize or make noise as you will, so long as it feels natural. Maintain a steady breathing pattern for an extended period of time before moving on, so that your energy may enter an altered state. Return to normal breathing once you feel a successful shift in your energy.

3. Now it's time to visualize. You are surrounded in darkness. Shadow permeates your being and is all around you, within and without. Blackness is all there is, and you are void of any light. Let the blackness fill you. Comfortably *embrace* it rather than fear it, for darkness is the essence of all creation. Feel its soft ambiance permeate your being, reminding you of your own mortality.

4. Begin to chant the name of the Angel of Death. The chanting should be deep and guttural, extended, and intense. Start with a whisper and repeat the sacred name louder and louder until you have reached your vocal peak, if circumstances permit: "AZ-RAY-EL…AZZZ-RAYYY-ELLL…AZZZZZZ-RAYYYYYY-ELLLLLL…" Follow by reciting in your mind any other invitations you feel are appropriate. Thought creates reality. Ask Azræl to appear before you and inform him that you would like to better understand who he is. Do not fully merge your energy with his, as you must keep connected to the earthly plane.

5. You will feel Azræl's presence around you. Keep your eyes shut. A shadow may form before you in your mind's eye, or you simply may be surrounded by the energy. Everyone's reaction will be different. Simply feel it for what it is, and know that you are safe. This is a glimpse of the hollow feeling of death, ultimate departure from the earth plane. You may feel tingling or coldness, joy or sorrow. Cry and scream if you feel the need. Shout and shiver, or remain perfectly still. React in whatever way feels right, dancing with the present energy. Be in the moment, and accept any visions, thoughts, and emotions that flow through you. *Just be.*

6. Pay attention to what you feel, as well as the information you are given, even if it's only in energetic form. Take note of what energies you are encountering. Simply be in the presence of Azræl, and allow yourself to learn from the energy at hand. Take time to experience his presence.

7. Now that you are experiencing Azræl's energy, communicate with him in your mind. Tell him why you invited him here, thank him for being the escort when your time comes, and tell him that you wish to know some of the mysteries of the afterlife while still in this body. Communicate mentally only, from your mind and heart, and approach him with utmost respect. This is your time to express what you are feeling and receive sacred messages in return. Do not question his need to take souls, and do not project upsetting or fearful vibrations. Simply bathe in the energy around you, ever minding death's presence at your side. Take as long as you need before moving on. Seek to understand death and the reality of change. Know Thyself.

8. You will feel when the time is right to part ways. When this time comes, thank Azræl for his presence and pay him proper heartfelt respect. Acknowledge his role, and inform him that you will walk beside him in peace when it is time for you to leave this earth. Gratefully ask him to depart, making sure that his energy is dissipating. When you feel his energy begin to fade, close the ritual by saying aloud, "Thank you…hail and farewell."

9. Any images around you now are fading back to normality. Your energy is becoming calm, centered, and stable. You are becoming aware of your body and the space around you. Sink into the present moment, knowing that you just experienced a brush with death, and that you are stronger, less fearful, and more aware as a result. You have danced with magickal darkness and have come out a being of light. Speak of this experience only to those who understand, and remain silent to those who won't. The experience is yours and yours alone, because it was this that you have willed.

10. Allow yourself enough time to ground and come back to the present time. Close the circle as you normally would, and smile, knowing that life and death are one and the same. You have made a connection with the unseen, and your spiritual sight has expanded to one degree or another. It's a good idea to take a bath after the meditation, or hit the sack and sleep like the dead!

Náuþs Galdr

(A Gothick Need-Fire Lighting Chant)

Digis dugann dráibiþái bláuþjái;
Gaqiwidédun nahts jah náuþs niþandó fón.
Riqis garaíhtiþ, reiks, ahmeins;
Sauil duþþé sniw, sigisláun Austróns!

Creation began in a troubled void;
Night and need gave life to a helping fire.
Rectify darkness, powerful, the spirituous;
Sun hasten to that end, prize of Ostara!

A hymn from the **Gothic liturgy** of the Germanic Gothick religion,
c. 400–700 CE. Reconstructed by Albareiks. Documented in
Gutiska Hunslastaths Razda. Théod Publications, 2003.

Bibliography

Agrippa, Henry Cornelius. *Three Books of Occult Philosophy*. St. Paul, MN: Llewellyn Publications, 1995.

Apuleius. *Metamorphoses: The Golden Ass*. Edited and translated by J. Arthur Hanson. Cambridge, MA: Harvard University Press, 1989.

Bardon, Franz. *Initiation into Hermetics: The Path of the True Adept*. Salt Lake City, UT: Merkur Publishing, 2001.

Belanger, Michelle. *The Psychic Vampire Codex: A Manual of Magick and Energy Work*. Boston, MA: Weiser Books, 2004.

Betz, Dieter Hans, ed. *The Greek Magical Papyri in Translation*. Chicago, IL: University of Chicago Press, 1986.

Blavatsky, H. P. *An Abridgment of The Secret Doctrine*. Wheaton, IL: Theosophical Publishing House, 1967.

Buckland, Raymond. *The Witch Book: The Encyclopedia of Witchcraft, Wicca, and Neo-Paganism*. Canton, MI: Visible Ink Press, 2002.

Cicero, Chic, and Sandra Tabatha Cicero. *The Essential Golden Dawn: An Introduction to High Magic*. St. Paul, MN: Llewellyn Publications, 2003.

Cohen, Kenneth. *Honoring the Medicine: The Essential Guide to Native American Healing*. New York: Ballantine Books, 2003.

Coughlin, John J. *Out of the Shadows: An Exploration of Dark Paganism and Magick*. Bloomington, IN: 1st Books Library, 2001.

Coyle, T. Thorn. *Evolutionary Witchcraft*. New York: Penguin, 2004.

Crowley, Aleister. *The Book of the Law*. Boston, MA: Weiser Books, 1976.

———. *Magick, Book 4: Parts I–IV*. Boston, MA: Weiser Books, 2004.

———. *Magick in Theory and Practice*. Secaucus, NJ: Castle Books, 1991.

Davida. Michael Alexandra. *At the Left Hand of the Goddess: Radical Rituals and other Workings of the Mary Magdalene Coven*. Boulder, CO: CLSM, Inc., 2004.

Del Campo, Gerald. *New Aeon Magick: Thelema Without Tears*. St. Paul, MN: Llewellyn Publications, 1994.

Dumars, Denise, and Lori Nyx. *The Dark Archetype: Exploring the Shadow Side of the Divine*. Franklin Lakes, NJ: New Page Books, 2003.

Faraone, Christopher A., and Dirk Obbink, eds. *Magika Hiera: Ancient Greek Magic and Religion*. New York: Oxford University Press, 1991.

Farrar, Janet, and Gavin Bone. *Progressive Witchcraft: Spirituality, Mysteries & Training in Modern Wicca*. Franklin Lakes, NJ: New Page Books, 2004.

Farrar, Janet and Stewart. *A Witches' Bible: The Complete Witches' Handbook*. Custer, WA: Phoenix Publishing, 1996.

Fortune, Dion. *Practical Occultism in Daily Life*. London: Aquarian Press, 1971.

Gordon, Leah. *The Book of Vodou: Charms & Rituals to Empower Your Life*. London: Quarto Books, 2000.

Graf, Fritz. *Magic in the Ancient World*. Cambridge, MA: Harvard University Press, 1997.

Greer, John Michael. *The New Encyclopedia of the Occult*. St. Paul, MN: Llewellyn Publications, 2003.

Grimassi, Raven. *Encyclopedia of Wicca & Witchcraft*. St. Paul, MN: Llewellyn Publications, 2000.

Harner, Michael J., ed. *Hallucinogens & Shamanism*. New York: Oxford University Press, 1973.

Harris, Stephen L., and Gloria Platzner. *Classical Mythology: Images & Insights*. Mountain View, CA: Mayfield Publishing, 1995.

Hicks, David, ed. *Ritual and Belief: Readings in the Anthropology of Religion*. Second edition. New York: McGraw-Hill Higher Education, 2002.

Hodkinson, Paul: *Goth: Identity, Style & Subculture*. Oxford: Berg, 2002.

Homer. *The Odyssey*. Translated by Samuel Butler. New York: Barnes & Noble Press, 1993.

Johnston, Sarah Iles. *Restless Dead: Encounters Between the Living & the Dead in Ancient Greece*. Berkeley, CA: University of California Press, 1999.

Jones, David E. *Sanapia: Comanche Medicine Woman*. Prospect Heights, IL: Waveland Press, 1974.

Jong, Erica. *Witches*. New York: H. A. Abrams, 1981.

K, Amber. *CovenCraft: Witchcraft for Three or More*. St. Paul, MN: Llewellyn Publications, 1998.

Kaldera, Raven. *Pagan Polyamory: Becoming a Tribe of Hearts*. St. Paul, MN: Llewellyn Publications, 1996.

Kaldera, Raven, and Tannin Schwartzstein. *The Urban Primitive: Paganism in the Concrete Jungle*. St. Paul, MN: Llewellyn Publications, 2002.

Kemp, Daniel. *The Book of Night: Legends of Shadow & Silence*. New York: IRAYA Publications, 1990.

Kilpatrick, Nancy. *The Goth Bible: A Compendium for the Darkly Inclined*. New York: St. Martin's Griffin, 2004.

Konstantinos. *Vampires: The Occult Truth*. St. Paul, MN: Llewellyn Publications, 1996.

Kraig, Donald Michael. *Modern Magick: Eleven Lessons in the High Magickal Arts*. St. Paul, MN: Llewellyn Publications, 1997.

LaVey, Anton Szandor. *The Satanic Bible*. New York: Avon Books, 1969.

Lehmann, Arthur C., and James E. Myers. *Magic, Witchcraft & Religion: An Anthropological Study of the Supernatural*. Mountain View, CA: Mayfield Publishing, 1985.

Leland, Charles Godfrey. *Aradia, or the Gospel of the Witches*. Franklin Lakes, NJ: New Page Books, 2003.

Lucian, of Samosata. *Philopseudes ("Lover of Lies")*. Translated by A. M. Harmon. Cambridge, MA: Harvard University Press, 1913.

Marciniak, Barbara: *Earth: Pleiadian Keys to the Living Library*. Santa Fe, NM: Bear & Co., 1995.

Mercer, Mick: *21st Century Goth*. Surrey: Reynolds & Hearn, 2002.

Metcalf, Peter. *A Borneo Journey into Death*. Philadelphia, PA: University of Pennsylvania Press, 1982.

Metzger, Richard. *Disinformation: The Interviews*. New York: Disinformation Co., 2002.

Moura, Ann [Aoumiel]. *Grimoire for the Green Witch: A Complete Book of Shadows*. St. Paul, MN: Llewellyn Publications, 2003.

Ogden, Daniel. *Greek & Roman Necromancy*. Princeton, NJ: Princeton University Press, 2001.

Penczak, Christopher. *Gay Witchcraft: Empowering the Tribe*. Boston, MA: Weiser Books, 2003.

———. *The Inner Temple of Witchcraft: Magick, Meditation and Psychic Development*. St. Paul, MN: Llewellyn Publications, 2002.

———. *The Temple of Shamanic Witchcraft: Shadows, Spirits and the Healing Journey*. St. Paul, MN: Llewellyn Publications, 2005.

———. *The Witch's Shield: Protection Magick & Psychic Self-Defense*. St. Paul, MN: Llewellyn Publications, 2004.

Pennick, Nigel. *Complete Illustrated Guide to Runes*. London: HarperCollins, 2002.

Pickering, David. *Cassell Dictionary of Witchcraft*. London: Cassell Publishing, 1996.

Plotkin, Mark J. *Tales of a Shaman's Apprentice: An Ethnobotanist Searches for New Medicines in the Amazon Rain Forest*. London: Penguin Books, 1994.

Rainier, Chris. *Ancient Marks: The Sacred Origins of Tattoos & Body Markings*. Santa Barbara, CA: Media 27 Publishing, 2004.

Ramsay, Jay. *Alchemy: The Art of Transformation*. London: Thorsons, 1997.

Roderick, Timothy. *Dark Moon Mysteries: Wisdom, Power & Magic of the Shadow World*. Aptos, CA: New Brighton Books, 2003.

Sangharakshita. *Know Your Mind: The Psychological Dimension of Ethics in Buddhism*. Birmingham: Windhorse Publications, 1998.

September [Lloyd Warren Ravlin]. *The Autumn Cemetery Text*. 1996. http://www.geocities .com/Athens/Delphi/4201/index.html (accessed May 2007).

Silverknife, Zanoni. *Lessons in Georgian Wicca, 101–104*. Class handouts and lecture notes. Missoula, MT, 1999.

Starhawk. *The Pagan Book of Living and Dying*. San Francisco, CA: HarperSanFrancisco, 1997.

Summer Rain, Mary. *Earthway: A Native American Visionary's Path to Total Mind, Body, and Spirit Health*. New York: Pocket Books, 1990.

Sylvan, Dianne. *The Circle Within: Creating a Wiccan Spiritual Tradition*. St. Paul, MN: Llewellyn Publications, 2003.

Thorsson, Edred. *Blue Rûna: Edred's Shorter Works, vol. III*. Smithville, TX: Rûna-Raven Press, 2001.

———. *The Truth About Teutonic Magick*. St. Paul, MN: Llewellyn Publications, 1989.

Tresidder, Jack, ed. *The Complete Dictionary of Symbols*. San Francisco, CA: Chronicle Books, 2004.

Trobe, Kala. *Magic of Qabalah: Visions of the Tree of Life*. St. Paul, MN: Llewellyn Publications, 2001.

———. *The Witch's Guide to Life*. St. Paul, MN: Llewellyn Publications, 2003.

Tyson, Donald. *Enochian Magic for Beginners: The Original System of Angel Magic*. St. Paul, MN: Llewellyn Publications, 1997.

Valiente, Doreen. *An ABC of Witchcraft Past & Present*. Custer, WA: Phoenix Publishing, 1973.

———. *Witchcraft for Tomorrow*. New York: St. Martin's Press, 1978.

Voltaire. *What Is Goth? Music, Makeup, Attitude, Apparel, Dance, and General Skullduggery*. Boston, MA: Weiser Books, 2004.

Wendell, Leilah. *The Necromantic Ritual Book*. New Orleans, LA: Westgate Press, 1991.

Whitcomb, Bill. *The Magician's Reflection: A Complete Guide to Creating Personal Magical Symbols & Systems*. Santa Fe, NM: Bear & Co., 1994.

Zell-Ravenheart, Oberon. *Grimoire for the Apprentice Wizard*. Franklin Lakes, NJ: New Page Books, 2004.

Index

introspection (introspective), 2, 11, 13, 23, 84, 133, 245, 248, 254
invocation, 146, 148, 206
Islam, 51
Italy (Italian), 190, 252

J

Jägermeister, 178
Japan (Japanese), 28–29, 48, 152
jewelry, 32–33, 38, 115–116, 137, 139
Jewish (Judaic), 72, 118, 241–242
John, St. (Saint John), 101
Jolly Roger, 240
Judaism, 234

K

karma, 202, 279
katoeys, 192
Kellner, Carl, 77
Kelly, Edward, 65
Kelly, Gerald, 76
Kelly, Rose Edith, 76–77, 205
Kether, 203
Kilpatrick, Nancy, 6
kitchen Witch, 70
kundalini, 181

L

labeling (labels), 3, 9, 12, 16–17, 34
lancets, 258–259
LaVey, Anton Szandor, 73–74
Law of Contagion, 254
Law of Reflection, 210
Legend of the Descent of the Goddess, 268
Leland, Charles Godfrey, 252
lemniscate, 120, 236

lemon house charm, 251–252
lesbian, 185
Lévi, Eliphas, 72, 238
liminal, 267, 269, 280
liquid eyeliner, 121, 123, 125–127, 129–130, 156
live action role-play (LARP), 261
Locks of Love, 133
Lolita, 28–29
lounge, 27, 155
LSD, 175
Lucian, 276
Lugosi, Bela, 46, 208, 259
lwa/loa, 79–80

M

magickal name, 208–210, 250
magickal tools, 148, 214
makeup, 9–10, 13, 15–16, 19–20, 23, 26–27, 29–32, 36, 38, 43, 45, 48, 109, 115–116, 118–130, 156, 158, 194, 196–197, 219, 228, 246, 256
Malice Mizer, 28–29, 152
MallGoth, 35
Manson, Marilyn, 34–35
Mansonite, 34–35
mantra(s), 89, 103, 134, 271
marijuana, 174–175
masochism, 182
masturbation, 178, 182
Mathers, Samuel Liddell MacGregor, 69
Maypole, 163
McMurtry, Grady, 77
McNevin, Estha, 121
media, the, 2, 9, 12, 14, 58, 78, 82, 108, 182
Mediæval, 24, 152, 240
meditation, 4, 50, 56, 82, 84, 86, 88, 103, 106–107, 109–114,

119, 142, 147, 153, 155, 170, 174, 209, 213, 228, 243, 245, 278, 280–282, 285
Mercury, 181, 189, 234
MetalGoth, 32
Metcalf, Peter, 268
methamphetamine, 178
metta, 110–114
Metta Bhavana, 110–111
Metzger, Richard, 213
Mexico (Mexican), 169–170
Middle Path, 83, 86, 166
Middleworld, 75, 82, 270, 272
miscegenation, 178
Mohawk, 23
monotheism (monotheistic), 51–52, 167
moon, 53, 55–56, 85, 105, 133–134, 148, 156, 165, 185, 206, 233–234, 237, 240, 245, 251, 253, 258, 271, 282
Moorcock, Michael, 230
MopeyGoth, 33
Morrison, Grant, 62
mundane, 1, 54, 75, 94, 117, 120, 142, 158, 200, 234, 266, 274
Murdock, George Peter, 49
Murray, Margaret, 68
mushrooms, psilocybin/ magick mushrooms, 170–171, 174, 176
Muslim(s), 6–7, 225
mystic(s)/mysticism, 2, 8, 10, 44, 49, 51, 78, 94, 101, 186–187, 219, 243

N

Napoleon, 38
Native American, 53, 75, 94, 141, 170, 190, 192, 197

Photograph Credits

Chapter I

Key to the Underworld—Model: Anna. Photograph © OakRaven Photography. Page 18.

Babydolls—Model: Nvwoti Atsasgili. Photograph © OakRaven. Page 19.

CasualGoths—Model: Jason. Photograph © OakRaven. Page 20.

CorporateGoths—Model: Karly. Photo © OakRaven. Page 21.

CyberGoths—Model: Shannon. Photograph © Rocky and Chromegirl.net. Page 22.

Deathrockers—Models: RazorCandi and Ponyboy: Photograph © RazorCandi and Ponyboy. Page 23.

FaerieGoths—Model: Wicked Mina. Photograph © Daf Productions. Page 24.

Fetishists—Model: Kitty. Photograph © OakRaven. Page 25.

GlamGoths—Model: Diana. Photograph © Visually Odd Photography. Page 26.

Gothabillys—Models: Sandi and Logan. Photograph © Dan Havner Photography. Page 27.

Gothic Lolitas—Model: Kuro Bara. Photograph © OakRaven and Lady Datura. Page 28.

Gravers—Model: Raven Digitalis. Photograph © Brenna English Chapman Photography. Page 30.

GutterGoths—Model: RazorCandi. Photograph © RazorCandi and Ponyboy. Page 31.

MetalGoths—Models: Eddie and Sherri. Photograph © OakRaven and BlessidDoom. Page 32.

MopeyGoths—Model: Raven Digitalis. Photograph © Chris's Place. Page 33.

NotGoths—Model: Russ. Photograph © OakRaven and BlessidDoom. Page 34.

PerkyGoths—Model: Miss Rip Redrum. Photograph © Tyler Wilson Photography. Page 36.

Rivetheads—Model: Timo. Photograph © OakRaven. Page 37.

RomantiGoths—Model: Analisa. Photograph © Analisa. Page 38.

SkimpyGoths—Model: Jamie the Metal Goddess. Photograph © OakRaven. Page 40.

SophistiGoths—Model: Karen. Photograph © OakRaven. Page 41.

TraditionalGoths—Model: Gashley. Photograph © Terry Mac Photography and Gashley Darcane. Page 42.

ÜberGoths—Model: Anna. Photograph © OakRaven. Page 43.

Vampyres—Model: Eden. Photograph © Eden Prosper. Page 44.

VictorianGoths—Model: Melissa. Photograph © Kronos Dega Photography and Velvetscars.com. Page 45.

VintageGoths—Model: Stephaña. Photograph © OakRaven. Page 46.

WhiteGoths—Model: Lady Datura. Photo © Tyler Wilson Photography. Page 48.

Chapter II

Formatron—Photograph © OakRaven Photography. Page 80.

Chapter III

Chapter IV

Chapter V

Chapter VI

Chapter VII